P9-CFE-993

A WOMAN OF JUDAH

A novel and fifteen stories

BY THE SAME AUTHOR

Winter Journey
Sandmouth

A WOMAN OF JUDAH

A novel and fifteen stories

RONALD FRAME

W · W · NORTON & COMPANY
New York   London

Copyright © 1987 by Ronald Frame
First American edition, 1989.

All rights reserved.

Published simultaneously in Canada by Penguin Books Canada Ltd.,
2801 John Street, Markham, Ontario L3R 1B4.
Printed in the United States of America.

Library of Congress Cataloging-in-Publication Data

Frame, Ronald.
    A woman of Judah: a novel and fifteen stories/Ronald Frame.
        p.   cm.
    I. Title.
    PR6056.R262W6   1989
    823'.914—dc 19
    88-33272

ISBN 0-393-02692-2

W. W. Norton & Company, Inc.
500 Fifth Avenue, New York, N. Y. 10110
W. W. Norton & Company Ltd.
37 Great Russell Street, London WC1B 3NU

1 2 3 4 5 6 7 8 9 0

Contents

A Woman of Judah is fiction. Names, characters, locations and events are finally the work of my own imagination, although their provenance – the source of inspiration – is another matter.

I should like to acknowledge my thanks to Mrs L.M. Turrin and Mr Leonard Beemy for their recollections of certain remote happenings in pre-War 'Wessex'. I am also grateful to Mrs Dinah Weaver, curator of the Davenham Collection at the County Museum of Ethnology in Dorchester, Dorset: and no less to Mark Fitzgerald for the hours spent patiently reading the local press of the period. Jane and Tony Pitton-Reed of Flitch Farm, Linmere by Sturminster Newton were the most hospitable of hosts.

R.F.

"And so an innocent life was saved that day."
Daniel and Susanna, Apocrypha
New English Bible.

*"So the summer went by and the nights of
shooting stars were over."*
Effi Briest, Fontane.

A Woman of Judah

For Stella and Patrick

1

We lunched late, on partridge and port, followed by Stilton and coffee: how I have always imagined a judge would dine.

But there are judges and judges. He seems bemused by this mild version of fame that has come his way in the 1980s. His verdict on it? 'A celebrity of the fourth calibre, I should say. Or just possibly the fifth. A man with his future behind him.'

We discuss his output of work in the past couple of years: articles, radio talks, television appearances, one book about the Winstanley trial and a second (topic unspecified) in preparation, ready pronouncements for the press – as requested.

I unchivalrously ask the question: and my host courteously and wryly replies that he is two months short of his seventy-fifth birthday.

'So much for the three score and ten. I don't know what I've done to deserve this.'

I sit a little uneasily in my chair, realising that the only terms of description that are occurring to me are clichés: 'lively', 'animated', 'keen-witted', 'spruce', 'spry', 'irreverent', 'ironic', 'self-deprecating'.

The housekeeper, Mrs Lloyd, opened the door of the dining-room and hesitated when she saw us. Her employer politely requested her to come in – we had finished eating – and, given the nod, she began clearing the table.

He was silent and pensive as Mrs Lloyd worked, passing between the two of us. At last, when the tray was laden and had been carried from the room and the door closed, he spoke again. 'There's something I should like to tell you. But it's on a certain understanding —'

I immediately nodded compliance.

'The story should wait until my death. If you wish to use it.

It may not seem very much, not much more than an anecdote to you. But —'

I provided him with assurances.

'Not here, though,' he said. 'Somewhere else, I think.'

He rose from the table, and I followed him out into the hall. We walked towards the back of the house.

'It's a long story,' he said. He pushed open a door; we stepped into a corridor, which brought us to a conservatory. 'If you're in no great hurry, that is, I could tell you —'

'Yes,' I said. 'Please. I should like to hear.'

As if in readiness, two cane chairs had been positioned in such a manner that either the distance between them would seem appropriately formal or, alternatively, their relative proximity would induce a sense of intimacy.

'All the time my wife was alive,' he said, 'I forgot about it, more or less. In the past couple of years, though, it's come back to me.'

He indicated which chair was which, and asked me – if I would – to sit down, please.

'In one sense,' he continued, seating himself, 'it's a memory.' His hands fell into his lap. 'In another sense it's much vaguer than anything you can recall. There seems to be a great doubt attached to it. As if – as if everything then took place in another element, almost. In ether, or beneath water.'

His hands closed round an invisible globe.

'It all seemed vivid enough at the time. But there were things I knew I didn't understand, and I was steering my way between these. Or being steered. That is the moot point, isn't it?'

I raised my eyebrows: an enquiry.

'If Hamlet were alive now, he might be asking his question differently: "to be, or to have your being done for you?"'

I smiled: meaning to be encouraging.

'Anyway,' he said, bypassing my smile, 'this isn't getting the story told. In hot countries old men sit in the shade and tell their tales, and that's their privilege. But the old don't have many of those. Privileges. I just take any opportunity that comes my way. You're too polite, I know, not to let me indulge myself.'

His hands continued to fumble with the subject.

'What you do ... What you do with this when I'm not here

*to recount my own party-pieces is up to you. You have a
living to make — rather a perilous one too, I should think,
no? — so everything's copy, grist to the mill. Maybe you can
give it a shape, and there'll be some point to it. Maybe in its
own way it will have something to say of the time and the
place.*

*He settled back in the basketwork chair: an old man com-
fortably accommodated in the shade, although his story was
to be of heat and the confusion of sunlight.*

*

False start. I meant my story to be at a remove from myself,
but the *he said*s somehow lack conviction. I meant my story
to be a short one, but I don't see now how that can be. I have
to explain how much I fail to understand of the events I'm
going to relate. (Stories should always be 'related', which
dates me to a period before I even announce my setting —
inland Wessex, in the middle years of the 1930s.)

Begin again, then. For life is lived, and endured, in the
perpetual hope of the new beginnings we might make.

2

I can't use the characters' real names. I'll give them
names of a different origination.

The town was in a western county. It perched on the side of
a hill. Those who could afford to (or who had the sort of
history and 'connections' and manner about them that
allowed them to get by on credit) lived in the upper part; the
lowlier sort muddled through their lives howsoever they
could, at their own level.

The town regularly features in guidebooks and on calen-
dars: its appearance is considered very photogenic. At that
time, in the mid-1930s, we thought rather less about its
aesthetic charms. I *was* attracted to it certainly, but rather
more by its air of dwelling apart. (I remember the morning I
went down on the train to meet my father's cousin, a lawyer
and my future employer. I suppose the town was looking its

best that day but I was more conscious that it was unlike any other place I'd ever seen before.)

There were cars, a few, and modern conveniences such as electric light and decent sanitation to some of the houses, but those almost seemed fripperies gauged against the old stone and fraying thatch and high narrow windows like sly eyes and the trodden horse-dung on the streets and the sheer persistence of myths and legends in that corner of the country.

Sometimes, at regular dates on the calendar every year, fairs were held on Pack Street: later I went to spectate at some, and the faces that came to hear the hawkers' hard-sell and waited till they were watching by lantern-shine were centuries old, the women's squashed under felt hats secured by long pins and the men's framed by bushy Victorian side-whiskers. On windy nights, very late, I might walk downhill, and I'd listen to the creaking signboards the length of Pack Street and I was suddenly in a tale of boyhood adventure by, not Thomas Hardy, but Robert Louis Stevenson.

The lawyer's office where I spent my working days was housed on the ground floor of a former Abbey house, in the small close called the Abbey Green. Beams twitched on the walls, mice scampered overhead, the three musty rooms reeked of quiet, circumstanced gentility. The dust that settled on our desks might have been the mortal sort, such as lay beneath the pompous tombstones in the Abbey. The only sounds to listen to other than our own breathing and the scratching of pens were – that first autumn and winter – the flames licking in the grates and the apportioning of the seconds on the grandfather clock in Mr Botterel's room.

When I moved there, to the town, I was young, twenty-three, which was far *too* young. I didn't know that such places are for those in the mellow autumn of their years, who welcome the boon of time to reflect and recollect; I didn't know that, with buildings too, 'prettiness' only goes skin-(or stone-) deep. I wasn't aware that you have to be strong-willed to live in such a community as – let me call it – Ivell Abbas, without the natural advantage of having been born there. In those days Ivell Abbas seemed even further from the rest of the world than one might imagine it is now. Maybe the worst of the age's political unrest and agitation passed us by: what

14

was less easy to adjust to was the backwardness of the spot, its traditions, everything turning in on itself, the lack of curiosity about what went on outside, a certain spirit of vindictiveness that had its roots in native intolerance, in jealousy. The counties of the west are profoundly sceptical: I learned that what other people don't know about you or cannot discover they will concoct for themselves, fabricate, and then have passed around just as they see fit. Nowadays we find the customs quaint, the pace nostalgically slow. From the cities we can't perceive the equivalent faults of such places: the numbing tedium, the narrowness of view like tunnel vision, *the unconcern to understand* – which becomes the very opposite, the negation of charity. We avoid the real and actual issues which haven't changed so much in fifty years: the exclusivity of the locale, the precision of social distinctions (even among the least favoured), the common refusal to forget or – usually – to forgive, the distrust of newcomers and a sixth sense for taking advantage of them.

This was the town of Ivell Abbas. It was hardly exceptional in any of its attitudes. Possibly it was more fortunate than some in its location: it faced south, it was fed by clearwater springs, storm-rain ran downhill. There were particular *dis*-advantages of the physical kind, most notably in the matter of health: Ivell Abbas suffered the normal country-town in-stances of fever, botulism and salmonella poisoning, diphtheria, scarlatina, poliomyelitis; also, every four or five years, an outbreak of consumption would occur, when the meads at the foot of the town became shrouded with miasma clouds. But ills of that kind chiefly affected those who lived below Pack Street: it might have seemed a good argument for social ambition at least (God helps those who help them-selves), but of course people had long memories for family history and even if someone were to make the fairy-tale jump in a generation they weren't allowed to forget their origins and the expectations they'd been born with in this life.

Time hung heavy, I discovered soon enough. It was every-where. There was nowhere it hadn't got to before you: it chose both the dank shadows and that ripe, saffron stone which was supposed to hold the sunlight of centuries past. You *smelt* it walking into rooms, it had you opening the windows to let it out, but it was persistent and canny, sneaking down chimney-flues and leaking through the cracks between floorboards. At its most harmless it manifested itself in the dates inscribed over doorways, but it also caught you unawares, in the familiar angles of a hallway or bedroom, or suddenly as you walked up a staircase or, out of doors, as you turned a street corner or walked from sunlight into shade. Even beyond the town, in the fields of the Castle estate and on the bridle-tracks, it wasn't dissipated or diluted: there was the graft of generations worked into those tilled furrows or stacked up high on the haycocks, it had worn the mud tracks flat to their hard flinty dryness. Away from the town time seemed even more pressing and pervasive: I could appreciate why Thomas Hardy had likened his characters to ants on the green baize top of a billiard table.

Some days time slammed down. Then the sky was vast, like the convex, distorting interior of a domed cover suspended above a salver. I would see it with the eyes of a tiller in the Dark Ages, or a Roman centurion's, or a hunter's as he returned to his camp, to the rings on the hill. Excepting the case of the grand Elizabethan manor house where the leaded mullions fetchingly framed views of the ruins of the old castle, the mood of 'history' in that place was one of pure, inbred desolation.

*

At any rate, this was where I found myself, with no one to blame but myself, you could say. But everything worked out well enough, to begin with. I had rather cramped but decent accommodation, in rooms above Pomfrey's the ironmonger's, halfway up Pack Street. I continued to find the job interesting and my work varied. I even found time to have a crack at what had been an ambition for the past four years, to write a novel – I began it at least, working on an outline and sketching in the characters. I liked Botterel, his wife was considerate and kind, and their daughter Lettice didn't insist on her dignity as someone soon to be married; they treated very fairly all told, considering I probably had something of the patronising air of the other city folk who'd settled in the place, believing ourselves crucially 'different' (which was only, in their case, a synonym for 'superior').

The social distinctions in Ivell Abbas in 193–, among some four or five thousand souls, were well-nigh feudal. I was able to find them entertaining, only because I considered myself to be outside their jurisdiction.

The 'primus inter impares' was our local baronet, resident (when he wasn't up in London) in the sixteenth-century 'modern' castle with his faded six-foot wife. Lesser specimens of nobility and relations of nobility occupied some of the larger houses dispersed about the upper hillside. Just beneath them, socially and geographically, were the best-connected of the commoners (if they were really that), without actual 'bona fide' handles to their names but familiar with the routine of country weekends and London balls. Beneath *them* were numerous strata and sub-strata, each meticulously distinguished.

You were supposed to know your place in the Order of Things, and to be aware of the perils attendant on your venturing too far out of it.

The professional class was as vigilant – and as complexly composed – as the others. Commerce was its great bugbear, and its social aspirations were always strenuously directed *upwards*. It was that group with which I principally came into
contact.

If the 'peasant' levels were the most exclusive, the most petty-minded and savagely condemnatory of themselves and others, the professionals were only narrowly outdone on each score. It seemed to be a custom of mind with them to judge harshly oneself as one would one's peers, but to show undue favour to social superiors and to judge *them* by more lenient standards than oneself, and to take an even sterner stance on the behaviour of one's social *in*feriors (the lowest knew no better, but there were some brazen upstarts among them who deserved to be kept in check). As they'd assumed what were imagined to be superior manners ('airs and graces' might be nearer the mark) they'd shown a more palpable falseness in their conduct, which could be either trivial or more serious and had something to do with a general condition of nervousness: being professionals they were uncomfortably aware that others with equivalent training and experience to theirs could tackle a similar job, doubtless to equal effect, and they believed themselves under constant pressure to maintain appearances and status in the face of continuous encroachments and transgressions from (as it were) the flanks and behind.

I don't suppose I ever felt other than uneasy, even apprehensive, in their company. I tried to think it had nothing to do with my being counted among their number. I was conscious that some of them or their 'betters' might presume I had my own share of the same neuroses: that only proves that I too had that regard for the opinions of others which I recognised as prominent among their failures of character as a class. Certainly I wasn't married or engaged, which marked me out, and I had no claims on the town or – so I chose to think, at first – *it* on *me*; I had no blood relations in that area except the Botterels, no friends, no responsibilities or obligations even.

I suspect that from the outset I was viewed chiefly with suspicion by all parties. I was someone who had rather too high an opinion of himself, and who had a mistaken conviction in his own independence. I did my level best (or I imagined that I did) not to cause major upset, to play pretty much by the rules, and yet – however hard I tried to *look* like a lawyer – I don't believe that at any time during my sojourn in the town I was considered much better than a misfit square peg insisting that I fitted into an incontrovertibly round hole.

*

I was invited up to the Botterels' again, to Moat House, for a family tea on the Sunday afternoon in the first week of October.

The weather had turned freakish, very sunny and warm, and we stayed out of doors. At some point Mrs Botterel and her daughter went inside to supervise preparations of the tea-tray, and her husband and I sat on the top lawn in deck chairs. Then the telephone or front-door bell rang and Mrs Botterel called from the house. Botterel hauled himself to his feet, inviting me to 'look around' until he came back.

He was gone a long while, but there was an acre and a half of garden to inspect. I wandered off. The tidy rose-beds and neat pergolas of trained climbers didn't interest me as much as the wilder areas. The lawn at the bottom, furthest from the house, roughened to long grass, and a path snaked through the wilderness to sprawling fruit trees. I followed the track, pleased enough just to find some shade.

I examined the fruit still left: greengages, the kind of pear that used to be called a 'Good Christian', and – in such profusion that the branches had sagged – firm russet apples. The windfall lay in the grass, softening to pulp in the heat.

I sat down on a bench beneath one of the trees. The branches fanned from the trunk like parasol spokes.

I leaned my back against the gnarled, knobbly, mossy wood of the trunk and closed my eyes.

Time passed. I wasn't aware how long. I'd drifted out of the here and now, into the sort of doze that's only inches below the afternoon, where sounds still register, but vaguely – birdsong, leaves turning in a breeze, insect-drones.

I woke with a voice snagging whichever thoughts I'd fallen into, pulling at me, hooking me very gently. My eyes opened.

I sat staring in astonishment.

I was being watched, smiled at, by a young woman dressed in pleated cream cotton and wearing a white cotton sun-hat.

She was quite unlike any other young woman I had encountered in Ivell Abbas. She had style, and – I couldn't help noticing at the same time – self consciousness: a good deal of both.

Her smile widened at my confusion. She raised one hand and brushed lazily at a fly. I remember the gesture seeming to inhabit its little moment perfectly: now I believe it must have inhabited it rather *too* well.

I stood up.

'I'm sorry,' she said, after another delay.

I shook my head.

'No.' I had to lower my voice. 'No, not at all.'

She walked forwards in front of me on the scythed grass, from left to right.

'But I've disturbed you.'

'No —'

She reached the long grass and stopped.

'It was so hot,' I said. 'So close. I just sat down.'

She turned round, and smiled again.

'I'm Vivien Davies.'

I should have held out my hand but she didn't offer me hers.

I introduced myself. I told her I was apprenticed to Botterel: that I came from Bristol.

'Bristol?'

She laid the fluttering hand on her shoulder. She spoke with the crisp and expensive enunciation of one born with 'advantages' in life, but without the excesses of some of the town's other Well-Born. 'And you've come *here*?'

I explained that Botterel was my father's cousin and that he had always shown an interest in what I was doing, my law studies.

'Yes,' she said. 'I dare say he always has.'

I must have looked puzzled by her reply.

'Knowing,' she continued, 'that he would find himself an able assistant one day.'

I shook my head and tried to make light of her assessment of circumstances.

'I don't know about the "able",' I said.

'Humility is very becoming, Mr Pendleton.'

'Eh . . . Pendle*bury*.'

'Mr Pendle*bury*. A very Christian virtue.'

I shook my head again.

'You're either not humble,' she said, 'or not Christian. I shan't enquire which.'

I'd just noticed the wedding ring on her fourth finger when another voice spoke. I had to turn myself round one hundred and eighty degrees to see whose.

The sun was behind him, and he stayed motionless, but the image – after two or three seconds – became clearer: a figure full-set rather than stocky, some years older than myself. He was wearing a Sunday-best tweed suit not at all appropriate to the day's weather. A surprise puff of breeze that had rustled the grass fell away to nothing and in the uncomfortable silence his eyes passed between the two of us. Her husband, I surmised, although the relationship wasn't instantly perceptible.

She stood saying nothing. He smoothed the hair on the back of his head with several slow sweeps of his hand. Wasps murmured about the hanging fruit.

I felt I might have turned the page in a book and there the

three of us would have been: trapped in the embarrassment of those moments, contrived by someone's writing pen.

'I wondered —'

His voice, deep and solemn, cut out.

'I thought you were talking to Botterel,' his wife said, with something sharper in her tone.

I was standing outside the diagonal of conversation.

'So...' she added, more coyly, 'I just walked on.'

'And here you are. I've found you.'

I was aware that, notwithstanding its baritone depth, the voice lacked confidence.

'Obviously you have,' she said, with more of the briskness. She pulled at a stalk of the long uncut grass.

'Good. Well...'

'You've done your business then?'

The man took a couple of steps forward.

'Davies,' he said. 'Frank Davies.'

I remembered the name from Mrs Botterel's potted guide to who was who in the town.

'*Doctor* Davies?'

He took another few steps towards me and held out his hand. I walked forward and offered my own. He had a firm grasp; I felt too how cold and damp his fingers were. He loosened his grip, let go my hand and backed away.

'We'll leave you in peace,' he said.

I shook my head.

'This – ' His wife aimed her voice at me. '– it's much the nicest part of the garden, don't you think, Mr Pendlebury?'

I turned round and gazed at her – but only very briefly; an instinct made me focus my eyes instead on one of the trees in the middle-space between them both.

'I do like it,' I ventured. 'Yes.'

'We'll meet again,' she said, with what might have been off-handedness after her amiability. I watched as she picked her way very carefully through the grass to the point where her husband was standing. They both looked in my direction and I had to screw my eyes up against the sun to see.

'It's – unseasonal weather,' I said.

'Yes.' She spoke before her husband could find a reply. 'It happens here.'

I nodded, as if keenly assimilating the information.

'You can't be a native, Mr Pendlebury,' she continued, 'and not know that this place is a law unto itself.'

Davies touched her elbow with his hand. She glanced down, then turned away.

'Mrs Botterel invited us to stay for tea,' he said.

His wife appeared to hesitate between steps.

'Sadly, though,' he continued, 'our time is otherwise accounted for.'

I stretched my arms and hands wide, merely to sympathise. At that Davies seemed to pull himself straighter.

'Good afternoon to you, Pendlebury.'

They left, and I remained in the orchard for a few more minutes until I sensed that they must be gone from the garden. I sat down on the bench and heard – or I imagined I heard – over-ripe greengages and blood-flush apples dropping from the branches and splashing into the grass. I convinced myself I was listening to the fallen fruit bursting and oozing where it lay, returning into the earth, soaking through the dry, cracked crust: pulp-rot, a riot of unstoppable death and decay...

Someone called from the house.

'Tea! Tea-time!'

It was Lettice Botterel's voice, not her mother's.

'Will-iam! Tea-time!'

A hand-bell tinkled: very politely, but also – so I recall myself fancying, sunk in the breathless, torrid, sere quiet of the orchard – with a persistence bordering on urgency.

*

I collected what information I could about the Davies'.

The doctor was in practice with an older man, Goodden. He was considered to be reasonably adept at his job, no better or worse than the various locums who had stood in over the years, and for the most part courteous, in a professionally formal way; sometimes he was less polite, when he felt his time was being wasted. Socially he didn't have a great deal of small-talk but he said the right things to his hosts and was inoffensive when conversations reached to arguments. He was generous in buying drinks at the golf clubhouse, and didn't exaggerate in totting up the scores in an afternoon's play. Everyone could see to the future, what

at the stile, as if she sensed a presence in pursuit. I
. The gate rattled behind her, and her heels squawked
oss the cobbles: to my (aspiring, overstraining)
t's inner eye, the seams of the stockings and the gusset
ankles punctuating the episode with two ironic
nation marks.

rsuaded myself that the men dreamed about her, in very
right, masculine, even animal, fashion. When the
en dreamed, the encounter ended in violence, with the
mer trouncing the doctor's wife for a particular offence
e dignity of her sex.

nd yet I gathered that Mrs Davies had done nothing – in
one's knowledge – to justify any kind of opprobrium. She
sn't becoming any more sociable, and she had been
ucated far from the town (although she couldn't help her
ckground), and her husband still had to win his laurels,
d certainly neither of them had the warmth about them,
e easiness, which made the imparting of a confidence to
hem very likely. But *technically*, so general opinion had to
concede, Mrs Davies – to this point, to date – was, well . . .
blameless.

We started to meet, the Davies' and I.

I spoke to them after an Abbey service, *hellos* and anodyne
remarks about the weather. I had a few words with them in
the crush after a charity musical evening in a house at the top
of the town; they'd arrived at the interval, and neither of
them seemed particularly taken by the pianist's Liszt selection. They were already seated when I arrived at the
Botterels' one Sunday for tea, and I wasn't able to get very
close – or even to see or hear much – round the side of the
settle that had had to be manhandled into the room. We
passed later on the steps of the bank: they clearly had other
matters on their mind, but this time we went a little further
than *hellos* and comments on the weather, and Davies even
sympathised about that 'bloody bench thing' I'd been 'shoved
on to' for tea at Moat House: I didn't mind, I said, and the
Botterels were very kind. 'Yes, I think they *are*,' his wife
replied. 'Frank,' she added, her smile frosting, 'doesn't know
who our friends are in this town.'

I once saw Davies drinking alone in The Plumes, and I

he must look like in another twenty years' time: that he
would still be here, employed in much the same way that he
was employed now, wearing his tweed suits and heavy, steel-
tipped brogues, with more bulk about his middle and a
prosperous man's jowl.

Mrs Davies was envied for starting off her married life in
such an attractive house, one of the handsomest of the smaller
sort on Laud Street. It had been the home of old Mrs Lattimer:
the property hadn't been publicly auctioned, but instead
offers had been made to an actuary and then considered by
Mrs Lattimer herself, after she had interviewed the interested
parties. She had declared herself impressed by the new doctor
and his local wife, the Antrobus girl, and she had invited
them to call a second time, for tea. In the end their offer on
the house and its two-thirds of an acre was topped by at least
three others but it was the one that the old lady accepted. 'I
want the two of *you* to have the house,' she told them.
'Houses aren't just stone and mortar and wood, other lives
live on in them, and I know my spirit will be free to come and
go if *you* are the occupants when I'm no longer in this world.'
Davies had admitted later that doubts had crossed both his
mind and his wife's as they sat listening, but they only had to
look around to remind themselves what a splendid home this
would make, even allowing for ghosts.

After the purchase Mrs Davies turned out to be not as
gregarious or hospitable a châtelaine as had been calculated
on at first. But that too seemed to fit with the house and its
recent reputation: Mrs Lattimer had preferred to be more
and more reclusive as the years passed. The doctor's wife
didn't host tea-parties or sponsor garden sales-of-work,
although she *did* entertain selected town company to dinner,
which was no more than the decent thing of course. On such
occasions she was well turned out, she smiled, was perfectly
agreeable – and yet, so her guests thought, she didn't fully
enter into the spirit of the event, she was always just a little
aloof, not snobbishly so but as if . . . as if she were an on-
looker. She gave too little of herself away, I was told. Later I
understood for myself: it was as if she shadowed herself,
passing judgement internally on her own words before she
spoke them, *if* she spoke them: either she seemed to be
concentrating very hard, as if she were afraid she might smile

at the wrong place in an exchange, or the conversation lapsed and she seemed to go drifting off...

From my preliminary investigations I learned that she was regarded as a woman difficult to fathom – rather 'odd', in short. Very presentable, but not quite like anyone else, not to be predicted in the way most people can be, not *dependable*. What she was like in private with her husband was endlessly speculated upon. The resident maid and the daily house-help who sometimes cooked and the gardener had very little to offer on the subject of domestic relations. In public the pair tended not to look at each other (well, perhaps they did, but only every so often and just for an instant), they didn't even correct one another in conversation as husbands and wives usually did, which was a little fishy: and yet on arriving anywhere and departing there was nothing in their appearance or behaviour to suggest they were not harmonious.

I was told there wasn't, and had never been, any great performance of affection between the couple, not even at the wedding. It was the general opinion (or guesswork?) that, for both parties, the marriage had come at a fortuitous juncture. The marriage might well have been the end of the matter. In time the couple would have settled into being the archetypal young-ish doctor and his wife.

But...

But Dr and Mrs Davies had never settled into the rôles of stereotypes, and keeping their lives as much their own as they could they both of them continued to escape the common knowledge.

*

With the weeks I continued to learn for myself.

To a few, the more naïve, they *did* seem to be more or less all a young doctor and his wife were expected to be, and they were spoken of by them with respect but also impersonally, as if the pair were principally functions, cog-wheels in the greater machine of the town. In certain quarters they were regarded as bonuses, in the social sense. Others saw Davies as a newcomer who had to justify himself in the community before doors could be opened either to him *or* to her, even though she had been born in Ivell Abbas. To many people, those living further down the hill, the couple's 'social' value

was of no consequence, an relation to doctors and their s

Two years after the marriage other wives were less excusing able in their appraisals. Hadn't herself? At the same time their hu of her presence: when she walke stance, they noticed her and re dressed, how she walked, if she wa The years actually seemed to be *im* That's not surprising, their wives wo probably has the life of Riley in that ho finger, what does *she* have to go sh children.

She was most to be envied on the la circumstances childlessness was conside town, in others a blessed relief and free thought that Mrs Davies flaunted that ca dependence, but they knew she was still you most probably – she was only conserving he wife of all people couldn't choose *not* to bear

Eyes of both sexes narrowed to see her, in he plush flush of her salad days. The men talk among themselves, glossing over their wives' o women also discussed her, but only with each unwilling to permit their men-folk the indulgence. the men talked lewdly: sometimes the women also more frankly sexual way about her, but without any of wonder or even of admiration.

In The Plumes I overheard a couple of young they'd seen Mrs Davies looking over a bridge, with the tugging at her skirt. Another time I caught one of the many spinsters squinting disapprovingly at the doctor's as she leaned across a barrow in the market, breasts al resting on a heaped mound of plums. Older men on st corners stared, chewing on their pipes, their eyes a myste Once I spied her in the porch of the Abbey when there was one else there, stopping to adjust one of her stockings a suspender height, then letting her slip fall and straightening her skirt and continuing on her way. I followed her across the Green, watching the roll of her hips, until she half-turned

her hea
stopped
off ac
novelis
at the
exclar
I p
forth
wom
drea
to t

an
wa
ed
b
a
t

once saw her in Trip Lane, closing a green wooden gate in a high wall, turn the key in the lock and throw the key over the wall into the garden. I saw Davies having an altercation with the boy at the petrol pump on Tallow Street, and in the post office one day I watched his wife as she despatched a telegram. He sometimes bought cut flowers from the Farmers' Institute, and once I caught sight of her collecting a pair of gent's shoes from the cobbler's. I noticed him on two or three evenings setting out by himself for a walk, and once I glimpsed her standing on Tallow Street, looking over at the unattended petrol pump. At the end of one afternoon I saw him sitting alone in the Abbey, and one lunchtime I watched her lean on the door jamb of the flesher's and remove a shoe to shake out a stone, massaging her foot and ankle before she replaced the shoe.

*

Her looks are difficult to describe.

She wasn't either of the conventional English 'types': tidily pretty with a peaches-and-cream complexion, or with the sharp angular features that are handed down from generation to generation, along with the clear, white, thin skin. She was more sensual than either, and resembling only herself she was her own woman.

She wasn't conventionally 'pretty', and so she couldn't aspire to anything beyond that, to beauty. But she was striking in a way I hadn't ever come across before.

The dresses she wore, looser and shorter than the belted, pencil-line fashion, only drew attention to all that this Mrs Davies was not.

*

Any description wouldn't properly account for the *effect* she had.

Long eyes, set quite far apart, with vividly green pupils. High cheekbones. A short nose, broad rather than narrow, the nostrils visible and not quite symmetrical. A large mouth with full lips (any larger or fuller and they might have been defects instead), and a lopsided smile that showed a generous proportion of her white, unevenly arranged teeth.

But there was something in the distribution of the features

27

that drew your attention to that face, and held it: an elusive quality to the eyes, which might have been owing to their pronounced almond shape or just the very speed with which their expression seemed to change, the suddenness with which they would look away from you – and something about the mouth, an omen of petulance, as if (to contradict its width) it was always threatening to contract to a straight concluding line, but didn't. You never quite knew *where* you were with her: in the space of just moments perfect propriety could turn to sultriness and back again, and you were left blinking. In one of the notebooks I kept at the time I wrote down *'glowing, well-scrubbed voluptuousness'*.

Her face, I suppose, didn't belong to the 1930s. She wouldn't have looked out of place in the 'sixties, among the modern girls of King's Road, or even in the 1980s. When I knew her – if I properly did, which is the point – she wore her fair hair in a very unfashionable style: she'd let it grow, quite naturally and without the vigorous discipline of perming or crimping or even bobbing, and had it pulled up on to the back of her head and fastened with silver filigree-and-tortoiseshell combs. The town's taste ran to hennaed hair, or the favourite brassy colour of the day, but she had resisted the trends and let her fairness bleach however it would in the sun. (The light tan on her skin was a feature unfavourably commented upon by some.)

A long neck, fine medieval hands with tapering fingers, slim hips (but you noticed them because her waist was so narrow), long legs and slender ankles.

But this is only telling half the story.

*

Or Davies.

He was a couple of inches taller than I was, about six feet. Broad-shouldered and well-built, but with his stomach kept in trim. At a guess, rugger-player's legs. His hands were less delicate than doctors' often are. His hair had begun to recede and already, in his early thirties, grey was flecking the black.

He had good looks of an anonymous kind: very pale blue eyes, a nose which had been broken in a rugger accident and just missed being Roman, thinner lips than his wife's, a cleft chin. His looks were wholly masculine; his manner – his self-consciousness, the lack of assertiveness – would have prevented other men from envying him, though. Women might have pitied him the nose, and also seen it as dignified, nearly patrician.

*

But two half-stories don't make a whole, least of all with the Davies'.

*

He smoked a pipe; he wore 'shaggy' tweed suits with a crisp crease in the trousers, and always on his rounds a hat. He was a younger man than his habits suggested, thirty or thirty-one.

She must have been a few years older than I first judged her to be: perhaps twenty-four or twenty-five. At the age *I* was however, twenty-three, even that small difference seemed vital.

*

During the winter, just as I was finding my way in the office, my father fell seriously ill.

My mother died when I was in my teens, and I was an only child, so the onus of responsibility became mine. Botterel proved very understanding, and I left Ivell Abbas to return home.

I was away for ten weeks altogether, until my father came out of hospital and agreed to share the house with a nurse.

When I returned to Ivell Abbas I was told that I'd missed the snow and the floods after the thaw, that I wouldn't have recognised the place: snow piled up on roofs like stove hats, three-foot-long icicles hanging from drainpipes, the country folk forced to walk along the tops of hedges to find their directions. When the melt came it was the cheek-by-jowl cotters' houses at the bottom of Pack Street that took the full fury of the tide, as they always did: the hill had looked just like a mud-slide.

I readjusted as quickly as I could. I was a sponge for all I could see and hear. I settled down to work, I immersed myself in it, so that I might forget the worst moments of the past two and a half months. In the evenings I mainly kept to my rooms above Pomfrey's, scribbling, or – if I was feeling the want of air and movement – I went for energetic walks, to the barrow called 'The Dumpling' on the Yelton road, or across the estate fields, up to Hang Wood.

I'd been trying my hand at writing for a couple of years – only as an interest, but a fond one – and now I toyed with some ideas I thought I might turn into The First Novel. I scoured the newspapers every day to find snippets that could provide me with additional inspiration. For inspiration of the literary *and* the sexual sort I pinned up some photographs of paintings I'd salvaged from my old room at home. Titian's 'Venus', Manet's 'Déjeuner sur l'herbe', Courbet's 'Femme couchée: le repos', Ingres's 'La Grande Odalisque', Cranach's 'Nymph of the Fountain'.

I could sit in front of the wall for minutes on end, speculating on the painters' subjects but failing to ask myself why I should happen to be so fascinated by these images in particular: denuded women so candidly reduced to their essence. Meanwhile the Abbey bells rang and from my window I learned to hear and see it all. The man who'd been born with only one eye somewhere near the bridge of his nose cycling up and down Pack Street hollering; Mrs Vintrey arthritically playing Schumann on her upright piano while her son, the Canon, played athletic games of 'tig' with his favourites from the town's brownie pack; spades breaking the soil and forks and hoes ventilating as gardens behind high walls were assiduously turned for sowing; and on evenings when windows were opened the pretty, younger Miss Hartley screaming abuse at her infirm, helpless sister because both their lives had gone sour. On the same sort of evenings Mr Cartwright from the bank who called himself a widower (although there was no grave or headstone known to be extant) would lift Audrey Mills' skirt in the kitchen while her husband practised an anthem for Sunday on the Abbey organ. There were rumours in the air that, after such an arduous winter, it might turn out to be a long, fine, dry summer ahead of us.

With my table I called a 'desk' pushed against the window, I sat with the nib of my fountain pen poised above a clean sheet of paper, ready – always ready and waiting – to begin.

*

In March or April invitations started to come my way, after I'd been put through my paces at the Botterels'.

Later, in the first phase of the summer that was to prove a

vintage one, came the first of the invitations from Dr and Mrs Davies: a couple of handwritten lines on a postcard printed with the address of the house (on the first was a PS in a more florid, feminine script – 'Laud Street = Day-wear!') With no less alacrity on each subsequent occasion of an invitation – increasingly surprised on my part that they chose to have me, and embarrassed that I was failing to offer *them* hospitality in return (but how could I, in my quarters?) – I wrote my schoolboy's acceptance note.

*

A story was running in the newspapers, about a young man in Norfolk who had murdered his fiancée and buried her in the garden of his mother's house. The police had had their suspicions and promptly acted on some hunch about the garden.

The murderer had admitted his guilt the moment he was charged with the deed. He'd done such a thing for the sake of love, he explained: because he'd been convinced that their happiness together could never have exceeded what it was but only, with time, diminished and fallen away from that ideal apex they'd reached.

Three months later police found the bodies of two young people, a woman and a man, in a locked room in Camden Town. They were lying in bed, in each other's arms. Two tumblers contained a mixture of whisky and arsenic. There was no accompanying note, but a newspaper cutting about the Norfolk man's strangled fiancée was discovered in a drawer.

'Suicide' was the coroner's verdict.

The metropolitan pair were not necessarily more or less sane than the countryman who had committed his murder. But *they* had improved upon the deed by denying the police the convenience of a tidy, cut-and-dried murder charge. In the rapture of a love that could aspire no higher than the peak finally attained, they too achieved its continuation *and its stasis* in their shared death.

*

The Davies' lived on Laud Street, along whose length the Abbey had dispensed some of its wealth in times gone by.

Their house was seventeenth century, of local stone with a high roof, and a more modest property than some of its neighbours. From outside it was deceptively small: a dozen or fifteen strides carried you past its frontage.

The ground floor was below street level. You entered by three or four steps into a stone-flagged hall; several rooms led off that, in different directions. A staircase gave you a view of upstairs, a long landing with a balustrade and a number of doors left partially open.

The downstairs rooms had low ceilings but were quite capacious. The effect was of a warren of rooms, since each could be entered either via the hall or from the next one, by way of a connecting door.

The dining-room was arranged in formal fashion. I learned that Davies had inherited a few pieces but had bought most of the furniture. Nothing was new, however. Everything carried the patina of age: the mahogany dining-table, the shield-back chairs with needlepoint covers, the six-legged sideboard, the coffer, the blotched and sun-faded print maps of the county on the half-panelled walls.

The sitting-room was at the back of the house. Flowers were arranged in fat copper cider measures. The floorboards smelt of wax polish; pot-pourri, heaped in bowls, gave off a musty, musky odour as you walked past. The furnishings were a mixture of formality and the opposite. There were a number of stiff-backed side-chairs with arms; two high-sided wing sofas in a chintz print, with soft cushions which – even through the covers – shed tiny floating ducks' feathers. A gilt mirror hung lengthwise above the fireplace, and two 'matching' porcelain figurines were placed symmetrically on the mantelpiece: these represented 'Love' and 'Rejection', but they seemed to me rather too similar to be distinguished easily; also on the mantelpiece were two chiming clocks with their workings visible under glass domes, each telling the time differently, with ten minutes in dispute. Among the paintings was one of Victorian strollers on a promenade and a more modern portrait of a formidable, grey-haired woman dressed in black, standing with one scarlet-nailed hand on her hip and a querying, demanding expression on her face, as imperious as a Roman emperor's. Davies admitted that the subject wasn't a relation, they'd bought the painting from a gallery. The visit after the next one I started to ask his wife about it: she said the woman was actually a great-aunt of her husband, now dead. 'Rather a *grande dame*. She used to live in London. Mayfair or Belgravia.' Thereafter – on my next visits – I looked at the picture in some confusion, trying to believe *her* story rather than his, that the woman was a family presence: *I am a family ghost, I shall follow all of you down the years, you disregard ME at your very peril.*

From the sitting-room the view was of the garden. French windows took you out on to a paved terrace. Sunk in the middle was a square-shaped pond, which the Davies' had had built when they moved into the house: it was perhaps six feet long on each side, with a fountain mechanism submerged beneath a flotilla of decorative lily-pads. The fountain hardly had the force of a 'jet': water rose gently four or five feet in a three-quarters vertical arc and dribbled back down on to the surface, filling the walled terrace area with soothing aquatic sounds and, all through that most memorable of summers, the suggestion of relief from the heat – cool, temperate, tranquil thoughts.

A few shallow steps dropped on to the top lawn. Dense flower beds of the cottage garden sort proliferated on either side, sheltered by old stone walls at least fifteen feet high. More steps led to a lower lawn, with a glass-house and frames on the left and a sundial at its centre. Beyond that were outbuildings and vegetable beds, and further on again was a washing-green, and then wrought-iron gates that gave access to a lane.

'This is it, Mr Pendlebury, this is my home,' Mrs Davies said on the first evening I was invited, drawing me a little apart from the others as we stepped down from the terrace. I smiled, rather unsurely, and turned to look back at the house. The upstairs windows were open and early bees knocked drunkenly at the glass. A vine of budding wistaria covered one wall and I imagined what it must look like in the fullness of summer, a cascade of lavender blue.

It appeared to me to be an ideal house in which to embark on married life. But something in her tone of voice had alerted me, that she didn't accept the situation as being quite so straightforward after all. (Unless, it struck me, unless by having all this now you are giving yourself too little to strive for later?)

I told her what I thought of the house and the garden: at any rate I gave her my complimentary thoughts on all their most favourable aspects. She nodded without looking at me, seeming instead to inspect the buds in the herbaceous border nearest us.

'Polyanthus, philadelphus, phlox.' She indicated which was which. 'Bergamot, is it? Oxlips —'

Behind us the fountain discreetly splattered the pond with spray and the other voices made polite, demure, tinkly dinner-table conversation.

I turned and looked back again: first at the open bedroom windows, then at the terrace. In the middle of the group Davies was watching us both. I caught him out before he could look away. He removed his pipe from his mouth and seemed to consider the bowl for a few seconds before addressing some words to the woman at his side; she – accordingly – shifted her attention to the pond and replied, pointing at what they were discussing so studiously, with such earnestness, the water-lilies with their future blooms already showing white on top of their heavy knob buds.

*

One Sunday in the Abbey I opened the hymnal I'd been handed at the door and found that some of the pages were stuck together. I pulled at them, and they tore at the corners.

The stains were visible through the thin paper, blotches of old yellow shot with black where the ink had run when the stickiness was fresh.

The cause occurred to me before the first hymn reached its end: stale, dried, frustrated semen.

*

Perhaps my memory is playing tricks on me now, but what I remember of Laud Street are evenings of baking heat with the windows open and the fragrances of the garden tumbling into the low rooms and dusk a long time coming.

They were evenings that appeared to give the guests satisfaction; Dr Davies and his wife were accommodating, painstaking hosts, and the meal was never less than very capable, but I sensed that the social ritual put an amount of strain on

34

them both. Even in other people's houses, where we also met, they looked a little – I suppose the word must be – 'studied'. It was as if there was a split-second's delay in their responses every time we were all required to react, as if how they behaved was in the way of an echo, secondary to their impulses. A few times I interrupted an exchange of their eyes, effected almost subliminally, and whatever their expression at any particular stage in the proceedings I couldn't recognise it as being that of a couple professing their affection before us. I thought it possible that they might be loving with each other in private, but I knew my own inexperience didn't equip me to judge. When they were on display, as it were, what I felt I could detect was – in short – a tension. They were both wound up on elastic for the event.

In their own house on Laud Street they seemed to be on surer ground than elsewhere. It was as if there they could trust more to the effect they were causing to be made, they led us with smiles and nimbly steered the conversation wherever they would. I had a notion that certain directions had already been decided on beforehand, the words came out with such delicately prompted ease, with the verbal bridge established to the subject before. (The topics seemed to be those which – even if *we* didn't perceive as much – helped to establish the presumptions and prejudices of each of us.) I also had doubts about some of the gestures, as if those were performing functions we weren't meant to be aware of: when Mrs Davies placed her bare elbow on the old wood of the dining-table and pulled at her ear-lobe, or when her husband held the arm of his chair or rearranged the handkerchief in his top pocket.

Seated apart from them both as I frequently was, I imagined a fretwork of live, singing wires in the room, nearly invisible causes and connections.

*

One conversation in particular I remember, because our main course had consisted of skate with lemon sauce and shallots.

The discussion took up a legal case that was appearing in the newspapers every day. A trial had been conducted, the concluding arguments offered, but the jury's final verdict on culpability was still pending.

In a Devon sea town the owner of a harbourside fish

restaurant had been murdered. His body had been disposed of in especially gruesome fashion. First, a saw and several knives were employed. Then the bones were ground down and the chopped flesh, organs, muscles and yards of intestine dropped bit by bit into copper pans of fish stock to simmer and flavour the liquid; afterwards the stock had been strained and any gristle that was left crushed in a mortar, pulverised like the bones. Finally the debris, the de-solidified matter, was thrown into the sea, or buried maybe; not quite all of it, however, because minuscule amounts of powder had been found, inadvertently trodden into cracks in the kitchen's floor tiles.

It was Mrs Davies who embarked on the subject, one still, breathless evening when I was again (to me, inexplicably) included in the company gathered at their table. Various opinions were exchanged concerning the jury's, *any* jury's ability or inability – and their *lia*bility – to determine responsibility. Apparently in this case the identity of the life-taker was not in question, but he and the murder's witness were each loading the moral blame on to one another.

The subject returned to Mrs Davies. She started to recount the story as (so she told us) *she* imagined it to have taken place, with the man whom the jury properly acknowledged to be the actual perpetrator of the deed, a commercial traveller called Tatton, arriving in the port one dire and ominous day and setting into motion the tragic business. His end was not love, but coolly mathematical murder: his other purpose was the evil pleasure of turning the woman's head around. He began by persuading her that she was unhappy to be married to her husband and that she needed to unburden herself of that dragging shackle. Under the stranger's spell she was helpless to do anything. In no time she found herself swept up in a passionate affair of – she believed – body and heart. Tatton exerted such control over her that he even started to think her thoughts for her. It was he who devised the murder plan, cajoling her – perhaps threatening her – into going along with him. She, he'd decided, was to be the decoy, the bait. The unfortunate wife was so disorientated that she agreed, she forgot how to say 'no'. The deed was done by Tatton (a knife to the stomach); in the minutes of shock afterwards the woman heard her husband's killer's voice telling her how they must rid themselves of the body without leaving the kitchen, which was already awash with blood.

We all sat absorbed as we listened to Mrs Davies's retelling of the story, as *she* had construed the pattern of events to have been. She spoke with what seemed to me then great conviction, with no suggestion of embarrassment. When she'd finished there was an appreciative interlude of silence: I sat counting the seconds while I considered my moon face reflected in a spoon by the candleshine.

Then her husband put down his glass and begged that *he* be allowed to give a different interpretation of those same events. Mrs Davies placed her elbow on the table and pulled at her ear-lobe, smiling pleasantly at no one in particular.

Tatton, according to this second account, may technically have been the culprit (Mrs Davies continued stroking the lobe of her ear), but he was a man who had been compelled to the action by the brazen wiles of the victim's wife. She had fastened on to her husband's visitor immediately, luring him like a seaside siren, taking advantage of the solitariness of the man's trade. He found himself persuaded by her into believing that *he* was the only possible means by which she could be saved from her misery, her living hell with the husband who was secretly the devil's own. She staged a confrontation between Tatton and her husband, whom she had alerted to the salesman's naive fondness for her: the showdown took place in the kitchen of the prettily timbered restaurant on the waterfront. The two men set to with bare fists, but a little later in the broil – and crucially – the wife laid one of the chopping-knives within their reach. It was Tatton, pushed back against the table by a man stronger than himself and now in fear of his mortal breath, who saw the knife and grabbed it. The husband pinned him down by his other arm and so happened to become one of the instruments of his own death. Before Tatton realised, the blade – aimed at the shoulder – had slid into the man's chest and, remarkably, it found his heart. Death was instantaneous; the body crumpled, spraying blood. It was the wife, seeing all, who instructed what was to be done next, how the body had to be disposed of. Tatton was too distressed to know what was happening; he applied himself to the task with another man's hands, another man's mind. When the later accident occurred that caused the murder to be discovered, he wasn't quick enough to defend himself against the widow's accusations. He was left reeling with the shock of the betrayal.

When he'd finished, Davies took up his glass again. His wife continued to smile, somewhat abstractedly. For a while longer we discussed the case, none of us liking to attach ourselves to one version or the other. Were we meant to take sides, or was it our respective gifts of social tact that were being calibrated? Perhaps too the subject was meant to shock us not a little: it wasn't staple Ivell Abbas conversational fare, as the Davies' must have been aware. And notwithstanding the fact that he was a doctor, in the line of bodies and blood. . . .

'I think he got what he deserved,' Mrs Davies said.

Her husband was ready with his reply.

'He should have done the decent thing.'

'What was that?'

'Saved himself from the shame.'

'How?'

'Put the knife into himself.'

'What would that —'

'He'd have saved his nobility.'

Mrs Davies laughed.

'And saved his soul,' her husband said.

As I remember, no one panicked. The skate bones were tidily rearranged on our plates. In the rift of time before another topic was introduced to replace it, the words hovered about us, tangling with the garden scents and seeping into nightfall on the fringes of our group, where the candlelight didn't reach. The matter of the *crime passionnel* was insinuating itself into our memories of the evening, an ineffable mood of wistaria and corrupted hearts and the sour, vinegary after-taste of shallots.

*

For every act of martyrdom there has to be a persecutor and a victim, and perhaps we all belong to one or the other category.

A persecutor requires a victim. But might it not be a complementary equation that the victim both wills the act of martyrdom and, in a less direct manner, decides the identity of the executant/agent? Someone who denies himself, who – however

38

many layers deep down in the subconscious – holds the death wish inside himself, may also compel the act of persecution in the person fated to be his tormentor. A killer and quarry belong to each other in a relationship of eternal intimacy.

*

Davies had, in the common parlance, 'appeared from nowhere'.

'Nowhere', I guessed, was probably North Devon: there was just the trace of a burr left in his carefully demulcent accent. I didn't hear him say where he'd gone to school, if he ever did say, but he talked quite fondly, almost sentimentally, about the period when he was doing his medical training in London. His stories of rooming in Bloomsbury, in Dombey Street, with his accounts of a student's privations in the city, all had the ring of authenticity. His wife would begin to shift in her chair whenever the subject of London came up, as if she sensed that the chosen coteries who were invited to the house were not at all familiar with those aspects of life lived on a shoestring, nor necessarily wanted to be. I sometimes wondered if he wasn't actually rather proud of his achievement, knowing that he was able to include an experience of that sort in his comfortable, settled existence: but at some point in the narration, I observed, he would catch his wife's eye and the conversation would take a different tack.

A very comfortable and settled existence, I was aware. A young doctor couldn't have afforded to live and entertain so without private means. The house was furnished in immaculate taste, which – I had concluded – is likely to be an inbred feature of character, a sort of native intuition: but was the instinct his, or his wife's? Hers, I would decide during these interludes in an evening when I would let the talk pass me by: until Davies himself would pounce on me and ask – with an (apparently) indulgent laugh – I was being very quiet about something, did it mean that what everyone was saying about such-and-such a subject was just hogwash?

*

I learned that in the two years before he came to Ivell Abbas a couple of Davies's great-aunts had died within nine or ten months of one another and he'd been declared the principal legatee of both. He had barely known the two women but they had been concerned that their money should go to their long-dead brother's scion of family, 'family' being a noble sophism to them both. In that respect he'd been the only possible beneficiary, and he must have known liking had had nothing to do with the matter.

His good fortune became public knowledge, although – it seemed – he had no part in imparting the information himself and never understood how it had happened. It reached the ears of Mrs Botterel, then her daughter. Perhaps even with them too, as with the rest of the town, the doctor was subsequently seen in an altered light. People's attention was intended to flatter him, but he seemed unresponsive at first. He'd come to Ivell Abbas a quiet, withdrawn, even uncertain man, and the money made him little different: it was as if, despite his London training and his professional rank, he still lacked a degree of social confidence. Only very gradually did he begin to relax. Perhaps that was owing to the presence of one particular person, whose path crossed his with increasing frequency: the daughter of the widowed Mrs Antrobus, young Vivien, from the brewery house.

'I remember very well how it was,' Mrs Botterel replied to my query. 'The brewery house. Grander than you expected it to be. Or it *might* have been grander, but its best days were behind it by then. *Once*, perhaps – The hot water never seemed to work, and the bathroom was always so chilly, although there'd be a cake of some absurdly expensive soap from Paris in a chipped Limoges dish. The carpets had worn away to nothing in places, and there were cracks in the walls you could put your finger into, but Mrs Antrobus didn't seem to see, or to care. She'd talk of long ago, and how her own family had lived, in Devon. About the town she might have passed for normal, in her right mind – or reasonably so, at least – but I don't think she was, and certainly she wasn't when she was in her own home. If that's what she really thought of it as being, because you sensed it had been foisted on her, and the brewery life was less real than the one she'd come from. That was a mixture of farming and Navy, if I recall, with pretensions beyond that. She had a couple of dogs – otter-hounds, to be different of course: I *think* that's what they were – and they ran all over the house, and if *they* didn't make the puddles on the carpets then the rain leaks did. I was never sure. Upstairs, at the end, they used to walk about with umbrellas over their heads if it was raining. When Vivien was small, it wasn't so bad, but her mother lost interest after that, when she'd gone off to school, and maybe her father couldn't do anything about it. I think he was a weaker man than anyone imagined he was, and his wife wouldn't have been able to forgive him for that. She should have had the whole field to choose from: and when she thought of who had died in the War and never come back. . . . Some people lost almost all their circle, among the men, and they never got over it, and so the time on the other side of it, the War – the life before – it seemed infinitely better, and beyond compare. That's the problem, when you think your best days are lived; they only come once in your life and then when they're gone it's for good.'

Mrs Antrobus's husband died – to paraphrase what I heard – from a terrible weakness of constitution, the mental sort not the physical. To state the case in the fewest words: the will to live was beaten out of him.

He had never taken to the responsibilities visited on him by his father and grandfather, to attend to the running of the brewery. The finer points of competitive business eluded him. It might have seemed to him that his wife imagined herself a cut above him; he always appeared ill-at-ease in the company of her friends and relations. His rôle in the town – in business, social and Abbey circles – was defined by his lack of enthusiasm, by the absence of even a token kind of faith. His silences were a heretic's; they caused people to be awkward with him, and perhaps he detected their hostility gradually building.

It seems paradoxical that he had made some very generous benefactions to the town when circumstances at the brewery least favoured such expenditure: a new wall plaque in the Abbey (in white Purbeck stone) to the fallen of the War, structural and sanitary improvements to the Sheep Row almshouses, new gates and pillars into the Abbey Green, half the funds towards the building of a bandstand in the municipal Coronation Park. And yet, for all that, he gave no evidence of wanting to share in the spirit of a community. He was only too aware that certain persons in the town (did he include his wife among them?) looked down their noses at anyone in trade, that others actually envied him, or else resented his inherited lot, that a few disapproved of a brewer's line of work on moral grounds.

Which is all to say (or I'm saying it for him), he believed he saw through the specious myth the rest of the country was turning to as the years of the 'twenties grew dark – a tranquil, backwater English town at peace with the world and itself.

'I'm not sure their daughter ever quite believed *her* life had properly started,' Mrs Botterel continued. 'The brewery business started getting into difficulties, at the very time it shouldn't have, of course, when Vivien was growing up, and I think that was bad for her confidence, the worst thing. I don't know what she told her friends. But the fees for her education were paid somehow, and it *was* better that she was away from home. It must have been awkward for her later too, because she couldn't talk about her father and she couldn't *really* speak about her mother either, because in one sense they belonged together. She *was* odd. I do believe so: the mother, I mean. I think she felt history had conspired against her. It does, of course, against everyone, but somehow – well, you have to live with that. And she'd also had the possibility of a choice – in marrying – but it hadn't *really* turned out to be that after all. She'd imagined the opportunities might not last, so she'd snatched at the young Antrobus fellow before anyone else did and because her own family had lost some of its grandness too, because her own father had gambled some of the family money away, I believe. Because he was bored probably, and had a gentleman's fine white hands maybe instead of an honest farmer's. He gambled at one of the French resorts, I heard.

'So it was history repeating itself for Mrs Antrobus, I dare say, with her husband weakening and not able to help himself – and that made her worse. After all the War unhappiness. And somehow Vivien had to cope with it, as well as she could. She got quite close to her mother, closer than she'd been although she'd always taken her side. There *was* a choice, of sorts, after John Antrobus died: she and her mother could continue to live in the brewery house, *or* somewhere else, and *she* wouldn't marry. But she was always too – too smart and modish, and attractive in her own way – so that wasn't *really* a possibility, not to marry. So she decided to find a husband, for *practical* reasons, but people usually do anyway, if they've any sense. They "find their own".'

*

I used to watch the summer visitors, wondering if they knew as they consulted their erudite guidebooks or refreshed themselves in the 'Willow Plate' tea-rooms: that the meads of cowslips and bog myrtle at the bottom of the hill were very possibly still miasma-ridden, that some children in streets and lanes they didn't visit walked barefoot, that the ancient Romans had uncovered a tradition of primitive, barbarous rites and put down the men of sway with all the righteous fury of their own official methods of violence; that medieval devil-worship used to have as strong a hold as the godly (sometimes even the Abbey served two masters), that straw effigies of adulterers used to be burned in the streets in the time of the Georges, that there was a tradition of child-drowning in the Yel stream.

In 1912 a house in the town burned down and, in the smoking ruins, the bodies of a middle-aged sister and brother were found, sharing the same bed.

Eight years later, at the outset of the enlightened 1920s, a grisly discovery was made in the basement of the house where the bookseller and his young wife lived – a naked boy child, skeletal and scarcely alive, whom the woman (although no one knew or as much as suspected) had had by a soldier sometime in the War. The child had been locked away by his mother's husband, the seller of books, and had never seen the light of day. As so much white sunshine suddenly flooded his lair, he survived for a couple of minutes, shivering in an uncontrollable spasm, and then he gave up his ghost, wordlessly, in the hands of his rescuers.

*

I had an outstanding promise from Botterel that, when he had time, he would tell me about Antrobus, because it seemed to matter to me to know.

'Not "matter",' I said. 'I'm just interested.'

'Well, sometime . . .'

He took up the topic one evening when his wife and Lettice were going to be late home and he preferred to put off some time in the office.

'No one really knew what was what about Antrobus,' he began. 'Adeline Antrobus's husband rather, that's how he came to be called even. Lots of brewers *do* make money and are very respectable. But he lost the knack. He didn't drink much, which you might have thought he'd allow himself, a perk of the job. He gambled, though, which made up: the horses. Kempton, Newmarket, Sandown Park – when he could get away. He borrowed money from his wife, he was always borrowing. Until she just stopped giving and instead she spent it, bits and bobs from legacies, filling the house with flowers when really the chair-covers and curtains needed replacing, and so on and so forth. I suppose he hated that.'

'And the brewery really didn't pay?'

'In another person's hands maybe it would have. Who can say?'

'Why didn't he sell it? Cut his losses?'

'Oh, he had pride too. It's most people's undoing, one way or another. They're too proud, of what they *ought* to be.'

'He stayed on here?'

'In a manner of speaking.'

'How?'

'He was two men. Or he was more than two men maybe. Here – he was the browbeaten brewer, and as suspicious of his wife as she was of him. But when he went somewhere else he could – he could invent himself again. And if he told people he was a brewer, he was a successful one and he either hadn't a wife or he did – in which case they were very happily married, blissfully happy.'

'They were both to blame? Do you think?'

'She'd cared for him once, I'm sure. But he turned out not to be the man she'd married. It happens. And *he* came to think he was trapped, and he had to make himself believe all

44

the more that it *was* a trap and she – she was the hunter. And anyway . . .'

' "And anyway"?' I prompted him.

And he went on to explain (so I understood it) how he had countered humiliation of the social kind with the sexual.

'With his lady friends. Women friends, rather. He wasn't going to run the risk of hoity-toity manners, I suppose: and there wasn't much chance of it there.'

' "There"?'

'In Bournemouth. Weymouth too, I think. And Lyme Regis.'

Like in Thomas Hardy's stories, I said: you went to the seaside resorts to find sin and freedom – or the illusion of them.

'Oh, it was real enough, I dare say.'

'And Mrs Antrobus – she put up with it? She didn't stop it?'

'The stopping was done *for* her, soon enough.'

'How?'

'He died in Bournemouth. A coronary attack. In unfortunate circumstances.'

'With one of his woman friends?'

'It was worse, I believe. With two. Between them they got him out of the house and dropped him on a street corner, but people saw and it all came out. In the end. Only *we* weren't supposed to know anything about it. But they used to light torches on hillsides in these parts, the news spread as quickly as that.'

'What about his wife?'

'She went from one extreme to the other. And back again. The wake was almost jolly – except for young Vivien. His wife – *widow* now – she talked about him. I suppose she had to, with the brewery still on her hands – and you could refer to him in those days and she didn't clam up and she didn't get teary-eyed at all. I mean, you didn't speak about Bournemouth, or his end, or even his usual way of behaving, just about the good he'd done with his gifts. And several times after that I saw his photograph in a nice silver frame on the mantelpiece. Then – when she had to get rid of the brewery, and the money in 'twenty-nine was nothing – that all changed. The photograph disappeared, and she didn't talk about him any more: if *you* did, she just closed up and her mouth shrank, and that was the feeling – a shrinking sensation – you got it in your stomach, that you'd say the wrong thing, the very worst, and that speaking to her at all was like crossing a minefield.'

'And her daughter?' I asked.

'It was the same. If you said, if something slipped out, you felt she was staring you into the wall. It made it difficult to have a conversation, so people stopped looking for opportunities. I don't suppose they meant to cut her, Adeline, although it must have seemed like that. So probably *we* made it happen, mother and daughter becoming so close.'

'Were they?'

'Maybe not naturally. We forced them to be, though. They relied on one another, and they had the bane of that silence about the man who'd died. Because he hadn't been a proper husband and father after all. Maybe we made them look to find reasons to belong to each other, I don't know.'

'But that's what you must think, isn't it?'

'We gave *her*, Vivien, her excuse – perhaps. That's all I think, really.'

'What excuse?'

'To have to protect her mother. And everything was sort of channelled into the relationship when it hadn't been before. Well, not like that. Worrying about the state of the house, for instance, because Adeline Bennett had always been house-proud, even though she had maids for the job. Or she'd *had* maids for the job.'

'And now her daughter has a maid,' I said. 'And a daily.'

'It was awkward for them. And maybe she has inherited her character half-and-half from her mother *and* her father. It might not have happened in the natural way of things, she and her mother might have had a – cooler relationship. But that's a hypothesis, which isn't how the world's business is attended to, is it?'

Botterel stopped for breath. Possibly he believed he had spoken enough about the Antrobuses, as much as propriety would allow him.

'What happened to the brewery?' I asked him, before the topic could be changed.

'It was sold. Did I say that?'

'Yes, you did. But it was sold at the wrong time, was it?'

'I think *any* time would have been the wrong time probably. The firm that bought it got into difficulties later, and *they* really ran the place down. It's just used for storage now. It's becoming a bit of an eyesore.'

'Could things pick up?'

His shoulders lifted and fell.

'Maybe. Or maybe not. I can't believe it'll be how it *used* to be.'

'No?'

'Well, that's just my feeling. Things don't work backwards, not in a positive way, I mean. Looking back is how you justify yourself, or commiserate. I don't feel the brewery will recover, not in my bones. It looks as if it belongs to another age now anyway. It's just what happens, and I think it's going to be passed by. Because there isn't the will perhaps. And Laud Street's not really the place for it. John Antrobus's memory will be like a ghost. Because *he* couldn't make it work and pay for itself.'

'Because he didn't *want* to. Did he?'

'This town is heavy with the past.' (It had been Botterel who first explained to me, in the very same words.) 'You can't avoid it.'

'You said, "looking back" —'

'I know. But the buildings – the stones – *they* hold it.'

He didn't finish, but I guessed what he meant: that the people of the town and the country surrounding it were intrinsically apathetic and incurious, most of them had a sort of leaden indifference to what lay on either side of today and beyond their ken, how it was that the events of their own lives fitted into the oppressive continuum of history in those parts. Which isn't to say that they couldn't be mercenary: but in the majority of cases that instinct faltered, confronted by the dwarfing totality of centuries and lives lived out before theirs.

That perspective induced a form of complacency perhaps, a trust in the tradition of centuries that precluded comprehension. '*Déjà vu*' and premonition were aspects of the local mentality, reaching back generations into the lives of the ancestors. All of which might have caused a certain streak of recklessness in people's behaviour, but it seemed to do the opposite: they gave themselves up, haphazardly, to faith in coincidence, to procrastination – what would happen *would* happen – and to the inevitability of time's passing.

Not all thoughts of ambition and self-aggrandisement were driven out, not by any means. But it was as if in the local character there was a fatal, mesmerising attractiveness about submitting yourself – at the first indication that a hope would be thwarted – to the dictates of the other, superior will. Guilt generally kept a low profile roundabout, and drew as little attention to itself as it could. The might-have-been was left where it belonged, in the dim and distant far-away-and-long-ago.

'And that is really all I know about *that*. For what,' Botterel concluded (cryptically?), 'you think the information may be worth to you.'

*

The rest of the town had watched the 'romance' of the young doctor and the Antrobus daughter with as much curiosity as it wanted to give the couple. *He* was an un-known, and the girl's mother had become quite superior, as if she only put up with the place on sufferance. No one was matchmaking, except Vivien Antrobus, which was enough: and possibly Davies himself, with the involuntariness of a moth to the flame, or the rabbit unto the serpent. The wisest knew he wouldn't be able to help himself, that he'd be snared, limed.

Apparently, Mrs Botterel told me, there were others before Dr Davies. A young man who was supposed to come into money but didn't because it was tied up in rubber plantations and the place went up in flames or something, or melted, and he never recovered from the desertion and became a curate in some out-of-the-way parish in the back of beyond, Hereford-shire, although it *was* said he was touched, the way of her own mother, and the religious business was only a disguise for something much worse. And there was supposed to have been a brother of one of her schoolfriends, but he went cold when he realised the financial situation and made some other splendid match, which must have dumped young Miss Antrobus no end, just as if she'd been bilked.

48

And so it came to pass. . . .

A peal of Abbey bells, handfuls of flung rice for luck, curious detonations from the organ (it was discovered afterwards that inflated prophylactics had been introduced into the mechanism's workings, by person or persons unknown). The bride forgot to thank Canon Vintrey and walked straight past the Marsh Street urchins with their outstretched hands, but it must have been difficult to remember everything.

Her schoolfriends of yore came to the reception in the garden of the brewery house, and evidently some of them had looked a little sniffy about the arrangements, as friends are not meant to do: the new Mrs Davies couldn't have expected that her wedding feast would be the occasion for the gleaning of her true friends from the fair-weather sort. An aunt and uncle of the groom attended, out of respect to his late parents; they said little, in their mousey Devon voices, and clung (metaphorically) to the canvas walls of the marquee, and looked lost, like babes led into the wood, and both took refuge in cups of hot sweet tea. A Davies cousin in a mustard waistcoat, of a cut the doctor later took to wearing, spoke at fortissimo pitch about the hunting round about his home town, Bath, but he was the exception among Vivien Davies's new relations-in-law: it was thought he must have a close connection with the dead great-aunts, who had been Davies's salvation in life. Mrs Antrobus was back in her element, for that one day, and the brewery lowering in the background might have been just an accident, a kind of dream, a dream you feel happy to wake from.

'Well,' Mrs Botterel concluded, 'Vivien *did* find herself a husband at last, but he wasn't *properly* "her own" kind, not *quite*, was he? Almost, but ... Mr Davies – *Doctor* Davies – he's a figure in the community of course, and he has means, which was all to the point. But, beyond that, no one *really* knows, and I don't suppose his wife is quite sure, either. I can't decide about them: they hold back as much of themselves as they ever give, that's how *I* see it. Sometimes you feel everything else is quite incidental to them except themselves, and its's all a bit of a – a "chimera", is it? I think they're quite wrapped up in themselves. I don't mean – well, I doubt if it's

49

"love": so it must be something else. But what it is, I don't know. Can *you* guess what?'

*

The Davies' were photographed once in a newspaper. They were attending a Tory junket in Taunton, and the newspaper of the district featured the event on its society page. I noticed the surname first – mentioned among five or six others printed beneath one of the photographs – then I switched my attention to the faces.

Davies in dinner-jacket was standing, predictably full-square, with his weight evenly distributed on each leg, his hands and cuffs by his sides. His lips were slightly apart, as if he were preparing to speak. His wife stood beside him, in an evening gown, one bare, braceleted arm by her side and her other arm placed across her stomach with the hand holding the forearm that hung down straight. She wasn't looking at the camera but at the activity in the room behind it. Her mouth was closed, shaped into the enigmatic semblance of a smile.

I cut the photograph out of the newspaper and pinned it up above my desk, alongside the reposeful nudes of antiquity. The room and the town would eventually fall silent (more or less) about me as I sat at the window contemplating those stilted stances. It seemed to me that the later I stayed up to stare at the wall, the sharper my hearing became: till I could pick up the merest sound, even the shifting and falling of dust between the layers of stone that kept the building standing around me.

*

I cut an item of news out of another newspaper. It was lost to me for a long time, but I tracked it down a few years ago.

After sharing the same house with her father for forty-one years, since her birth, a woman beat her father to death with a red-hot poker from the fire.

The event took place in North Cambridge. The father was a highly respected classics don, eminent in the field of the New Sophistic rhetoricians. His daughter had been his amanuensis for as long as anyone could remember, and acted as his hostess on the occasions when other dons were entertained at the house.

The two of them had lived in an atmosphere of sedate refinement, disciplined routine, erudite causerie.

The years had passed, each as exactly similar to the others as possible, only allowing for the encroachments of old age and middle age respectively.

But there was the rub for the daughter: a man like her father became more 'distinguished' with age and was held in still greater respect, while she (she surely had the intelligence to real-ise) found herself more and more the victim of other people's pity, because of what she was assumed to have 'sacrificed'.

Self-sacrifice is the means by which certain (frequently in-telligent) persons justify and demonstrate a fundamental failure of nerve. This degree of self-awareness only provokes those same victims to feel *more* bitter: they will believe their fears and self-doubts to have been present in them from birth, inherited from a parent who showed no evidence of such weakness of character.

The mental torture is a slow death. The murder of the other is more than simple revenge: it most emphatically levels the equation.

The effect is, as it were, denying itself by returning to eliminate the cause.

*

The heat all that long summer was persistent, consistent. Day after day after day of temperatures that reached the upper eighties. The skies darkened now and then, and a little rain might fall, but mostly the clouds were harmless, high and thin like carded fleece, and hardly moving in an afternoon.

Sometimes it seemed to take too much effort to try to think straight, and the temptation then was not to think at all, simply to let your mind slip its moorings altogether... You coasted by, with as little application of any kind – mental or physical – as you could get away with. By the end of the working-day your limbs felt leaden, all you wanted was the little energy left to find shade. Your head became too heavy for your neck, and felt like a wooden bowling-jack.

Gardens dried, flowers wilted, and the evenings were filled with the clatter of tin watering-cans. Everyone had a constant thirst. Jugs of cooling water were left to stand in water in deep wash-sinks; children gathered round pumps in the streets and splashed themselves; I regularly saw two middle-aged twin-sisters in pebble glasses and florid print frocks come out of The Yel Tap carrying between them a watering-can filled to the brim with frothy farmhouse cider, a concoction you had to drink with closed teeth, otherwise you swallowed the apple pips and the detritus of the cores – a mind-numbing beverage that had been known to cause, in several instances down the years, brain seizures and irredeemable, first degree paralysis of limbs and the internal organs.

*

Fourteen months after the wedding, a loose stair-rod had sent Mrs Antrobus tumbling down the staircase in the brewery house.

Her son-in-law had provided the new carpet to replace the threadbare runner that had been there for decades. The fitter had suggested brass stair-rods to complement the fine quality of the carpet, and so it was that the fatal train of events was auspicated.

It didn't prove fatal until the sixth week of Mrs Antrobus's confinement in hospital, a private nursing-home in Taunton, afforded by her daughter's husband. The end was quite sudden, and came without additional pain to the patient.

Her daughter wasn't present on the fateful, fatal afternoon in question. Dr Davies drove her over to the hospital in the evening. Apparently her demeanour was solemn, deadly serious, but she also seemed quite detached as she attended to the formal details.

The funeral service was held in Ivell Abbas, in the Abbey, on a day of lashing rain. The aisles smelt of moth-balls and sodden wool and crape. Canon Vintrey spoke of God's mercy, the word 'salvation' was repeated several times. Mrs Davies fixed her gaze on one of the windows and – those who saw her discussed the point later – she might have been hypnotised. The guttering leads were running with water, the gargoyles peering and leering from the roof spouted the over-flow from their mouths, and there were moments when the softly spoken, intermittently smiling Canon Vintrey could hardly be heard. His smiles were a mite more restrained and seemly that day, but he was in his element, with a large, respectful congregation in black spread beneath him, and no restless, rustling, slithering children to distract from the beauty of his heavenly images. All the time Mrs Davies alternately sat or stood with her eyes trained on the high window opposite her, and throughout the service her husband would turn on her the same look, which everyone knew to be one of utter helplessness.

At the graveside Mrs Davies kept herself to herself; an umbrella was held over her head but she seemed oblivious to everything as she pulled at the fingers of her gloves and looked down, tearless, at the wet grass. People were remembering her on the morning of her father's funeral, when she'd seemed so hostile in her sorrow; then she'd stood with her arm linked through her mother's (although no one had believed a very deep bond existed between the two to date) and she'd most curtly, with a teenage girl's defensive pride, shaken mourners' hands at the end while avoiding their eyes and words. At her mother's funeral she seemed again not to be attending as she held out her hand and the mourners, beneath their umbrellas, filed in front of her: the faces were the same ones as on the previous occasion, but she wasn't noticing. Her coat and hat and handbag were new, some of the women observed, and possibly the shoes too; they were able to remember the days not so long ago when she used to go about the town kitted out in some of her mother's glad-rags, as if it must be her fate to always live – as some seem chosen to do – in her mother's shadow.

The headstone which appeared in the weeks afterwards was a more elaborate edifice than the usual. It was sculpted in marbly imitation of an unfurled scroll: 'wife of' and the deceased's husband's name were engraved in smaller letters, and it was noted that there were no familiar words of comfort from the Bible or the Book of Common Prayer. The starkness of the wording caused quite a deal of comment. For two or three months flowers were regularly placed in a granite crock: out-of-season forcing-house chrysanthemums and roses instead of the common-or-garden daffodils and narcissi. Then, as the summer months progressed, no more flowers appeared: the same spray of dahlias withered, and the spot was clearly unattended, like the dead woman's husband's grave. Mrs Davies no longer paid any of her brief, businesslike visits of an afternoon to the hillside, to empty and refill the water in the stonemason's urn. She wasn't seen in that graveyard ever again.

53

She *did* make an appearance at another graveside in the town – I witnessed the occasion for myself – in the spring of the year after the next: but it was at the opposite end of the town, by the walls of the Castle Church of Saint Jerome, in circumstances much more under her own purchase and heft.

*

I wasn't seeing her always in the *same* company, her husband's apart, which may have made it easier for her to exchange enthusiasms as effortlessly as she did.

Maybe none of the details are very vital ones. Her favourite colour was sapphire the first evening, but emerald on the second. Her favourite composer was Rachmaninov, but later she announced with great assurance that she couldn't be having anything to do with the Romantics and Bach was whom she liked listening to best. One evening she enthused about capons, on the next occasion she said she thought she must be one of those cranky new vegetarian types because she couldn't bear to eat anything that had had a life in a farmyard. (Prospective hostesses concentrated on the information, eyes narrowing, seeming to remember that they'd heard she liked veal, or was it venison...) She took a teaspoonful of salt on her plate on the first evening and on the second waved it away, saying she never did. She explained why she preferred Toledo to Seville, and another time I overheard her say it was a dream of hers to go to Spain. (Davies appeared not to remember anything that had been said previously: his face registered no surprise, only – at best – polite, affable, mild interest.) She wore her hair up, she wore it down. One Sunday lunchtime, at the Botterels', she refused a cigarette with a laugh and a vigorous head-shake, but in different company (minus the Botterels) on a subsequent evening – my last such meeting with them – she calmly accepted a cigarette from my silver case and leaned forward for a flame as intimately as she might have done for a confidence.

I do recall one habit that was unvarying. When the pudding or fruit plates had been taken away and the crumbs cleared, she would perch her elbows on the edge of the table-top, straighten her arms, and place her chin on the back of one or other of her clasped hands, and listen to the others' talk with her eyes trained on the silver or the glasses, smiling at the voices. She was retreating from us. Her breasts beneath the material of her dress dropped to within a few inches of the table's waxed wood.

She might have been thinking anything then. Every time I waited for the moment of her deep silence to come, when her breasts would drop. My eyes were keen and peeled even when someone was talking to me: I sat waiting and watching. However many contrasts and contradictions she'd offer in the course of a meal, I knew when the crumbs were cleared away and she set her funny-bones on the table-top that this was truly the one and the same Mrs Davies.

*

The brewery hadn't officially been closed, but work there had been suspended for the past three or four years. The high wooden gates on Laud Street were chained and padlocked, but I could see through the crack between them and the pillars.

Already the yard was seeded with grass. Tiles had fallen off the roofs and birds flew in and out of the attics. At night, walking past, the effect was ghostly. A hoist arm stuck out of a wall like a gallows' jib. The main building was vast, proportionless, as high as an ocean liner. The wind rattled the loose panes in the windows and disturbed the roof-leading; a weathercock spun round and round, if the wind was strong enough, and some piece of idle machinery inside the building would turn, groaning and clanking and setting my teeth and nerves on edge. By moonlight it was a spooky and unnerving sight.

*

That may not have much to do with anything. But, in my mind at least, how I *felt* did add *some*thing to those associations I inevitably made between the brewery yard (the brewery house on Laud Lane was similarly out of bounds and hidden from my view by a high wall) and the former Miss Antrobus.

It was hard not to believe that *she* also had a haunted quality. Her past life was outmoded, already antique, and she was attempting – against the full knowledge of the town – to re-work herself in the terms of her new life.

So my evening perambulations may not have been wholly

beside the point. They prepared me for what was to come inasmuch as they unsettled me, they had me viewing the obvious from a wary, tangential standpoint. Of course that couldn't make matters very much easier in a town like Ivell Abbas where, among the professional class, appearances were indeed of the essence.

*

I remember those Laud Street evenings as if they were a regular element in my life. They weren't, though. I don't suppose I paid more than six visits to the house *in toto*.

I guessed I was invited because I was closer to their own ages than those they entertained. *They* were being indulged, I came to see, because they were of some so-called 'importance' in the town, they had cachet and also some influence, and it paid – at the cost in money and time of seven or eight servings of dinner – to be on the right side of them.

I could offer my hosts nothing like that. But I did have my legal career ahead of me, however it might turn out; I presumed they were both of the opinion that I was an investment of their time, as someone else who might prove a useful acquaintance in their future.

*

I don't think Davies would have appealed to me as a friend in the normal run of events. (Living in Ivell Abbas was an aberration from normality, I see that now.)

Our instincts guide us to friendship. Do we feel natural with a person, do we share interests and hold our convictions in common, do we have an equivalent 'eye' on the world? Can one feel natural with a person who himself appears *not* to be natural, who seems to assume that such a friendship – although untried and untested – exists?

Davies appeared to be a certain sort of person, in the externals and by virtue of his profession. He supported the political status quo and was unfailingly conservative in the other opinions he admitted to having. It was my surmise that he had become a doctor less for idealistic reasons than to assist his own rise in the world. If so, he was no different from many others of his calling in that respect. What I felt distinguished him was his essential seriousness and the man's privacy, his introversion, which couldn't fool me with its sociable ha-ha's, those camouflaged digs to my ribs when he joked across the table that, for *one* of us at least, it seemed to be well past our bedtime, or was this too much like having to sit up late with the adults?

Whatever was taking place on the surface of the moment, he was always busy beneath, reading it in a different way. What he *meant* for us was what appeared on his face, which told a different story: *many* stories. *I'm intent, I'm sympathising, I'm amused, I'm being ironic, I'm listening to you very hard, I'm actually disbelieving you but I'm also being a polite host, I have a doctor's reserves of discretion, I enjoy filling this house with such august and responsive (please note, Pendlebury) guests as my attention flatters you that you are.*

He was quick-thinking and was seldom surprised in conversation, he would keep one step ahead, and often it was as a means of showing his own cleverness, which perhaps he didn't realise – although he might have done if he had happened to glance at his wife at precisely the moments I did, when a terrible impatience seemed to deep-freeze her eyes and her mouth and I could see the pressure of one hand on the other leaving white marks on the skin as not a single muscle in her body flexed.

I am a responsible man, judge this book by its cover, how could I refuse friendship, how could you? I might see him looking at me and the golf-clubhouse smile would be lost until a second or two too late, because the mechanism working beneath the obvious was on overtime, stretched to capacity, all mental resources concentrating on this singular subject of William Pendlebury, myself.

*

'We should have a round some time.'

'I'm sorry?'

'On the greens. The golf course.'

I had to explain I didn't play.

'Then we'll have to teach you, won't we?'

I made a very feeble joke out of it: who knew if *I* was capable of being taught anything?

'What's that?'

'Who knows if I'd be worth teaching?'

57

'Splendid game,' he said. 'Gets you out in the fresh air. Empties your mind.'

I asked him if he played with others, or by himself.

'Oh, I can play by myself,' he said. 'Often do. Good discipline. Try to beat your own best, no cheating.'

I attempted to look approving.

'I go when I can,' he said. 'When I'm not working.'

His accent was more clipped than usual and there was no hint of the country burr, he was getting into an easy stride. No one could demur that today he wasn't as he appeared to be.

'Wish Vivien would take it up.'

His wife smiled, tolerantly. She must have heard the remark dozens of times.

'Chasing a ball over grass with a little stick?'

It didn't seem to be the reply she'd made dozens of times previously, because Davies's face – unprepared for once – showed his puzzlement and, in the next instant, irritation.

'Not "a little stick", dear.' He squeezed out a smile. 'Hardly that.' His lips thinned, till they were like a scholar's.

'No?' She shrugged. Her own mouth, with those ominously full lips, was equally determined not to smile.

'Damned great bag to lug around,' Davies said. 'It'd be easy if it was just "a little stick".'

'You could get yourself a caddy.'

Momentary pause.

'Well, of course that's why I'm trying to get Pendlebury interested, isn't it?'

His, and my own, stilted laughter. But then the subject is let go of, like a stinging nettle.

*

When I went for a walk and took the lane past the old brewery, which came out on the Conduit, I was directly behind the houses on Laud Street.

They all had long gardens, running down to vegetable plots and high stone walls. Some of the walls were inset with railings. It wasn't railings but two padlocked wrought-iron gates which allowed you to see into the Davies' garden.

At one time cars and carriages must have driven in that way, but the track behind the gates was now grassed over. In common with the other gardens, there were strips of

58

vegetable beds and several rows of stakes supporting sweet peas and hollyhocks. A low wall separated the bottom part from the first of the two lawns. Beyond the elevated top lawn you could see another wall, clad with floribunda roses, and just visible through a stone arch was the paved area with the house on three sides of it. It was there, in the enclosed inner sanctum like an atrium, that the fountain dribbled into the pond.

The bottom section of the garden, at the lowest level, was also where the household's washing was pegged out on lines. Perhaps the trees that flanked either side of the rusty gates had had fuller branches at one time and had kept the washing fully hidden. Now it was possible to see the contents of the lines. It may only have been coincidence that Mrs Davies' underwear was invariably placed furthest from the view of the house and closest to the spot where anyone walking along the lane might – theoretically – have cast eyes on the items, if so inclined.

I looked in, on windy days and still when they either flapped wildly, turning somersaults, or hung loose and slack from the pegs. Everything was put out to dry, by whoever organised the business: underskirts, knickers, brassières, girdles, stockings, suspender belts. They were in several shades, flesh pink, rose pinks (Coral Satin and Albertine), ivory, cream, glaring snow-white.

On my wash-day walks, which had to take place in the interval I was allowed for lunch, I would find some pretext for stopping outside the Davies' gates – a pebble in my shoe, or shoes, or loose laces – and I would perch on one leg, looking in. The washing was usually attended to twice in a week, sometimes three times, and was hung out in the morning; I chose to time my passing for no later than one o'clock, at the outside. The underwear would still be obligingly displayed, either slapping blithely in a breeze or becalmed and pendant. I coundn't decide which sort of day I preferred, there were advantages in both: when a wind blew there seemed to be life in the various garments, and when they were quite inert I could concentrate better on their colour and shape and function.

On a couple of occasions I spotted the Davies' maid-of-all-work making her way down from the house with a wicker washing-basket of linen and other assorted items cradled in her arms: only once, I think, did *she* see me.

I can't say why I was so drawn, but maybe I don't need to be apologetic. I was young, a bachelor, and (I thought) free; there was something very pleasantly clandestine about coming so close, literally, to the objects of my fascination. Also, I should admit, there was an added frisson: my uncertainty *why* Mrs Davies's underwear should so consistently be pegged out on that further line of the two, where no one looking from the house would be able to see but where a passer-by on the lane *could*. Surely the washing's being a potential social embarrassment, provocation even, must have occurred to the maid? – or am I bringing my own inherited Puritanism to bear on the matter? The one time I was noticed was when the maid appeared from behind the tree, unpegging some articles, and chancing – was it? – to look over her shoulder at precisely *that* moment: she must have been afflicted with deafness if she didn't hear the breath catching in my throat.

Whenever I saw Mrs Davies in social circumstances, even just making her way down Pack Street, I found it difficult not to make a mental connection with what I couldn't – now – see but which I *did* view hanging from the lines on washing-days.

It didn't matter what she was wearing on top: I saw right through that, a dress or costume in some fashion I couldn't put a name to, and I was imagining instead the swish and sheen of the underskirt-slip, the controlling tightness of the girdle, the dependable tension of the suspenders, the uplifting support of the brassière.

No other woman in the town carried herself quite as Mrs Davies did; she held her back very straight, certainly, but she also walked languidly, with – at the same time – a sensual over-emphasis on each of the movements, so that feet, ankles, calves, knees, thighs, hips, buttocks, torso, arms, breasts, wrists all seemed to function by a strict harmony of rotation, multiple manoeuvres meticulously subdividing what appeared in other people to be the simple taking of steps from a point A to a point B. Her hips rolled – that was especially noticeable – but all the other movements, within split-seconds of one another, contributed equally to that effect.

Watching her, I was reminded of those photographic diagrams where some straightforward (one had imagined) human activity is catalogued frame by frame, split into a sequence of progressive sub-actions: a naked man doing nothing more extraordinary than climbing stairs, up and then down again, or making a running jump.

*

In the house on Laud Street, of course, I was closer, viewing her across the dining-table. (Always across it, from the opposite side, where I was bid to sit: so that I had both a fuller but more distant compass than anyone else.)

I watched and I listened, and a few times I was able to catch a glimpse of a thin satiny or lacy strap, just the frill or edge showing, and the faintly ribbed outline of some underlying structure beneath whatever she was wearing in honour of her guests.

It didn't occur to me, not until much later when I lived somewhere else, that perhaps I was only giving myself away, that the thoughts might have been written on my face, or in balloons above my head, no matter that I congratulated myself on being so discreet. I was inexperienced and naïve and green, in that town that was half as old as the hills.

But 'later' I couldn't do anything to excuse myself: if her husband had noticed it would merely have confirmed his distrust of me, but how could such a discontented man *not* have noticed? – while all the time I was considering myself much too smart, much too shrewd for Ivell Abbas.

*

There's the story of the man who ached after his best friend's wife, but who was too righteous – or afraid, and maybe ashamed – to declare himself to her: *she* who seemed hardly to notice *him*.

At night, though, he had his way with her, in his dreams. There she knew exactly what was what, she succumbed and surrendered, with perfect willingness and wreathed in smiles.

While, in another world, the woman continued as before, welcoming this best friend of her husband to the house, with exemplary politeness and a manner of chaste indifference.

At night the man's dreams became more exotic. Directed by shared intuition, he and his adored one fled the attentions

61

of the husband, they travelled to all manner of exquisite places – the Alhambra, Fez, Fiji, the Caribbean coast of Colombia, Zanzibar, Bali.

While, in another world, the woman continued as before, making this best friend of her husband welcome to the house, with more of her exemplary politeness and that nunnish nonchalance. Until one evening, casually and in the general conversation, she mentioned the name of a secret valley they'd chanced to discover in his dreams of Bali, where – when she clapped her hands – the hillsides shivered and shook and thousands upon thousands of butterflies took hovering to the air.

*

The fourth or fifth evening I was at the house, when we were taking our leave, I had returned to the sitting-room to find my cigarette case.

I heard the rustle of a dress behind me and turned round. She stood holding out the case.

'You found it?' I said. 'Excellent.'

'You'll have to be more careful, Mr Pendlebury.'

'Yes. Yes, I will.'

I took it from her. The silver felt warm, as if it had been held in a hand or against the skin for some time.

I must have been staring at a photograph.

'Guess who?' she said, picking up the silver frame.

It had been taken at her wedding. The shot included her and several of the guests, standing in social poses inside the tarpaulin marquee.

I wished I could have the privacy to examine the details, to tilt the image this way, that way. I muttered something to her, polite and appropriate.

'No, look again,' she told me.

I duly looked again.

'It's the bride's day,' she said.

She took the photograph from me and lifted it to the light from the window. She pointed to herself. I looked closer.

The others, I noticed, were watching her. She stood in front of a table laid with a white cloth and covered with the breakfast food. She was holding out her arm.

'See?'

I bent forward. A butterfly had settled on the sleeve of her wedding gown, on the long buttoned cuff.

'It flew in from the garden.'

Now it was she who was peering more closely.

'I just looked down and there it was.'

What is her point in telling me, I was wondering.

'It made me think of the marriage at Cana,' she said. 'And the miracle. The water and the wine.'

I nodded, but I didn't really comprehend.

Afterwards — weeks later — it occurred to me that the important word might have been 'miracle': perhaps that was why she had entered into the marriage, in the hope of achieving her own miracle — the amelioration of her lot.

That still left one question open and unanswered. Why had she chosen to tell me, or at least suggest such a possibility to me? Did she want her marriage to be verified, to become 'real' in some particular way, which no one else was willing to do or was quite equipped to do?

And why — I asked myself — why should that task have been settled on *me*?

I stood smiling. I turned over the cigarette case in my hands.

She replaced the photograph frame on the side table.

Tonight she had been at her most elegant and her most elusive. Every so often a sultry expression would pass across her face, a *wanting* look that would seem in those seconds to be the clue to her, holding her features in a unity, something to do with the intensity of that expression. And then it would fade, submerge, as she remembered to do her social duty by us all.

*

I dreamed in my sleep that she confused me for her husband.

I was passing the house one midnight and she called out, 'Frank!' The interior was in darkness and I can't say what drew me in, other than the obscure rationale of a dream.

I closed the door and she took my arm. I followed her upstairs, like a blind man, to the bedroom at the back. She ran her hands over my face before she kissed me.

She left me and I heard her freeing herself from her clothes, letting them lie on the floor.

She walked across the room, contours stippled by moon-light, and always so that shadows fell on particular spots.

'Let's not talk,' she whispered.

She pulled back the top sheet on the bed and slipped beneath. She lay back on the pillow. She lifted her hands to her hair and her fingers began to pull out the combs. The hair winnowed about her face against the white of the pillowcase. A vision of her mother passed in a moment. The moonlight through the window, through the wistaria, showed me she was smiling. She had her eyes closed. The fingers of one hand rested on her throat.

Her eyes stayed closed.

Still watching I raised my foot from the floor and fumbled with my shoelace to unknot it. One shoe, and then the other.

*

'What do you think of her?' Lettice Botterel asked me.

'Of who?'

'Mrs Davies.'

'Ah.'

I was as evasive as I could be in the reply I gave.

'And you?' I asked her.

'Oh. I think she's – unique.'

'"Unique"?'

'Well, isn't she?'

The question had returned to me.

'Yes. Possibly.'

'We agree on that,' she said.

'And – and what else is she, do you think?'

'I think *she's* the one to know that. If she can —'

'I don't – quite follow you —'

'Does she understand her influence? *I* see it, though.'

'What "influence"?'

'She could turn this town upside down on its head, if she wanted to.'

'Yes?'

'Oh yes, she *could*.'

'How'd she do it, then?'

'I can't say, "how".'

'*Why*, then?'

'She doesn't *believe*, does she?'

'"Believe"?' I fished.

'"Accept" it, then. She's a sceptic.'

'There must be others – just like that —'

'They hide it. Under stones. Or in dark rooms. At the backs of cupboards.'

'If she did that – I mean, turned the town upside down —'

'Then – the town would right itself again,' she said. 'And it would turn *her* – into a sort of legend.'

'A *"legend"*?'

'A myth.'

'Would it?'

'Don't sound so impressed. You don't understand —'

'No, maybe I don't.'

'She wouldn't stand a chance then. It would be like being – being possessed by people's memories. Of course you can get up – *one* can get up – and go. Leave the town. That's the theory.'

'Leave it?'

'Or do you think she'll pass her years here? Her three score and ten?'

'I don't know. Maybe she will.'

'No. No, she won't.'

'You seem very sure —'

'It's just a matter of *how* she goes. If people will remember.'

'And will they? Remember her?'

'Oh, yes. Only too well. So she can't win, you see.'

'She can't?'

'She thinks she has a choice.'

'Maybe she does have —'

'A choice?' Lettice shook her head. 'Nobody really has a choice. You must have guessed?'

I didn't reply. *You* have no choice left to you, it occurred to me, not about that schoolgirl's snub nose, and too much space between that and your mouth, and a top lip that's too thin. You wouldn't be talking like this if you did, Lettice Botterel.

'It's all been worked out for us long before,' she said. 'In the past. What it's made us to be.'

'You mean – predestination?'

'Sort of.'

'That's pretty hopeless,' I said. 'Then your life's a closed circle, surely?'

'Yes. Something like that.'

'But can't you break it?'

'If you're made that way. In which case you're only made that way anyway. That's the catch: or the logic of it.'

She smiled.

'You can imagine choices,' she said, 'where there aren't any. And *not* see what's only obvious and intended and *meant* for you, when it's right there in front of your eyes.'

Maybe, I thought, maybe you're only talking religion, in another guise.

'I – I'll have to consider it,' I told her, trying to make light of the moment.

She crossed her arms. She smiled directly at me. I had a momentary sensation of *déjà vu*, a twice-told tale, of Davies's wife standing in the sitting-room in Laud Street, turning a smile directly on to me, after she'd taken back the wedding photograph: as if she were daring me to some action. Then Lettice moved, back into the sunlight from behind me, and the features of her face became clear again.

She had made her choice, hadn't she, with her spouse-in-waiting, Charles Allingham? If she was warning me, 'Vivien Davies has made her choice too, her husband, whatever you think about a handful of words spoken at an altar,' I wasn't going to hold that against her.

I collected something like gravity back into my face. So far as I could be, I wanted to let her see I was *grateful* at least, because she'd had the courage and concern to say to me (at her father's instigation?) what no other person in the town had or would have done.

*

The stillness of those days! Heady like wine.

But in the background, turned down low, the crystal wirelesses were crackling: tunes – American melodies, the 'Swing Time' songs, 'Body and Soul', 'The Continental' from 'The Gay Divorcee', 'It Ain't Necessarily So' – and also the stories of Europe's troubled season in the sun and, if we'd heeded the signs properly, the first rumours of a gathering war.

*

I heard a story about Mrs Antrobus.

Apparently two of her brothers and a favourite uncle were killed in the First War, within seven weeks of one another. Back in Devon she attended three memorial services in close succession. At the third she had something like a brainstorm: she swept a pile of prayer books from a table-top and sent a vase of summer flowers flying. The incident was all the more alarming to the congregation because she wasn't sobbing but looking much like her usual everyday self. She marched out of the church as the organist struggled to play a voluntary, and never in all the years after that set foot inside the building again: not even to view the brass plate that was screwed up on the wall beneath the Flanders window, where a stained-glass infantryman knelt on impossibly green grass, covering his face with his sleeve.

*

They say that those who betray their country, the spies and the fifth columnists, are infected with a terrible boredom, a desperate sense of 'ennui'. It may be that that grows out of just such disillusion and faithlessness as the kind that afflicted the brewer's wife.

Her daughter, I also heard, found it preferable for a while to spend holidays with her schoolfriends, in their parents' homes. Perhaps those seemed genteel havens of tranquillity compared with her own, in the sort of country where 'our sort', persons of a certain station, still passed their time hunting and playing mah-jong and stabbing threaded needles into canvas. I imagined her sitting in panelled rooms scented with the slightly bitter aroma of garden pot-pourri, listening to the slow ticking of a clock and the footsteps of maids, or the snick-snick of a gardener's boy's secateurs, while the rest of the world occupied itself somewhere else, over the hills and far away. In her friends' homes life was still conducted at the pace of the old ways, in the old days. But maybe the gaps between one beat of the clock and the next as the pendulum trailed precipitated a variation on her mother's imbalance, an upset in her own equilibrium, an unevening of the precious keel, a dizzying sensation that she was falling into those deep holes between the seconds.

Perhaps. There was also the consciousness surely that this

67

quiet life was being superseded by other events in the land and by the knowledge that she had a 'home' from which her visits elsewhere were only in the way of interruptions or deflections: diversions from responsibility, from a worse loneliness, from dependence and the facts of the brewery's financial plight. Life in the country houses was gracious, civilised, but maybe she also knew that it was really a glorious confidence trick: only luck had determined that a father or brother or uncle had survived the War, the town-men who'd fought had seen and suffered too much in other lands to think they could ever see their own in quite the same way again, the masters in London didn't know everything and the other masters in their houses and gardens were helpless to save themselves from being killed and drawing their last breath in a foreign mud bog.

I pictured the brewer's daughter starting to drift, into her middle teens, into hardly seeming to care, into the custom of thinking herself a victim. The walls of the brewery yard – seen from inside, with the great wooden gates chained and padlocked – must have seemed too high to scale in metaphor even. When her father died, maybe she concluded that she was being *acted against* and she was immersed further inside herself. Maybe she learned to extract some perverse pleasure from the constrictions of domestic life with her mother: she was enduring her suffering like a martyr, believing that it must end eventually. And all the while she was looking about her, with mounting panic, for the likelihood of an escape: failing the physical sort, her suffering unto an end had to become something else, a transcendent state where, if she couldn't *feel* any more, she would be able to disconnect and float free.

Purple prose thoughts in a young man's head. But perhaps they weren't so very wide of the mark after all.

Her earthly sufferings in her mother's house *did* release her in a manner of speaking. She was re-incarnated, several times over (it transpired), but without losing the memory of what life had been. Remembering only made her more determined in spirit never to find herself in such a situation again, where the buffetings could knock the very stuffing out of you. *She* would decide, and maybe men would be her revenge, and marriage turned to a tool, and it was to be for a specific end, for her own physical comfort and the dazed condition of scarcely having to think at all – of *being*, on a minimal level of consciousness – one with deep-pile carpets and hot water permanently on tap.

*

Then for a long while – it felt a long time – it became very noticeable to me that I was being cut by her, snubbed. She seemed to have a primed sixth sense for my presence, and if we both chanced to find ourselves on Pack Street at the same time of the day she would unfailingly cross the road in front of me, to the other side, or – if we were closer and she couldn't manage a natural enough angle – she would suddenly vanish into a shop doorway.

I had taken to attending the Abbey services regularly on Sunday mornings, and she succeeded in avoiding me there too. It seemed that she and her husband would place themselves wherever I was not. If I arrived *after* them and could choose my pew, inevitably they would finish their conversation with whomsoever they were favouring and then remove themselves to a point (almost) out of my range of vision.

For three or four weeks our paths didn't cross socially either. On Sundays I was expecting to encounter them at some of the houses where I was served – like a deserving, handless nephew – luncheon or afternoon tea. But they weren't there, and perhaps the company sensed my disappointment. I felt the spinsters across the table were observing me with steelier eyes, through slits even, and that sometimes the wives were betraying themselves with falsely demure, victorious smiles.

I didn't believe that we merely *chanced* not to meet: the town was too small for that, and I guessed already that it was like an echo-box. For a number of weeks I'd been picking up other people's suspicions on that score: a pitying look, the domino effect of nodding heads, a pithy enquiry as to the state of my health, all the eagerly selfless questions – how was I settling down? how did I amuse myself, was there enough to keep a young man occupied in Ivell Abbas? was I comfortable, which houses in the town had caught my eye? did I think of putting down roots here? The questions were like goads, little shocks of current: like pincer nips, it occurred to me, turning over the remains of crab on my plate whenever Mrs Botterel – originally from the Norfolk coast and a champion of shellfish – served them as an entrée.

'Ivell Abbas has a way of swallowing people,' Miss Midgley said – perhaps nastily.

'Refusing to let them go,' Botterel clarified, with his genial host's smile.

'It's give and take,' Mrs Reed said, vaguely majestic in the absence of her husband.

'Be careful how much it asks you to give,' Lettice Botterel warned at my side, *sotto voce*.

'What was that?' Miss Midgley asked, cupping a hand to her ear. 'I'm afraid I didn't catch that.'

'Mr Pendlebury,' Lettice Botterel enunciated, as if to the stone deaf who must read by the lips, 'is asking how long it takes to be accepted in the town.'

'You intend to stay among us for a while?' Mr Eustace enquired, leaning forward.

'You mean to settle here, Mr Pendlebury?' Mrs Wilson-Hall asked.

Suddenly a ring of faces was absurdly concerned about my intentions.

'Twenty years at least,' Miss Midgley told me – perhaps nastily. 'Outsiders have to serve their apprenticeship first.'

Lettice Botterel beside me sighed.

'Old Ivell Abbas still calls the tune,' she said.

'Oh, *certainly*,' Miss Conrad replied.

'Old Ivell Abbas exacts its dues,' Mrs Botterel opined, in an ambiguous tone of voice.

'How old is "Old"?' I asked.

Miss Midgley heard: her eyes, precision instruments, bored.

'Really *quite* old,' Mr Eustace offered, in his timid way.

'I should say, two generations at least,' Mrs Reed announced, swelling with confidence despite the absence of her husband.

'Oh, at *least*,' Miss Conrad retorted.

Lettice Botterel, sitting stoically beside the interloper, sighed again. But I didn't fully appreciate those condoling exhalations of breath. I was thinking other thoughts. How, by saying nothing, the doctor's wife – if she had been here –

would have scuppered their pious fraud, shown us it was moonshine, even though she was a fourth generation in the town and of more vintage stock than even the grand Miss Midgley.

With a single atheist's smile she would have demolished those certitudes Old Ivell Abbas prided itself on living by.

*

I used to wonder how anything could be kept a secret for long in that imagined backwater of the country.

For instance, a story did the rounds – emanating from a house called 'Wetherdene', owned by a Mrs Murgatroyd – that the doctor's wife had been spotted in Bournemouth one afternoon. She'd been walking down one of the zig-zag pedestrian ramps that lead from the level where the hotels and terraces are to the long esplanade overlooking the beach. She wasn't alone when she was seen: she'd been walking arm-in-arm with the Laud Street maid, perhaps only to steady herself on the gradient, so that her legs wouldn't run away with her.

In Ivell Abbas eyebrows were raised, in imitation of surprise.

One Sunday Dr Davies was sitting alone in the Abbey. I presumed his wife was unwell, but the next day I caught sight of her from the office window as she went about an errand, seeming not at all out of sorts.

I heard no more about her between then and the next Sunday when, again, she was absent from the congregation in the Abbey. Through the lessons I saw heads turning to look in Davies's direction, and the singing was used as an excuse to crane further forward and to mutter comments under the music. After the service Davies didn't wait to shake hands with the Canon, as he usually did; performing such minimal courtesies to the bigwigs in the congregation as were required, he walked off at a rate of knots, as if the Abbey Green was the last spot he wanted to be at that particular moment.

During the following week, as the weather warmed, I kept my eyes and ears open. Someone told me Davies had been short-tempered with some of his patients.

'Hay fever?' I suggested.

'Go and tell Davies now that you've got hay fever and he'll tell *you* it's a state of mind.'

I still went for my walks after work, and I felt the air then heavy with pollen. About seven o'clock the stone of the buildings seemed to be radiating the heat it had gathered during the day. The skies were duck's egg blue and clear, vaulting over the county and, in a sense, overpowering. I remembered when I was a child throwing my head back and trying to run, imagining all that blue waste as a great engulfing summer sea (like the bay) till I made myself dizzy and almost sick with the sensation of infinitude. That feeling came back to me, in a disturbing way, and along the lanes and backways I concentrated instead on what was closest to me: the stalks of frilly white meadowsweet that had seeded in every free corner, the hummock of grass between the wheel tracks, the laminae of green moss worked into every wall, spent matches thrown away, the discarded and outlived husks of butterfly cocoons.

I walked downhill past the railway station and on to the road that passed round the meads in a semi-circle. Long ago the verges had been planted with silver-barked plane trees spaced at an exactly even distance from each other: the effect of striped shade on the red tarmacadam road was attractively Mediterranean, Latin. I'd hitch myself over a low rusted fence into the Castle grounds and climb a steep field where horses were brought to graze. At the top was a push-stile and a panorama of more fields, with a bridle-path leading across the narrow valley, down this near side and up the far one.

I'd negotiate the stile's narrow metal gate and continue walking, on the humped track of grass between ripening cornfields. In the nook of the little valley's 'v', beneath some beech and oak trees, the path widened as it joined a farm road of trampled flints; wooden gates led into fields where half-defined horse-tracks disappeared into the distance, but there was no confusing the bridle-path, a chalky white trail curving uphill and gouged out of the corn-yellow and the green of the grass verges.

Three-quarters of the way up the incline was another stile, of a different sort, the climbing variety. I'd sometimes sit on top of it to look back the way I'd just come and to consider. In a later season, when the corn had been harvested and sold and turned into millers' grain, the fields were given over to flocks of partridges, which the estate bred, and the game-keepers did their rounds then carrying shotguns over their shoulders. But that was in the time to come, and much would have happened in the human sphere before I smelt the burnt fields and understood that the winter had come and gone and a tragedy or two had befallen us, before I realised – as if my reactions were delayed – that the earth, tilled after the scorching, wasn't just earth but was covered by legions of scrabbling, twittering partridge fledglings at their feed.

After the fields I took to coming back along Laud Street, not by the lane behind. A third Sunday had gone by and, again, the doctor's wife hadn't appeared in the Abbey. I turned my eyes to the house as I passed and glanced into dark rooms six or nine inches below street level. But there was little to see. The rooms appeared to be empty. Only once was I made to stop in my tracks. From my awkward vantage-point on the pavement I spotted a pair of legs: two bare feet in espadrilles crossing stone flags, ankles and calves without stockings, and the edge of a blue dress, the blue of corn-flowers. The feet stopped just as mine had stopped a few seconds before. She must have spotted me. I hesitated, forgetting at first that I would be as obvious to her as she was to me. I started into motion, failing to remember that there was a possibility she would be unable to identify me from what was visible to her: my shoes, and the cloth of my trousers, and the waist-tail of my jacket. I moved off, jerkily, most uncomfortably aware that I'd been bested.

On the evenings that followed I kept to the same side of the pavement – realising I'd be fully visible if I crossed over – but I didn't let up on my pace as I walked past. I didn't even turn my eyes to look, in case she'd positioned herself beneath one of the windows or upstairs. I varied the times of my walks to convince myself I wasn't surrendering so soon to a domestic ritual: but it was also done, I knew, in order not to leave myself more of an object of suspicion than I needed to be. It should seem as if I only happened to be passing that way....

But how had it come about that, after so short a time, I now found myself viewing my actions like a man outside himself?

*

Was it ever the case, as the tellers claimed, that Mrs Davies's maid was seen in the vicinity of that hamlet past Heyton where the woman who made babies lived?

The woman had inherited the gift from her mother and grandmother. She contained a headful of knowledge about herbs, the leaves of plants, root extracts, leeches, poisons, animal saliva, and about particular combinations of all or some of them which would induce fertility in the womb of a woman previously unsuccessful in conceiving.

The *savante* was famous, or – rather – infamous. Her skin was like an old lizard's, one which had lain too long in its life under a hot sun. She had graceful, almost lady-like gestures, but a mouth of rotten yellow stumps for teeth; the smell of her trade hung about her, and she could only be visited (in secret consultation) with an extreme effort of will. Her potions, it was said, only failed with those who chose not to believe. In a special sense she was a faith healer.

Someone very much like the maid in appearance had been spotted once in proximity to that hamlet beneath Heyton Woods. If she had been carrying a spray of catkins, or prim-roses, that would have been one thing, a pretence at least. But she'd had her hands in the pockets of her summer coat, and if it positively *was* her, she seemed to be going about her errand very purposefully.

*

My colleague at Botterel's, Hoyle, told me a story.

In those parts, about the year 1910, a woman made a good marriage. Her husband wanted a son, and the presumption was that she would bear him a family. She had no alternative: that was only a wife's function. But it became clear to her that her body was unable to conceive.

Physical relations started to depress the woman. On one occasion the husband, in sheer frustration, succumbed to temptation and had his way with one of the maids living under their roof.

As a result of the encounter the girl, who had come to the house a virgin, found herself pregnant. Her mistress dis-covered but it wasn't long before she overcame her anger: indeed she soon hatched a plan, which she necessarily had to tell the girl, placing herself in her trust as she, the maid, was originally supposed to have been placed in hers.

The consequence of the pact was that the maid was sent from the house, on the excuse that her mother was sick and required her services. A little later the wife made a show of absenting herself from the town for a day. She spent the hours at a seaside resort shopping with the maid for what they would need, but when she returned home in the evening she told her husband that she had visited a doctor in the next county: he was a specialist in gynae-cological matters and had stipulated that she be put on such-and-such a course of treatment. She persuaded her husband that she would like to visit Switzerland, on the 'specialist's' advice, and he agreed. Privately she arranged how and when she would rendezvous with the maid for the journey to the Continent.

In Lausanne, in her grand hotel, the wife placed padding beneath her dress and passed as an expectant mother. In a modest pension in the same city the maid swelled and swelled until the day she bore her child. The wife wrote a purposely equivocal letter home, informing her husband that her own 'progress' (underlined) was much better than she had dared to expect: she felt a different woman, and – she told him – he would surely appreciate the results. She dissuaded him, how-ever – at length, in four paragraphs – from thinking of paying her a visit.

The wife returned home with the baby in her arms and the maid in meek tow consoling herself with a fancy watch her mistress had bought her from a jeweller's. The husband was incredulous: a boy, a son, his wife had borne him an heir! Rapidly he calculated in his head how many months, but he realised that nothing untoward could have happened between his wife and any Swiss Lothario to cause *this*. Any-way, he began to see the resemblances in the baby's face and hair colouring to his own.

The maid came back to the house, and because the husband thought he must be soiling his mothering wife to make love to her as he would have done to a woman of the streets, he transferred his attentions back to the pretty maid. His wife wasn't unwilling to accept the (unadmitted) situa-tion however; and the maid, who was being paid generously,

75

felt in herself a certain – inevitably secret – bond to the man who'd brought her with child.

The incidents were reckoned to make a happy-ending story, for its time, which was already supposed to be as far away as history from our own, in the liberal, humanistic 1930s.

*

Walking across the Abbey Green one afternoon I spotted her ahead, making her way towards me. It was too late to change my direction and avoid a meeting.

Our paths were destined to cross?

We slowed as we approached – and stopped.

'We – we meet again,' I said.

'We meet again, Mr Pendlebury.'

Cautious and alert smiles.

She was wearing a dip-necked summer dress with short sleeves, and no gloves. Her eyes looked sleepy, with the lids only half-opened in the glare.

'I haven't seen you,' I made so bold. 'On Sundays.' (*Too* bold?) 'Lately, that is. At first I —'

She rested her pannier on her forearm and drew back her hair with both hands.

'Do you think there *is* a God, Mr Pendlebury?'

The question took me aback and I couldn't conceal the fact. She ran her tongue over her teeth and left a little trail of lipstick on them.

'Do you think He's watching and disapproving?'

'Watching?'

She repositioned one of the combs.

'Noticing I've absented myself.'

I searched for words to say but she interrupted, in what might only have been light-hearted, carefree fashion.

'I doubt that, don't you? He has other things to think about, to plan.' She pulled back some strands of hair with supple, tanned fingers. 'An earthquake somewhere. A hurricane. A few fires. Motor accidents. Drownings. Did you know a little girl drowned in the pond of Hintock House, ten years ago? My mother told me.'

I shook my head.

'I read in the newspaper last week,' she continued, 'five nuns were killed in Portugal. Going over a railway-crossing, in a horse and cart. The horse survived, by some miracle. I suppose it's amusing even —' She was speaking with the diction and grace of Anna Neagle in *Bitter Sweet*. '– in a perverse way. What do *you* think?'

She stood straightening her strings of blue beads, then checked the matching clips on her ears.

The beads stopped just beneath her breasts.

'When I was young,' she said, 'it always seemed to be raining on Sunday mornings. I mean, often enough for me to realise. I had one pair of shoes that kept leaking, so I'd know I couldn't wear those. I remember standing in my bedroom at home trying to choose. I think I have to content myself with believing that the Good Lord was testing our faith.'

I felt the only reply must be a smile.

'The other people here,' she said, 'why do *they* go? Do they all believe? Do you know?'

I couldn't do anything but shrug.

'What is it,' she asked, 'that they need saving *from*, do you think?'

If I'd had the nerve I would have looked into her eyes and raised my eyebrows, the way of actors in films I'd seen. Instead I looked over my shoulder and whom should I have caught sight of but Mrs Wills, Mr Fishlock's stout, po-faced sister with her very persistent curiosity. She didn't look away in time and I saw her blush and pull her white gloves tight and then begin searching furiously in her willow basket.

Mrs Davies must have noticed too. She didn't move off immediately. She stood with her weight on one hip, balancing on one heel and tapping lightly on the cobbles with her toe.

'I expect,' she said, 'religion's about the last thing that gets discussed here.'

She looked round about her, around the Abbey Green, avoiding the direction of Mrs Wills, who still hadn't passed on.

Then she laughed, and lifted her eyes to the Abbey tower. A bright, optimistic party laugh that gave the lie to what she had been saying.

Mrs Wills walked by, giving us a wide berth. Her head was turned a little sideways, but she didn't speak. She picked up speed and hurried off, to tell her friends and others about the rummest sight she'd just seen.

*

77

Once (I heard) in the previous winter a fog had come down, so thick that you couldn't see from one side of a street to the other. It had hung about the district for three days.

In the midst of it someone walking along the Shaftesbury road had almost been killed. He *heard* first, what he thought was a car being driven at speed, but couldn't understand *how* on such a day, when the little traffic he had encountered was moving little quicker than himself.

The noise came closer, turning to a roar. He felt it was almost upon him and he had to throw himself into a hedge as headlights dazzled and a car raced past.

He had enough presence of mind left, just, to be able to recognise the car: a Talbot, like the only one in the area, Dr Davies's.

The doctor, it was discovered, had been in his surgery all that afternoon. His wife's whereabouts had been unknown; no one had seen the maid either. Nor could anyone remember about the car.

The story circulated about the town. In one version the man who'd been walking along the road was sent flying by one of the car's mudguards as a woman's laughter – *that* woman's laughter – made fun of him. (The laughter of *two* women it became in time: uncaring, daredevil, scathing laughter.)

*

Davies telephoned the office one day and asked to speak to me.

'I've been meaning to ask your advice,' he began.

'Advice? Yes, certainly.'

'I'd be grateful —'

'Don't think about it.'

'It's about a will.'

'I see.'

'I suppose I *ought* to see Botterel.'

'I don't —'

'Maybe it'd be awkward.'

'I —'

'Any possibility of your coming over sometime to discuss it?'

'Yes, certainly.'

Whereupon Davies was interrupted and the conversation was suddenly terminated, with no more than a brusque 'goodbye'.

*

I decided to forgo my constitutional and called in at Laud Street one evening about seven o'clock.

The maid admitted me into the hall, and requested that I kindly wait. I said yes, of course.

The windows were open on to the street. The house had the enclosed, muffled silence of felt wadding. I looked about me, at the coffer and the wheelback chair and the polished copper measure holding an arrangement of polleny Californian poppies, larkspur and tiger-lilies. There was panelling on the walls, to two-thirds of their height: old, smoky wood with an amber shine from beneath. The flag-stones seemed to have a film of moisture on them. Upstairs the doors along the landing were each a few inches ajar.

The maid returned.

'This way if you would, sir.'

She took me behind the staircase, into a corridor which ran towards the back of the house. A side door led out on to the paved terrace. The maid turned the handle, pulled on the door, and stood back to let me go through.

I walked outside. The door closed behind me.

My steps became slower.

Davies's wife was sitting by the pond with her legs bare, dipping her toes in the water.

From so far away in time I can see her and hear the fountain's splashing. The evening is hot, listless, still, like all our evenings in that season. I remember a feeling in the air I could call either 'hesitation' or 'expectation'. We were all of us, separately, waiting for something to happen. We knew ourselves to be dissatisfied and unfulfilled: but maybe it took those particular moments on the terrace for me to realise fully. Time had dragged on in an otherwise pleasant and unexacting way: we were willing to put up with it because we recognised that things would not always be so, but change they must, for better or worse.

I started out of my reverie. She got to her feet, pulling at her skirt, and I looked away.

'This *is* a surprise, Mr Pendlebury.'

'Please excuse —'

'How nice to be visited out of the blue.'

She came towards me — I turned and stared — in loose, slapping espadrilles.

'I'm afraid he — my husband — he's not back yet.'

The dress — jade green — had very short sleeves, exposing most of her arms. I saw she'd been sitting in the sun, which other Ivell Abbas wives did not do.

'Do — do you know —'

'He's out on one of his calls, I expect.'

She was wearing no lipstick or powder.

'I – I'll —'

'I always feel,' she said, 'I haven't *quite* got used to time here. After all these years.'

'You — you haven't?'

She passed her hand across her brow, languidly. A thin hand, with fine impractical fingers.

'It doesn't seem to work how it does in other places, have you noticed?'

'I —'

'Although being married to a doctor —' Her voice was becoming lazier, almost somnolent. ' – I should *expect* – never to know. Isn't – isn't that so?'

'I don't really —'

Her tongue appeared between her teeth and moistened her lips.

'Maybe – *your* clients are more – punctual,' she said.

I thought she sounded disinclined to believe it.

'Now – now you come to mention it —'

'Sometimes I think he's been – dragged back – into the last century. Or – something just as absurd.'

'Yes?'

She scraped the hair back from her temples. I couldn't ignore the colour of the sun on her arms, which didn't seem to stop on the line of the high cuff.

'He's been spirited away,' she said.

I attempted to smile.

'Now, what shall we do with ourselves?'

Her lips stayed parted, for breath.

'Shall we wait in the house, Mr Pendlebury?'

80

'Yes. Yes. If you're —'

'This heat is unending, isn't it?'

Her dress had buttons on its front. The bottom ones, the lowest eight or nine inches above the hem, were undone.

'It just goes on and on.'

I watched her fingers pushing between two of the buttons at the top. She wasn't wearing either her engagement or wedding ring.

'*Is* it ever going to end?' she asked. 'Do you think?'

She didn't wait for an answer but led the way indoors, through the french windows into the sitting-room. I followed, watching the correspondence of the components of her walk, those that were visible to me: knee, calf, ankle.

'As *my* husband *will* insist on saying, take a pew. Please.'

She pointed to one of the two wing sofas.

I sat down. She seated herself on the other sofa, at a right angle to me, on another wall. She looked over at me, smiled, crossed her bare legs, and sighed perhaps.

'It's difficult,' she said, 'finding anywhere out of the sun.'

I nodded agreement.

'Probably the curtains are going to fade. We need blinds, I think.'

I nodded again.

She looked over her shoulder at the open french windows. 'Still...'

She didn't finish the remark. What did she mean: the blinds would be bought, or the blinds wouldn't be bought, or maybe it didn't matter either way?

She spoke like a hybrid, a Carib Mademoiselle crossed with a debutante banished to the shires: a sitter on verandahs and stoeps, with the sort of voice and accent to suggest a life invoiced on charge accounts.

She slipped her feet out of the espadrilles.

'Did you know – you wanted to stay here?' I asked her. 'In this house?'

She looked down at her feet and shrugged.

'I had no thoughts about it really. When you're just married, it's supposed not to matter.'

Supposed. I puzzled about the word.

'Everyone here tells me I should count myself lucky.'

'Ah.'

She leaned back in the sofa. Her toes curled and uncurled on the rug.

'Do *you* think I'm lucky, Mr Pendlebury?'

I coughed; I said I didn't think it was my place, really, to —

'But I'd like to know.' She brushed away a fly. 'You *once* told me. Do you see things any differently now?'

I stared at the fly, not aware that it had landed on her knee.

'It – it's a very nice house. Very nice indeed.'

She smiled, in a private and *crafted* way that seemed to confirm I had missed the point, she had beaten me hands down for astuteness.

I focused away from her, on the shelves of books. I screwed up my eyes, to let her see I was reading the titles.

'I don't read much,' she said.

'No?'

'I don't have the span of attention. Isn't it called?'

'Ah.'

I looked at her. She noticed, and shrugged again as her eyes skimmed over the objects on a side-table, including the wedding photograph.

'Those books are your husband's?'

I pointed. I'd looked along the spines on another evening: Stendhal, Rousseau, Flaubert, Turgenev, as well as World's Classics.

'He may have read them,' she said. 'Once.'

I repeated her. '"*May* have read —"?'

She sighed in the heat. Even indoors the day was muggy, sticky, and the air thick, close, stuffy, clotted.

The subject of the books vanished, just as she intended, into the ether.

Quarter of an hour passed.

We talked, seemingly about little, but with depths vaguely suggested and the silences as probing charges.

She had just tucked her legs beneath her when I looked round at a sound and caught sight of Davies standing in the doorway.

She was sitting opposite the door and she must have seen, but she carried on talking – in a livelier voice – as if he wasn't there.

'I like flowers in the house – they're civilising – but gardening is quite different. Those conversations people have about it, and I can only think: if you dropped down dead, your gardens would show you no gratitude, you know, they'd just run wild and turn into jungles.'

'Well,' Davies said, stepping forward, 'I haven't heard you impart those *bon mots* of wisdom.'

'Perhaps you weren't listening.'

'Perhaps I wasn't.'

'I shouldn't intrude —' I began, and crouched forward to stand up.

'Sit down, Pendlebury.'

'Mr Pendlebury has —'

'Good evening,' I said from the sofa.

'Good evening, Pendlebury.'

'*This* is civilised too —'

'*Good* evening, my dear.'

Davies bent down, his wife leaned forward, and he kissed her on the brow.

Her expression was hidden from me in the vital instant before she sank into the back of the sofa and started talking again. Her face showed no comely, wifely delight.

'Don't you miss a garden?' she asked me.

'Oh, I . . .'

Davies stood tall, with his hands in his pockets.

'Don't you have one, Pendlebury?'

'No,' I replied, and shook my head.

'*Don't* you?' Davies said. 'I didn't know.'

'He lives above Pomfrey's,' his wife told him.

'I didn't know that either.'

'You should listen, Frank.'

'I wasn't *here* to listen.'

'But we haven't been discussing that.'

'No?'

Davies crossed his hands behind his back, like a 'paterfamilias'.

'You told us at dinner once, didn't you, Mr Pendlebury?'

His wife smiled – at neither of us – and toyed again with the two top buttons on her dress.

'I distinctly remember. My spouse must have been deeply engaged on weightier matters.'

'I doubt that,' Davies said.

'I always think you must be.'

'In *this* town?'

'It seems to me the talk becomes rather shallow at my end of the table. People paddling in my shallow rill.'

She glanced over at me. I shifted my eyes to Davies, who was looking down at his wife's sandals.

'I have to go out again,' he said. 'I've two or three calls to make.' The Devon burr was the most pronounced I'd ever heard it. His hands were by his sides now and I noticed that they were bunched, with the fingers curled up into the palms.

His wife stretched one bare leg in front of her and lifted her hands to her hair.

'I don't feel like eating,' she said, in the accent of her social tribe, but with less exaggerated, less stretched vowels than many used: an accent which would have opened doors to her anywhere. 'How can you *bear* to wear tweeds, Frank? Mr Pendlebury wears a linen jacket and an open shirt.'

'Not for work he doesn't,' Davies responded, burr-ing.

'Work –' – the word carried a little echo of Devon – '– work *stops* at six o'clock. For most sane people.'

'There aren't any rules about it,' Davies said.

'It's self-discipline that *makes* rules.'

'I'm disciplined enough.'

'Everything in its proper place?'

I saw a streak of perspiration trickling down Davies's temple. His neck was colouring inside the stiff white collar.

'Yes, you *are* mad,' his wife said; and I felt somehow that humour was being left out of the remark . 'Quite mad.'

'And what do you suggest I do instead?'

'I have no idea.'

'Go about in my underwear?'

'It's those tweeds —'

'Or in the raw?'

'Did you know that Edwardian *gentlemen*' – the word received the weight of her emphasis – 'they did without underwear in summer?'

We seemed to fall into a silence. We tumbled into it, as if the floor had opened. Seconds went by.

'*Very* interesting,' Davies said curtly.

His wife smiled.

'But is it interesting enough for your friends, Francis?' she asked him.

Davies stared at the rug, at its pattern. The perspiration trail had reached his cheek. His lips were moving: he might have been inwardly counting, under his breath.

'On second thoughts,' she decided, 'I think not. What do *you* think, Mr Pendlebury?'

'I'm sorry I have to leave the party,' Davies said.

'I – I have to go too,' I told them.

'Mr Pendlebury said he came here to see *you*, Frank.'

'Did he? Well, I'm afraid that will have to wait.'

'Of course,' I responded.

'*You* can stay, though, Pendlebury.'

'No, I really *must* —'

'Keep my wife company —'

'My husband is the public's servant, Mr Pendlebury. He is at their beck and call.'

Davies let out his breath; he must have heard himself, and then offered us instead a hangdog smile.

'I ought to be on my way,' I told them, and mumbled thanks for their hospitality. They were both watching me: she with a careless half-smile, he with an odd, perhaps obsessive sort of curiosity.

' – I've enjoyed —'

She leaned forward for her espadrilles. Another button had become undone at the top of her dress. I happened to look down at that very second and caught a glimpse of cleavage. I immediately guessed that there was nothing to hold her breasts.

My mistake was then to glance at Davies, who was continuing to watch me very closely, with one finger applied to the perspiration track. I looked away again and was suddenly shaken by a fit of coughing.

At the front door, in no less perplexing daylight, Davies said that he was driving out to a farm on the Heyton side, so he couldn't give me a lift.

'We shall meet again, Pendlebury.'

I turned my head on my neck and looked back into the hall. His wife was climbing the staircase; she was looking upstairs, and pulling one hand slowly behind her up the banister rail.

'If I don't expire of the heat first, of course,' I heard her say. Then I *thought* I heard her say, 'Would the town mourn me, do you think? With the gnashing of teeth –'

Her voice trailed away. Davies was watching from the doorway. His face was more troubled than I had ever seen it before: as if the mask had been forgotten, and he was finally at a loss to understand anything.

Or was the mask already too much of a character trait to be forgotten? Was he wanting to back me into a corner, where I would feel obliged to say something, to make some remark he would take for complicity and which he would later use against me?

I didn't say anything. Nor, which was even stranger, did he.

He returned to the car and started the engine.

The maid crossed the hall to the door – 'Good evening, sir,' she said – and closed it after me.

On the other side of the street an inquisitive face retreated at a window.

The car drove off, sputtering blue exhaust fumes behind it.

I turned in the other direction and took my first steps.

Simultaneously, downstairs in the house and quite audible through the open window in the hall, I heard music.

It sounded as if it must be coming from the sitting-room. A scratchy record of operatic voices, a soprano's and a tenor's in a duet: piling on top of one another, at a climax of their own public, conspicuous brand of emotion.

The volume was turned up louder, to fill the house with that brash farrago of love.

*

Davies telephoned the office.

'About the will,' he said, in his most refined, clipped, burr-less, self-confident tone of voice.

'Ah,' I said. 'Yes, I've been thinking —'

'Changed my mind.'

(Hail-fellow, well-bloody-met.)

'I see,' I said.

'Yes.'

'Would you like —'

'So that's that.'

'We could discuss it —'

'Not really any point, though, is there?'

86

'Mr Botterel could —'

'No. I wouldn't mention it to him. Might think I don't trust him or something.'

'I'm sorry,' I said.

'Nothing to be sorry about. Just changed my mind, that's all. For just now.'

'Oh well.'

'Another time maybe.'

'Yes. Yes, another time. Whatever —'

'You must come over sometime. To the house.'

'Yes. Thank you.'

'Let me know.'

'I – feel very inhospitable.'

'Well, that's what *we*'re all set up for, isn't it?'

'Ah.'

'Sorry to trouble you.'

'Not at all. My pleas —'

'Got a patient waiting.'

'Righty-ho.'

(Jesus, did *I* say *that*? Begin again.)

'Fine.'

'Goodbye, Pendlebury,' he said, at his most pukka and bespoke, and with the mockery left ringing in my ears.

*

Nature seemed to reach a hiatus about harvest time. The business of breeding had been completed and the cycle was in temporary abeyance; there was an abundance of food, fewer hazards threatened survival.

Stillness – more or less – reigned, in a perfect paradigm of summer. The heat shimmered in the fields and danced along the rooftops, and trees staggered under the weight and mass of foliage; birds and beasts and humans alike took to the shade, insects floated idly on currents of air; a skin of fine white powder gritted everything and there was perpetually the taste of dust on your lips.

*

The one exception among the species to this mood – this predisposition to inertia – was the herd of deer in the Castle grounds.

87

The time of the annual rut approached, and I oberved the mating ritual several times on my walks over the park land. Mostly the pairs kept themselves hidden but a few ventured out from the trees into the candid light of day. The buck would trail the roe, never further than a yard behind, often coming in so close that its snout touched the rump. The trailing was endless, simple circles and loops of eight and all manner of configurations flattening the grass. I didn't see the climax of the performance but it could only have taken one form.

A gamekeeper came upon me one day when my attention was rapt. He told me matters weren't quite as they appeared to be, that the sturdier buck wasn't mercilessly stalking the roe, harrying her so as to exhaust her and wear her down: it was the female that led the male, setting the pace and settling the patterns they trod on the grass. The roe was sharper, cannier, spurring the buck to the act of coupling whenever it was that *she* decided.

'*She* knows bloody well what's coming to her, and she leads him a merry dance all right. Mark my word. She's red hot for it, she is.'

3

The first I learned of the incident – or the incident that might have been, or the incident that never was – was from Lettice Botterel.

'And I *ought* to tell you since she's your friend.'

'She's *not* my "friend",' I said, immediately put on the defensive.

'She invites you to the house.'

'They both do.'

'I heard you were at the house when *he* wasn't there.'

'Well . . . ?'

'And *she* was.'

'For quarter of an hour.'

'Fifteen whole minutes?'

'Have you heard something?' I asked her.

'You've guessed?'
'No.'
'As it happens, quite a lot of people *are* talking.'
'About me being at the house?'
'Something else.'
'Oh.'
'Worse.'
' "Worse"?'
'People seem to think so.'
'Your parents – ?'
'They know *some*thing.'
'What – what about?'
'I'm sure it's all a mistake. Really.'
'You haven't —'
'They've muddled everything up.'
'Please. What is it about? Tell me.'
The story concerned Mrs Davies and two well-known and
'venerable' worthies of the town. I had already heard of them
before I'd – briefly – met them: two contemporaries, in their
early sixties, Bertram Fishlock (managing director of the
amalgamated family firms of building contractor and stonemason) and Frederick Gilbey (seedsman and horticulturist),
one a widower and son of the redoubtable Mrs Fishlock
(who, at eighty-five years old, was reputed to keep him still
firmly under her thumb, the habit of a lifetime) and the other
a long-established bachelor and Abbey warden-cum-vestry
clerk. They were friends of old acquaintance and wholly
respectable personages in the community. I had spoken to
each of them, only a few words, and watched them leading
the cast in a local production of *Iolanthe*. Somehow I'd
imagined they must be similarly inoffensive and unworldly,
but what Lettice Botterel was to tell me quite confounded any
such assumption.
    An encounter was alleged by the two men to have taken
place very recently at number 31 Laud Street. They claimed
that they called together at the house; they were intending to
speak to Dr Davies but found him absent. His wife invited
them on to the garden terrace to wait; in the course of which
short interlude of time –
    'Well what? Tell me.'
    'They say she meant to – to compromise them.'

'But how?'

'Making suggestions. Inflaming them. Oh, I *can't* —'

It was too much for Lettice Botterel, or so she pretended. But I picked up from another source that Mrs Davies had – apparently – said such things in the men's hearing as would imply she was offering them both sexual favours. According to some accounts the bride of two and a half years stripped herself semi-/almost/completely bare in front of them and leaned against the wall/crouched/lay on her back on the ground. There were further variations: that the two men had pleaded with her not to undress, that she had laid hands on them, that she had gone down on all fours, stark naked, like a beast of the field.

Even Fishlock and Gilbey denied that she'd been naked: she had used verbal means and certain lascivious movements of her limbs and the tongue in her mouth to indicate her purpose, without actually undressing. But they had both been there to witness the woman's behaviour for themselves, and it had gone far beyond impropriety and (Gilbey's word) 'decadence', to be tantamount to an act of gross indecency.

'It was the heat,' Lettice Botterel suggested.

'How was it the heat?' I asked her.

'Their brains addled.'

'Whose brains?'

'That's the question.'

'What is she to them?'

'A siren?'

'How, though? *Why?*'

'Oh, she doesn't have to *do* anything.'

'You've seen her and spoken to her. She wouldn't *say* such things. Would she?'

'You'll have to put that question to yourself.'

'If it was the heat, they could have imagined it.'

'Could they?'

'Hysteria,' I said. 'Siriasis. Delirium induced by the heat, by their proximity to her. Davies should know that. Two men without wives, driven ...'

I hesitated.

'Yes?' she said. 'You can tell *me*, William. I shall soon be a married woman.'

'Driven to a frenzy of desire —'

90

'Would she do that to *you*?'

'I'm not sixty, like them.'

'All the more reason, I should have thought —'

'I haven't lived here all my life,' I reminded her.

'Like me?'

'*You*'re not a —'

'I'm not a man, no. But what if it's not only men —'

'What? "Not men"?'

'I've heard women talking about her too. Quite intimately. About her body.'

'Heat hysteria,' I said. 'A paroxysm. Fired by the common talk.'

'They've lived here all their lives, Fishlock and Gilbey. They'll expect to walk the streets like heroes.'

'What about *her*, though?' I said. 'Mrs Davies?'

'So, what do *you* think?'

'That they can't charge her with anything.'

'Does that mean she's innocent?'

'I – How can —'

'Or *they*'re innocent?'

'How – how can two men of sixty be innocent?' I asked her. 'With all their lives behind them?'

'Or a woman of – what – twenty-six? Looking as *she* does '

'Why should they say such things? It – it's incredible. I just can't —'

'Before you start,' she said, 'on your Saint George adventure to save a maiden in distress – Charles was supposed to be taking me to the picture house. Now he can't go. And I'm —'

'He's stood you up?'

'I'm desperate. Please, William.'

'Which film is it?'

'*As You Desire Me*.'

'Garbo?'

'Mmm. Papa'll give me the motor, if I ask him nicely.'

'I can't drive.'

'But *I* can.'

I turned to the desk and swept my hands over the paperwork.

'Oh, just for tonight, William, please —'

*

91

When I should have been getting myself ready for our evening, I couldn't stop thinking of what I'd just heard. I moved from my desk, to the window on Clock Street, to a chair, back to the window, to my desk again.

When the floor-mopping started I left the office and walked back to Pomfrey's, unable to attend to anything going on around me. I walked upstairs and pushed each of my keys in turn into the door-lock. (Most doors in the town went unlocked; I had brought bad city habits with me.)

Inside, I stood at the window and forgot about Lettice Botterel's cancelled evening, about the film, puzzling how the situation with Fishlock and Gilbey could conceivably have come about, how they'd been able to imagine a thing of that sort: and how anyone might believe that such a fantastic story could have any truth at all in it.

*

At the fifty-ninth minute of the eleventh hour, Charles Allingham telephoned Moat House and relayed the news that he would be available for *As You Desire Me* after all.

Lettice telephoned Pomfrey's shop to pass on the tidings. Pomfrey was book-keeping and happy enough to eavesdrop.

'So, that seems to be that,' she concluded.

'Oh, well,' I said, cupping my hand round the mouthpiece. 'Sorry, William.'

'Another time perhaps,' I felt obliged to offer.

'Yes. Yes, we could,' she said, with markedly more enthusiasm.

'I hope it's good. The film.'

'You really don't mind?'

'I'm fine,' I said, truthfully enough.

'I wouldn't blame you —'

'This was what you arranged in the first place.'

'Yes, I know, but —'

*

I lost most of a night's sleep and couldn't concentrate on my work for most of the next day. I heard snatches of the tittle-tattle in the other rooms.

It was I who telephoned Davies, at his surgery. I hesitated, then asked, how were things?

'Not so good.'

I told him I thought I knew why. I could hear the sigh of breath at the other end. I took it to be his relief, which made my job easier; I'd imagined he would pretend he hadn't heard, or tell me he didn't need my sympathy.

'Would you – Would it be best to talk about it?' I said. 'In a professional capacity?'

Since the afternoon before, I'd felt my instincts directing me. I didn't know the couple *well*, they were acquaintances not friends, but they didn't deserve this. There had been some appalling misunderstanding.

'I'll try to get finished by seven,' he said. 'Could you come over? To Laud Street?'

I hesitated, then I told him, of course.

'Thanks, Pendlebury.'

If there was any mockery or irony there this time, I didn't hear it. I believed I was making myself *necessary* to them, as I'd always assumed would never happen.

*

Half an hour later Davies called back and suggested he came to my flat. Fine, I said.

I left the office early, to tidy up, to lock away in the drawer in the table desk whatever was requiring to be locked away. When Davies arrived he looked not at all dispirited. He smiled, had a careful look round the little sitting-room, at what I had pinned up on the walls (I'd remembered to pull off the newspaper souvenir of the Tory jamboree), the photographs of paintings and the clippings. He looked down at Pack Street from the window.

'You see everything from this window, don't you?'

I agreed.

'It makes a map from up here,' he said, pulling his pipe out of his pocket but not lighting it.

'I'm not sure that tells me so much really.' I was thinking of those prints of gazetteer maps that hung on his walls: rather mathematical for my own taste.

'So this is where you spend your time?'

'Some of it,' I said.

'Just some?'

'Well, I go walking. I try to keep *away*, if I can.'

'I'm sure Ivell Abbas has its eyes on *you*, though.'

I agreed.

'I'm sure it has.'

'Too clever by half.'

He returned his pipe to his pocket.

'I'm very sorry,' I said.

Then Davies changed gear, he launched himself upon the subject.

'Of course, all this is quite scandalous.'

'Yes.' I nodded eagerly. 'Yes, it is.'

'It's obviously a pack of lies.'

'Obviously,' I said.

'So, Pendlebury, what should we *do*?'

'We —' Then it was that I noticed his use of the first person. 'One – one could bring an action,' I said.

'I can't tell what the town thinks.'

'Does that matter?'

'Won't it influence things? – the outcome?'

'It depends where the case is heard,' I said. 'But – but you're not in doubt about the outcome?'

'No. I – I'm trying to be practical, that's all. I mean, to assess the chances.'

'We have to make clear what happened.'

'I see.'

'We have to say – well, that *nothing* happened.'

'Yes.'

It seemed to me that he sounded less than positive on the point.

'So,' I said, 'everything has to be quite clear in our minds.'

'Yes.'

'Does your wife understand that?'

'I believe so.'

'Very well. I shall do whatever I can. To – to prepare the ground. To help prepare it —'

It struck me that I was speaking out of a corner. I hadn't meant to find myself in such a position: where I was committing myself, and the obligation seemed to be mine. But if I hadn't *meant* it, was I not allowing Davies to put such a construction on what I was doing, what I was saying – namely, that I *was* making myself available?

'There'll be all sorts of questions, won't there?'

'Yes,' I said. 'Yes. Are you ready for them?'

'What – what sort of questions —'

'I can think of *one* —'

'What?'

'I feel – before we – before this goes any further —'

'Yes?'

'I've got to ask you – It's personal, I mean. If this goes ahead —'

'We *have* to go ahead, don't we?'

('*We*'.)

'To – to retrieve your wife's reputation, and your own, yes. Certainly.'

'Then ask away.'

'Well...Is – would you say your marriage – it's a happy one? A successful one?'

'I suppose – everyone calculates such a thing quite differently —'

'Can I ask you then, how do *you* calculate it?'

'For the person *I* am – I'm content, I believe. I have a very – "desirable", you could call her – young woman for my wife.'

He dug his hands into his pockets and dropped into a chair, watching me.

'Yes,' I said.

'I didn't *expect*...'

'I'm sorry?'

'I don't think it was my *expectation*: to marry such a person.'

'You – you value her appearance?'

'Not *just* that. It's what people see first, of course.'

'Did you always believe it would happen?'

His lips pressed tightly together.

'That you would marry?' I said.

'It's what happens, isn't it?'

I nodded.

'It's automatic. An instinct. It'll get *you* too —'

'Maybe, yes.'

'Of course it will. Even if you think it won't —'

'Did you ever? Think it wouldn't?'

'I don't think I knew what I was looking for. It's very abstract, you know.'

'Your wife isn't abstract?'

'No. Not at all.'

95

He seemed about to laugh at my remark, but didn't. He pushed his hands deeper into his pockets. I noticed a tic pulling in his right cheek.

'Were you – were you surprised – that it was *this* woman?'

'"Surprised"? Perhaps.' He lifted his hand to his cheek. 'I was proud, flattered. Maybe it *was* more than I expected.'

I sat down opposite him. He took out his pipe and I watched him stack it from his tobacco pouch. In another few years he would have filled out and lost more hair at the front, he would be starting to look middle-aged: while his wife would still be in the full, brazen bloom of youth. By then the town would have swallowed them whole, or else spat them out.

Davies lifted his eyes and shifted in the chair. He seemed uncomfortable, to judge by his gestures. There was that tic. Yet each time I'd caught his eyes since he came into the room they were animated, intense, *alive* in a way I hadn't seen them before, not even when they'd picked me out from the others at his dinner-table.

What was compelling him now was his *excitement*, like a courser after blood.

4

The 'solution' was owing to something I was told by Botterel, the story of an archaic custom in the town, one which had infrequently been put into actual practice but which *had* been performed (and witnessed by Botterel himself) as recently as 1921.

Where an act of trespass or defamation had taken place in the town which only concerned townsfolk, and where it was deemed either untimely or inappropriate (and perhaps not legally justifiable) that the case should be settled in a court of law in another town, tradition ordained that a civil court of assessment could be instituted in Ivell Abbas.

One essential premise and proviso was the co-operation and participation of (at least) the plaintiff and defendant. Additionally, each should agree that there might be such representation as either party decided on. Self-defence was permissible.

A quota of impartial notables – customarily a trio – would sit in judgement. Convention had it that they were presided over by a senior member of the local landed family, the Marlotts, presuming he had no direct involvement or stake in the case, or else by a deputee. The panel could (although it was also entitled not to) make a pronouncement: it was then a matter of honour, not law, for the participants to hold to that.

Usually the cases related to disputed borders on land, or grazing or fishing rights, or something of that order: access to a water well, the condition of lanes and tracks, wet leaves falling from a tree on to a neighbour's path, stubble burning or bonfire smoke causing a nuisance. There had also been several incidents of slander (domestic and public, to distinguish between them): I went to Dorchester to check for myself, in the records of the institution then called the 'Dorsetshire Antiquarium'. (These are now kept in the Davenham Collection, to be found in the County Museum of Ethnology, Plaize Street, Dorchester.)

I pondered the possibility for some days – and Botterel and I continued to discuss it – before I elected to mention it to anyone else. I learned that people in Ivell Abbas were well aware of the custom, although very few had observed in person its implementation; almost without exception they regarded it favourably, a response that smacked of a certain civic pride.

I ought not to have been so surprised. In a county given to especial inwardness, where self-dependence was the clue to the general character, a community had formulated its own institution to regulate on matters that could be seen to include, even indirectly, the interests of everyone. It was the town that must be best able to judge, not a body of faceless persons living elsewhere, wholly subject to the slow, laborious, cryptic workings of the national legal system. I dare say there had been instances of bribery and perjury not recorded in Dorchester, but most probably their incidence was less than occurs in courts of law. Presuming the best of it, this method saved time and expense and – paradoxically – it saved the honour (or dishonour) of the town in frequently delicate matters from becoming county gossip.

These centuries-old hearings had no binding code of conduct laid down other than the ritual-approved composition of the presiding trio who must hear the case. Care had always been taken that the procedure should not trespass anywise into the province of the constitutional courts. Anyone, whatever his or her standing in the community, could lay claim to the privilege, which was its chief democratic virtue. So long as both, or all, parties *voluntarily* presented themselves, a case could be heard. The three justiciars should be good men and true in the public's estimation. (Presumably in times past the custom had had to be abandoned whenever the baronet was known to be a man lacking in the proper qualities, yet I could find no reference in the archives to any replacement ever having been sought.) Witnesses might be called, but no more than a reasonable number of them, as good sense dictated: they need *not* be called, if none were thought necessary. Anyone had the right to spectate, so long as he or she caused no affray.

*

First I mooted the possibility (in roundabout fashion) to Davies. He was immediately agreeable, and seemed genial even to know that a solution of such a sort was possible. I had an impression that all was clarified in his mind and he had now no doubts about the outcome, a development which buoyed *me* up a good deal. He didn't seek to know why I preferred this arcane method to the full panoply and the financial risk of magistrates and jury in a crown court. He seemed wholly unsceptical.

'This will suit your wife too?' I asked him. 'She'll approve?'

'Yes. Yes, indeed. I think I can speak for her on this account.'

'Maybe I should speak to her first —'

'As you wish, my good fellow. Just as you wish.'

*

When I made a few preliminary enquiries after the maid, Mrs Davies told me that Martha had taken her weekly afternoon off that day, so that she was alone when the two men claimed to have rung the bell of the front door.

'Can you tell me what — what happened that afternoon, Mrs Davies?'

98

Her answer was that 'nothing' had happened: nothing whatsoever.

'My husband must have been at the surgery. Or the golf course maybe. I was upstairs, lying on the bed. I'd been asleep, I think. I had the curtains closed. Because of the heat —'

'You didn't see the two men?'

'Not at all.'

'Or hear them?'

'No.'

The maid couldn't remember where she'd been that afternoon. None of the Davies' neighbours had any recollection of seeing Fishlock and Gilbey arrive or depart.

'Perhaps I was reading something.' Mrs Davies closed her eyes to think back. 'But I don't normally. I'd only have leafed through the pages. It was too hot for the brain to function. On that sort of day it just — well, locks.'

'And...'

'"And"?'

'May I ask, Mrs Davies — what you were wearing? That afternoon?'

'Yes. I was wearing my slip.'

'That's — all?'

'That's all. I was lying on the bed.'

'Nothing else at all?'

'Beneath my slip?'

'Eh, on top.'

'On top of it? No. No, just my slip.'

'I see. I see.'

Her husband stood listening to her, with his hands plunged deep down in his trouser pockets and his eyes shining.

*

When I was preparing to confront Fishlock and Gilbey about a civic hearing, it happened that they contacted me and made the same suggestion. They consented in principle, they said.

I met them to discuss any reservations. We were served a genteel afternoon tea for three with cinnamon toast and Battenberg cake in the sitting-room of the elderly Mrs Fishlock's house. The two men recommended to me that neither Dr Davies nor his wife should be present at the time their testimonies were heard, 'for delicacy's sake'. That being

99

so, I then said, I believed that both *their* testimonies should be given separately, and that neither should be present in the room when the other spoke. They exchanged glances before replying, very well, and beneficently smiling at me their approval. (Their air of harmlessness, speaking frankly, quite disarmed me.) *I*, they said, would obviously be speaking on Mrs Davies's behalf, was that not so? I tried to appear as demure and also unconcerned and lawyer-like as I could before replying, yes, very probably I would be. And what about themselves? I asked. They told me they had only the truth to admit to, so they would be presenting their own case themselves. *Separately*, I reminded them. They exchanged glances again and nodded.

And it was as absurdly easy as that, in those essentials. More complex was securing the services of Lord Marlott and two others, the 'notables', but eventually that too was organised, for such-and-such a day.

*

News of the forthcoming hearing in the Old Schoolroom spread about the town, even into its darkest corners. It was *I* who was held to be the principal agent in the business, and I didn't know whether to be flattered or embarrassed. I wondered if it was correct for me to pledge too strong and partial an interest. I might pretend that, as an incomer, I was interested to study such an archaic, unique form of municipal civic justice, but no one seemed able to separate in their minds the prospect of the event to come and the concomitant abstract of 'justice' from the living, breathing, actual fleshly form of Dr Davies's wife.

Botterel appeared a little anxious on that account, but for my sake rather than the practice's. His own social contacts with Fishlock and Gilbey were continuing; perhaps, I thought, he was in doubt about the outcome, and he feared a fall in store for me? I acted with as much confidence as I felt I could get away with, which was done to inspire confidence in him but seemed to achieve the opposite end. His wife invited me to join them for dinner on a couple of occasions 'à trois' (Lettice pleaded her young fiancé as an excuse both times), and I felt I was being offered their sincere and heartfelt sympathy for my puggish determination to clear this woman's name. (Their talk on the matter was exemplary in its even-handedness, evading what I knew to be their true conviction – that the wife of Dr Davies had tempted those two gentlemen to give the go-by to the strait and narrow.) Maybe they were also wanting me to know, that in respect of this business and much as they felt for me, I was obliged to stand alone and, under everyone's gaze and by my own efforts, to outface my destiny *vis à vis* the town.

But it was a once-and-for-all situation I believed I was ready for.

*

The slandered had a right to be present, but also had the prerogative to decline to appear in person. Mrs Davies – to the town's surprise – declined. In her stead, it was learned, she had appointed *me* to speak on her behalf, and I had agreed.

I realised of course what must happen as a consequence: that the town would see me, the outsider, officially declaring myself against the word of two of the elders. For ever I must belong to the Davieses' camp, to a trinity.

If I'd been convinced of the absolute truth of her story and the falsity of the two men's, I think I could have accepted the situation. But I'd gradually lost that certainty I'd had. I felt *sorry* for the woman, that above all else. I'd persuaded myself she needed my assistance, she deserved someone to defend her, but I now recognised that what she was doing with *me* through her will was to effect an influence that bypassed the finer instincts. So, if it could happen in my own case, why not – earlier – with Fishlock and Gilbey as well?

I'll blame the heat then, our torrid equatorial weather. I have to remember that I was a young man, that Mrs Davies paid me the supreme compliment of her trust, that – after fourteen months in the town – I was spoiling for a fight and a showdown, and perhaps (as the Botterels realised?) I was nothing so much as a hapless innocent abroad.

*

Without warning, Mrs Davies presented herself at my office. She'd come voluntarily, she said.

I almost fell over in my haste to find her a chair and clear a space on the desk.

'Tea? A cup of tea?'

She started to peel off one white glove.

'No thank you, Mr Pendlebury.'

'Any – anything else?'

'Just a glass of water perhaps.'

'Of course.'

'And —'

'Yes, Mrs Davies?'

The glove fell from her hand to the floor.

'Perhaps if the window —'

'I'll open it. Yes. Yes, of course. With pleasure.'

*

Later.

'Is there – is there —'

'You have to ask me more questions, Mr Pendlebury. I understand that. So please go ahead and ask them.'

'I have to ascertain —'

'Yes?'

'— if there's any truth – any truth at all – in the statements made by —'

'I can't say how their imaginations work, what they're capable of imagining.'

'But they say – certain things —'

'Yes. Yes, they do.'

'I have to determine – you see – whether – whether there is any substance at all – in their allegations —'

'About my conduct, you mean?'

'Yes. Yes, precisely so.'

'The answer to that is quite simple.'

'And —?'

'There is *no* substance in what they say.'

'So...'

I took a clean, pristine sheet of paper and picked up a pen but I didn't write with it. I had no need to.

'You told me you didn't even see them.'

'I didn't see them, and I didn't hear them.'

'Of course.'

There was a pause. She coughed.

'I wonder—' she said, 'would you mind – do you think we might open the window just a *little* more?'

'Yes. *Yes.*' I jumped out of my chair. 'Whatever have I been thinking of? I'm sorry —'

I pushed up the sash.

'Thank you, Mr Pendlebury.'

'*What* weather it's been,' I said.

'Yes. Quite biblical.'

'I'm sorry – "Biblical"?' I repeated.

'What's to come next? A swarm of locusts maybe?'

'Do you —?'

'Yes, Mr Pendlebury?'

'Do you think the heat – may have some bearing? On this matter?'

'Oh, *I* think so, don't you? It *must* have. I *do* wish one could go about with one's legs bare —'

Another pause opened up in the proceedings. I found myself looking at her legs, crossed in front of me. They were sheathed in fine silk with a high sheen. Very elegant legs for a doctor's wife in a country town.

I lifted my eyes.

'Those men – does any reason occur to you?'

'None at all, I'm afraid.'

'Ah.'

I sat down. I applied my nib to the sheet of paper, behind books where she couldn't see: but it was only my signature, four or five times. In the silence of the room the scratching sounded businesslike.

'May I – may I ask you . . .?'

'Yes, Mr Pendlebury?'

'Do – do you like living here, Mrs Davies?'

She smiled.

'Living here?'

'In the town. *This* town.'

'I would tell you, but I'm not sure – that I *should* —'

'Oh you *should*, Mrs Davies. In the strictest confidence —'

'Yes, of course. But what I would say to you in the course of social conversation, and how I might reply to you in your office – I feel you must have to swear an oath in such a place —'

'It – I'm sorry – does it – intimidate you? This room?'

'A little.'

'I'm sorry. Really. I do apologise —'

'But *you* have no choice, Mr Pendlebury.'

'Your husband – has asked me —'

'And you have to find out. If I'm telling the "truth". In inverted commas. I understand that.'

She smiled again.

'Your husband – he's naturally —'

'— concerned.'

'Yes. Yes, indeed. He *ought* to be, oughtn't he?'

'Does *he* have any choice in the matter either? He's my husband, so he has to be seen to do the proper thing. And since I have been accused of an improper act —'

'It's a damned disgrace!' The words came out before I could stop myself. But I didn't *want* to stop myself. 'Ridiculous. It would only be possible in an end-of-the-world place like this.'

'I was wondering what your feelings for us were —'

'I don't —' I started again. 'Doesn't it offend you, what people think? How easily —'

'How easily I was disbelieved? Or *they* were believed?'

'Yes.'

She shrugged her shoulders.

'Those men are stalwarts. Pillars of the community. My husband has been here only a little longer than you. That isn't long enough to establish yourself, not in a place like this.'

She clasped her arms at the elbows.

'Of course,' she said, 'maybe it's worse to belong, because everyone then thinks they know all about you, your history. And what they *don't* know...'

I felt I was riding a roundabout, in the oven heat.

'Can I —'

'Yes, Mr Pendlebury?'

'Does it surprise you, then? What happened?'

'Or *didn't* happen, since that is our purpose?'

'Yes, of course.'

'I think it went through my mind. I foresaw.'

'When?'

'When I felt people's eyes were on me.'

She crossed her legs and – seeming not to realise what she was doing – raised her skirt an inch or two on her calf. She used the silence that followed to pull at her collar, to push two fingers between a couple of the fly buttons on her dress.

'I don't – I don't know how you stand for it.'

'What makes you think I *do*, Mr Pendlebury?'

Another of those enigmatic smiles appeared on her face. This time her eyes held mine. Several seconds passed before I thought to look away.

'I don't *think*, Mr Pendlebury,' she began, 'you would have interested yourself in such a matter if you judged me to "stand for" things as they are. Then I would have accepted my lot. But for some reason you saw me marked out: you knew I wasn't the ordinaire doctor's wife after all. Didn't you?'

During my time in the town, no one had spoken of its or their own affairs in such a disengaged way. I was heartened by her independence of mind: cheered and inspired. But she hadn't yet told me all I wanted to know.

'So how do you cope?' I asked her. 'You *are* a doctor's wife.'

'Yes,' she said. 'I am. But it does have its advantages, too, a few.'

'Such as?' I ventured.

'When I married Frank I knew it would allow me – a certain status, let's say.'

'Does it matter so much to you what people say or think? About *you*?'

The question came closer to the heart of the business than I was able to realise at the time. She just smiled again, politely: evasively, I can see now.

'It seems to matter to my husband,' she said. 'He tells me we have to clear my name. That we will try to do so with your assistance.'

I nodded.

'Apparently,' I said, 'he thinks I can.'

'Apparently.'

'Is your husband a good judge in such matters?'

'Frank has depths too. Everyone here has depths.'

I felt I was back on the roundabout, the turning carousel...

'That's what you have to learn...'

She leaned back in the chair. She turned her eyes away from me, towards the window. The street was empty of pedestrians and traffic. I watched the fingers of one hand undo the top two buttons of her dress.

'When do you think this hot spell will pass, Mr Pendlebury? Soon?'

Her fingers reached inside the collar, traced the outline of one shoulder.

'I – I don't know,' I said.

'It will end in thunder. Lots of thunder.'

'You think so?'

'Glorious storms. Electric storms. Forked lightning, and night as bright as day. We're well known for them here.'

'You – do you like the storms?'

'They wake me up, I think. It's very Gothic of me, but maybe I have Miss Havisham's blood in my veins.'

'Do you?'

'A brewer's daughter. She was jilted, wasn't she? Thrown over? And created her own monster – what was she called?'

'Estella.'

'All that sourness in her. Once...she was head-over-heels in love...but with the wrong person...'

She stretched out in the chair and closed her eyes. Her fingers stayed inside her blouse.

I stood up. I don't know why I stood up.

I left my chair and walked forward, making no sound. She kept her eyes closed. I moved towards her, where she sat in her stockings with her skirt pulled up to her knees.

Were her breasts loose inside the dress? I recognised it for the first time, it was the same dress, the cornflower-blue one I'd glimpsed through the window of the house, which had halted me in my tracks.

I turned my head and then I stopped dead still. Davies was standing in the open doorway from the hall. The light was behind him. He was watching us both.

'I didn't —' My voice came out as a croak.

He smiled drily.

'I wondered if you'd finished —'

'Yes.' I coughed into my hand. 'Yes, I —'

'If you haven't —'

His wife didn't open her eyes.

'I was driving past,' he said.

'I think – we've —'

His wife still sat – or reclined – with her eyes closed, in the fall of sunlight through the window.

'Whenever you like,' Davies said, with something eerily

close to enthusiasm, pleasure even, in his voice. 'Till we get this business over with.'

I walked to the door and stepped out into the hall. I felt his presence suddenly diminish without the advantage of his own secrecy, standing in the doorway watching. He looked hunched. It was as if, in an instant, I had the clue to him.

'Yes,' I told him, 'yes, we'll get it attended to.'

But I saw the same glitter of excitement in his eyes I'd caught the time before.

'And it'll be —'

Be back to normality, I meant. How you were. Before. Before I had anything to do with you both, you or her.

I stood between them, looking at neither. Through the open windows at the back of the hall I could feel the dead weight of the heat. I opened my mouth for breath and took little sips of it.

I looked down at the old flagstones at my feet — like the uneven floor in the hall in Laud Street — and I noticed that they were actually oozing a film of dripping moisture, as if (to my failed author's eye) they were suddenly all in a panic about something.

5

The evening before the hearing I saw Davies from my window and called down to him, inviting him up.

Oddly for a man of such a fit, hale appearance he had some difficulty with his balance and breathing on the steep stairs. His breath smelt of drink, I noticed, and the sweat was breaking out on his forehead. He had scratch marks on the back of one hand, and what seemed to be a recent bite on his neck.

He looked round the room with an unremembering expression: everything would surely be forgotten tomorrow.

Hiding inside himself was second nature to him by now and at only one stage as we talked did he open up, fleetingly: but in a way he never had before.

He seemed to lose track of where he was, in which room in

which town. From far away, but quite audibly, the Devonian was speaking.

'You know, I was going to do some quite noble things,' he said. 'Once upon a time.'

'You were?'

'That was the idea.'

'In what way?'

'What's that?'

'These "noble things"?'

'Oh. In my work.'

'You mean – research?'

'Maybe. Or just "serve". Humanity and all that. The poor as the rich.'

'But you do, don't you?'

'What?'

'Serve them?'

'No,' he said. His head lolled against the back of the armchair, his signal of defeat. 'No, I fucking well don't.'

*

'Cheltenham, someone told me.'

Botterel seldom 'talked' about his fellow professionals in the town, so that responsibility would usually fall to his wife and daughter. But maybe, I thought, maybe this evening will be different? He'd called round with his best wishes for me and encountered Davies on his less than sure-footed way downstairs.

We both stood at the open window watching his departure. I came out with the question and asked Botterel what the disclosure in our conversation could have meant.

'It was in Cheltenham. An elderly doctor took him on, I forget his name. In Montpellier. I don't think it was what he'd been expecting, Davies. Or so I heard.'

'How?'

'I know someone in —'

'No, I'm sorry. How was it not what he was expecting?'

'Oh, Cheltenham: lush life, pretty much. We'll give him the benefit of the doubt, say he was a man of principle. But principles become ballast to some people. What he used to think, back in London, maybe that wasn't what he found himself thinking in those old dames' drawing-rooms.'

A picture came into my head of grand but down-at-heel Regency villas, peeling stucco frontages and busts of heads in alcoves with chipped aquiline noses, cooling tea in the true black Wedgwood pots, shuddering water-pipes which had worked loose behind the walls.

'The old doctor went a bit soft – up in the head. Davies had quite a lot of the work to do. Then something happened.'

'"Happened"?'

'I didn't discover. No one did. Except that one of the patients died. The old man had been going to her for years, she was a hypochondriac, but she was quite robust. The family got interested, though, they sniffed something.'

I took my cue to ask the question. 'How did she die?'

'Wrong prescription. Tablets she shouldn't have had, and too many of them. It was written in the old man's hand, but – you know how stories start – no one could be *quite* sure.'

'"Sure"?'

'That the writing was his.'

'I see.'

'Davies was taking over some of his load. Maybe too much. Pressure of work. The old women paid, very handsomely: big services' pensions, colonial, diplomatic, that sort of thing. I dare say he was just like the old man, he didn't want to lose any of the – the rewards.'

'But – if she died —'

'Oh well, she'd mentioned the old boy in her will. Let's presume he told Davies about that. The old chap was very generous to Davies apparently. A bachelor, "not the marrying kind" as we used to say.' Botterel paused. 'Which usually had a sting in it. An implication, you know? Anyway, he gave Davies things, gifts. To keep him there, I suppose. Not a bad-looking chap, Davies.'

'No,' I said, twigging.

'A comfortable set-up, I imagine. At first.'

'Was he needing attention? The old man? Medical attention?'

'He went into nursing-homes eventually. Well, in and out of them. Cheltenham's chock-full of the places.'

'So,' I said, 'that had to be paid for?'

Botterel nodded.

'The old man died. Before Davies was ready, another

doctor pounced, moved in. Rich pickings. Davies *could* have fought it, I suppose.'

'But he didn't?'

'It must have been then he heard about Goodden here. On the look-out. Wanted to get shot of Cheltenham and those old women. Probably told it was still a pretty cushy billet, Ivell Abbas. Maybe it is.'

'Maybe,' I repeated.

'No one here knows about Cheltenham, I'm quite sure. Apart from me, and Elizabeth: and now you.'

'Yes,' I said, and nodded confidentially.

'Perhaps it *was* all just an unfortunate accident. A genuine mistake. The old boy didn't know what he was doing. Wobbly handwriting.'

'And Davies didn't land his nice little smack out of the woman's will – a present from his elderly male admirer who never married?'

I immediately sensed that I'd said too much, overstepped a mark I hadn't appreciated was there.

'We can't read too much into it,' Botterel said, resorting to his non-committal professional voice. 'And no one *can* know. Of course —' The tone became more excusing. ' – he could have waited a week or two. And picked any *other* small town in England, I dare say.'

In which case, I asked myself afterwards, would there have been a wife like the one he now had? Was he just unlucky here? – or was he one of those people who need to give someone else (it might be *any*one else) the responsibility of their conscience, to bullyrag and rack them, to feed them back their own self-distrust and their spite of themselves? *Was Mrs Davies just the objectification of his guilt?*

Boxes inside boxes inside boxes inside boxes.

6

The hearing took place in the Old Schoolroom, a vault-beamed hall tucked behind the Abbey, in its lee, for which most practical of reasons it had survived the scourges of the two Cromwells. Usually it was reserved for presbytery functions, or – once in a while – for purposes of a general election to Parliament.

When I made my carefully timed arrival on the day, after a phone call to Laud Street and some words on 'form' to Fishlock and Gilbey, I found between thirty and forty spectators sitting on rush-bottomed chairs in the body of the hall. They were later upstanding when the notables entered from a side-door: Lord Marlott, with a Madeira sun-tan, flanked by Mr Tremlett (patriarch in the family haulage contracting business) and Mr Dolce (retired senior Excises official and Baptist lay-preacher).

Lord Marlott seated himself on a throne-like structure carried in from the Abbey, and the other two lowered themselves on to substantial ladder-back chairs with arms, appropriated from the same source. The solid table behind which the testifiers were to sit belonged to the Schoolroom; on top of it was a tray of effects supplied by Lettice Botterel, namely a bible for the oath-taking and a jug of water and several tumblers. I was equipped with a lectern from the Abbey vestry, on which I importantly laid out my papers and prompts.

The windows had been opened in deference to the heat. Even mad King George the Third, imprisoned in a great gilt frame and stranded high on one wall, looked distinctly uncomfortable with climatic conditions, eyes popping and powdered wig slipping and all that flesh on his face the colour of undercooked beef.

A reporter from the area's newspaper bustled in at the very last moment. My heart sank. There were no chairs left and he had to join those who were standing, or slouching, behind. He loosened his tie in readiness – as reporters did in the films – and mopped his brow and neck with a handkerchief.

I was starting to itch inside my suit. I could feel a flood of perspiration beneath each arm, mapping huge tropical islands on my shirt. Already my back felt wet, and I couldn't stop myself inserting a finger between my stiff collar and my neck: it was the sort of day that would have rusted a collar stud.

Fishlock was summoned first. After he'd taken the customary oath of law on the bible, to tell 'the truth' and nothing but, he repeated his story very much as we'd originally heard it.

'I wish to establish,' I said, 'that, according to your own version of events, Mrs Davies initiated those – as you called them – "lewd advances".'

'Quite right,' Fishlock said.

'As she sat by the garden pool?'

'Quite right again.'

'Can you repeat – the precise nature of those "advances"?'

There then followed a show of false propriety, which I had to counter as best I could with paper-rustling and a monumental effort not to lose my patience.

'Mr Fishlock, you have made certain allegations concerning the – purported – behaviour of Mrs Davies. I would request that you now give an account of their precise nature, if you would.'

From Fishlock there was some coughing, adjusting the set of his waistcoat, tugging at his cufflinks.

'It was a very hot day.'

'We have established that, Mr Fishlock.'

'She – Mrs Davies – had removed her stockings. She had also – also – hitched up her dress. It wasn't clear to me – clear to me —'

'Yes, Mr Fishlock?'

'I wasn't sure – just what she was wearing – beneath —'

I glanced up at Lord Marlott on his throne; he too was mopping his brow with a handkerchief.

'And —'

Fishlock pressed his right hand flat on the table-top, as if he were trying to leave an imprint.

'Then she started to do – and say – certain things.'

I echoed him. ' "Certain things"?'

'Yes.'

'Will you tell us what?'

'I – I'm not —'

I reminded him. 'You have already told your friends precisely what, Mr Fishlock.'

'Very well. She – she ran her fingers – up and down her legs. And lay back, on the flagstones. She said – she wished a man would understand the things she wanted – that a woman has wants – and most of all what she needed was —'

Needed *what*, he wouldn't say. I cajoled him, threatened him, unsure of my ground I mentioned obstruction, perjury even: till Mr Tremlett on the dais took pity on him.

'I'm not sure if I heard the next words properly,' Fishlock said.

'But,' Mr Tremlett enquired, 'you did hear something?'

'I thought I heard – a most unladylike remark pass her lips.'

Fishlock refused to repeat it when asked: he declared it was against his 'religious tenets and convictions' to speak such a common, base expression.

I wanted to laugh out loud.

'Very well,' Mr Tremlett said, content to pass on the point.

I was allowed to resume my questioning.

'What did *you* do,' I asked, 'in the midst of all this most offensive indecency, as you claim it to have been?'

'I was shocked, of course. Very shocked. I didn't know *what* to do. The doctor's wife was – she was making all sorts of suggestions – bold and lascivious. She – she let her dress slip, up her legs. I tried to look elsewhere. Her feet were in the pool —'

'But you noticed that her dress had been pulled back and her legs were exposed?'

'Her legs, yes.'

'And more?'

'To a – to a birthmark. But I didn't want to look.'

'Of course not, Mr Fishlock.'

'I – I looked at her dress. Briefly.'

'Can you describe the dress?' I asked.

'The dress? I —'

His eyes turned to the seats and their occupants, beneath the dais.

'What colour was it?'

'Colour?'

'Yes.'

'Blue,' he said. Again he looked into the body of the hall. 'Like the colour Mrs Reed is wearing. More – sky-blue, I suppose.'

'Cornflower blue?' I put it to him.

'Cornflower blue has something of the crocus, a hint. A lighter colour, I should say.'

'*How* light?'

'Not speedwell. Sky-blue, I'd call it. Because of the reflection in the pond, I thought it odd at the time —'

'You managed to keep your eyes on the dress? For a while at least – while you continued to stand there?'

'I didn't know what else I *could* do. She – she seemed to have me hypnotised. Both of us. I'd never...'

'You'd never – ?'

'Seen such a brazen woman, I suppose.'

Lord Marlott sat nodding in the silence: then appeared to realise his faux pas, and looked down very soberly at the two pages of procedure in front of him.

I turned again to Fishlock.

'Might I ask what your previous opinion of Mrs Davies was?'

'I – I hardly thought about it, I don't think. She was Davies's wife —'

'*That* we are not in doubt about.'

'I usually saw them together. A neat, attractive woman, if I had to give a description.'

'Which wasn't what I asked. I wished to hear your *opinion*, Mr Fishlock. You've given a physical description.'

'I had no opinion, really. She was Davies's wife —'

'No opinion, that is, until the occasion, the purported occasion, when you chanced to come calling – with Mr Gilbey – to the doctor's house. In the hope of seeing *him*?'

'Yes.'

'And why was that?'

'To – to discuss the health of my mother.'

'Which was a subject he was already familiar with?'

'Yes. He has attended my mother.'

'But not as regularly as Dr Goodden?'

'Dr Goodden has been in Ivell Abbas forty years.'

'*Some*times Dr Davies attended your mother? Atten*ds*?'

'Sometimes. Some things are —'

'Yes?'

'— are easiest discussed with people you know less well.'

'There was no other place where you could have discussed matters? His surgery, for instance?'

'His house seemed a good enough place. Privacy was essential.'

Lord Marlott was nodding. I glared at him, and he stopped.

'You'd visited the house before?'

'Oh yes.'

'Since Dr Davies bought it?'

'No. I called on Mrs Lattimer a couple of times.'

'It was how you remembered it?'

'I should say so.'

'The garden too?'

'Again I should say so.'

'And the pond?'

'I hadn't seen that before. I believe it was the new owners' idea.'

'A round pond?'

'Yes. No. No, it had straight sides.'

'And now – and now you were calling on Mrs Davies. As on Mrs Lattimer?'

'That was for a different purpose. With Mrs Lattimer.'

'You called at Dr Davies's house to talk about your mother?'

'Yes.'

'Let us re-establish – you *had* discussed the matter with him?'

'Not properly.'

'"Not *properly*"?'

'Not in so many words. I wished to ask his medical advice.'

'And he wasn't there?'

'Unfortunately not. *Most* unfortunately.'

'You thought he *would* be there?'

'Yes, I presumed —'

'And then it was that you – you *both* – encountered his wife instead? This neat, attractive woman you describe.'

'Yes.'

'But her husband wasn't there?'

'No.'

'Who told you that? Mrs Davies?'

'Yes.'

'Not the maid?'

'The maid?'

'Yes, Mr Fishlock. The *maid*.'

'I don't – I don't remember seeing a maid that day. No. No, I didn't.'

'It was just Mrs Davies? Wearing her green dress?'

'A blue dress. Sky-blue. Yes.'

'You're sure about that? – the colour?'

'Oh yes.'

'*Quite* sure? When the experience seemed to shock you so?'

'I was thinking to myself – such a very innocent colour – and such profane thoughts. It seemed to me she must be a very unhappy woman —'

'So you *did* have an opinion after all. You arrived at an opinion very quickly, didn't you, Mr Fishlock? When you said you had none before.'

'Well, what else *could* I think? That was my – interpretation, yes.'

'Thank you for your co-operation, Mr Fishlock. That will be all.'

*

I requested that Gilbey be brought into the hall.

In recognition of the man's self-importance we had to wait several minutes until he had taken the oath and was finally seated, I had handed him the glass of water he requested, he had cleared a frog out of his throat and then coughed several times more, and was finally ready to answer my questions.

'Mr Fishlock asked if you would accompany him to Dr Davies's house, is that correct?'

'Quite so.'

'On what business, do you know?'

'That concerned Mr Fishlock's mother, I believe.'

'Why did he ask you to go with him?'

'I have known Mr Fishlock a long time. I have known his mother a long time. She requires some assistance now. Although she is a woman in full possession of her mental faculties. But – we have talked about the matter.'

'It had been discussed with Dr Davies already?'

'I dare say so. But I was not privy —'

'Dr Davies regularly called on Mrs Fishlock?'

'Yes.'

'As Dr Goodden has also done?'

'In the past, yes.'

'The matter had been broached with Dr Davies?'

'I don't expect either party would have cared to do so in the lady's hearing.'

'I see.'

'We had been waiting for our moment.'

'Your "moment"?'

'To enquire.'

'At Dr Davies's house?'

'It seemed the most suitable place.'

'Not the surgery?'

'Mrs Fishlock is *not* a run-of-the-mill patient, you must appreciate.'

'Ah.'

'Certainly not.'

'You meet Dr Davies in other circumstances? At the golf course, I believe? You are all three members?'

'He plays quite regularly, I have heard.'

'You meet him there?'

'We do sometimes, yes. In the normal way of things. On the greens.'

'Indeed "regular" is the word, is it not? For Dr Davies? I understand,' I said, drawing myself up, 'I understand that he plays on most Tuesday and Saturday afternoons. On the very same afternoons you yourselves do.'

'Yes. *We* play a little more often —'

'But this particular Tuesday afternoon you chose to go to – to consult him —'

'We'd forgotten.'

'It *was* a Tuesday, though? That's what you first claimed?'

'Which day of the week it was didn't concern us. We'd come to see Dr Davies on a pressing matter of business.'

'Had Mrs Fishlock's physical condition deteriorated?'

'I can't – I can't say. I'm not aware so. But Mr Fishlock seemed to regard the matter as quite urgent.'

'So, he kept you informed about certain aspects of his mother's health and not others?'

'As professional men – busy men – we have a lot of matters weighing on our minds —'

'I'm quite sure so, Mr Gilbey.'

'Bearing *every*thing in mind, it doesn't become *easier*. As the years go on, I mean.'

'I'm sure not, Mr Gilbey. At any rate, on this one day, a *Tuesday*, you decided to approach Dr Davies on the delicate subject.'

'That is so.'

'Only to find, of course – according to your version of events – that he wasn't present in the house. He was on the golf course.'

'So we discovered.'

'From his wife?'

'I – I can't remember.'

'*She* told you?'

'I suppose she must have done.'

'Or the maid?'

'The maid? Yes, I believe she *did* tell us. Her employer was not at home, she told us. Dr Davies was playing golf —'

'Although you might have remembered that beforehand? For yourselves?'

'We don't play the greens with Dr Davies. Not regularly.'

'Yet you *might* have remembered.'

'As I said, Mr Fishlock —'

'Of course. The mind being overburdened, I recall —'

'It slipped our minds.'

'Slipped your minds? I see. *Then* you remembered —'

'Yes, Mrs Davies *did* mention it to us. She said her husband might be there.'

'Not the maid?'

'I *mean* the maid.'

'I see.'

Gilbey coughed several times, and had to ease his throat with water.

'The house was familiar to you, Mr Gilbey?'

'I had been there in Mrs Lattimer's time.'

'It seemed the same to you?'

'I – I wasn't thinking to look —'

'Mrs Davies spoke to you where?'

'She was outside on the terrace.'

'Mr Gilbey, will you now please explain – the sequence of events on that auspicious, indeed – by now – notorious afternoon?'

'That is *your* expression for it.'

'Yes, Mr Gilbey, my own merely.'

'I doubt if I can "explain", Mr Pendlebury.'

'I'm sorry?'

'How could I *explain* – ?'

Now I felt *I'*d been caught off my guard.

'Relate that passage of events, then. Adumbrate. If you please, Mr Gilbey.'

'From which point?'

'Let us say, from – as you claim – your going into the garden.'

'"Claim", Mr Pendlebury?'

'It is my job —'

Mr Dolce coughed, rather pointedly.

'If you *would* kindly, Mr Gilbey —'

'Let me remember —'

I dutifully waited.

'Mrs Davies was in the garden. The maid showed us out. She was sitting beside the pool. The ornamental pond.'

'You remembered the pond? From Mrs Lattimer's time?'

'It was new. I'd heard about it —'

Gilbey stopped, tightened the knot in his tie, reached out for the glass of water.

'It was a new pond,' he repeated.

'A square pond? A round pond?'

'I can't – I can't remember that. Square. No, round. Perhaps —'

'Mrs Davies was sitting? In a chair?'

'On the ground, on the stone. Beside the pond.' (This detail corresponded with Fishlock's account of events, barring the maid's part.) 'She had her toes in the water – and her ankles. Mr Fishlock and I stood there —'

'Do you remember if the fountain was playing?'

'I think so.'

(Fishlock had denied any recollection of a fountain.)

'And then?'

'And then Mrs Davies started talking to us.'

'"Talking"? In a normal tone of voice?'

'No. No, quite softly.'

'But you could hear her?'

'Quite distinctly.'

'Even though the fountain was playing?'

'A *quiet* fountain. I heard, yes.'

'You heard the same as Mr Fishlock?'

'I should say so.'

'Even though you heard the fountain and – according to what Mr Fishlock has just told us – *he* didn't?'

Gilbey straightened his back.

'I don't know about that. *I* heard the fountain.'

'And you heard what Mrs Davies was saying? Quite distinctly, didn't you tell us?'

'*Too* distinctly.'

'Exactly *what* did you hear her say?'

'Unspeakable words. Unspeakable for a lady.'

'Recognisable words, however? You weren't unfamiliar with them?'

'Sadly, I *have* heard them, yes.'

'In Ivell Abbas?'

'From some rough elements. In the lower orders, of course.'

'I see.'

'But *never* in such circumstances.'

'Can you remember any of the words to repeat to us?'

'*Not* to repeat, Mr Pendlebury.'

'They were being addressed to *you*? To you both?'

'Who else?'

'Over the plashing of the water, you knew that she was – what? *Why* was she saying such things?'

'I haven't come here to explain "why", Mr Pendlebury. I leave the niceties to you.'

'"Niceties" perhaps being somewhat of a misnomer? Given the situation?'

'Indeed. I can't say *what* her purpose was.'

'You find yourself unable to repeat the words?'

'The worst expressions you can think of: that *any*one could think of. Dredged from the – the sump of human experience. Quite disgusting.'

'Where does that "sump" exist? In a region apart? Or, could it be said, inside each one of us?'

'That is philosophical speculation, Mr Pendlebury: or sounds amazingly like it.'

'Very well. You use the word "sump"; you say you were "shocked". What was your previous opinion of Mrs Davies, before the events of the afternoon in question?'

'She seemed to me...'

'Yes, Mr Gilbey?'

'Well brought up. She – she looked the part, I should say.'

'She was respectable, decent?'

'Being a doctor's wife . . .'

'You've known her far longer ago than that, though? When she was Miss Antrobus?'

'Yes.'

'Did you know her well?'

'I knew her father. To some extent.'

'You had no – no closer contact? With Vivien Antrobus?'

'"Contact"?'

'Acquaintance.'

'I took an interest in her progress. As I heard about it from her father.'

'Until his death?'

'I suppose so.'

'You knew Mr Antrobus well?'

'Not – no, not "well".'

'*Mrs* Antrobus?'

'I – she wasn't a woman to —'

'With the knowledge you had of Vivien Antrobus's life —'

'Hardly that.'

'At any rate, you had no – no forewarning at all of Mrs Davies's alleged behaviour on the day you claim – you say you called on her, with Mr Fishlock?'

'I should say not.'

'Mrs Davies, it's your assertion, spoke those unrepeatable words. Can you describe to us her *actions*, Mr Gilbey?'

'If required to.'

'Please feel free.'

'I should describe them as being of a very *loose* sort. Flighty. Not becoming her standing.'

'Her standing is important to you?'

'It must have some bearing on how I regard her, how *everyone* regards her.'

'How "loose" and how "flighty"?'

'It hardly seems proper to —'

'Please feel free.'

'Very well.'

With that, Gilbey hunched forward in his chair. His eyes seemed to be seeing back to that afternoon.

'Some of the buttons on her blouse were undone, if I recall.' (Fishlock too had mentioned buttons.) 'Her legs...'

'They were bare?'

'Yes. Quite bare.' Gilbey licked his lips. 'There was water on them, runs of water. They glistened.' The tumbler was raised, and Gilbey sipped from it. 'She – she sat caressing them. With her fingers. She'd pulled back her dress. She seemed –' He replaced the tumbler on the table and stared at it. 'She seemed to be naked beneath. I could –' He spoke more softly. 'I could see her thighs. Her thighs. And just a little more –'

'What did you see? Her buttocks?'

'A glimpse –'

'But you *did* see?'

Gilbey lifted his eyes.

'How could I not?'

'We can't really presume to judge on that matter, Mr Gilbey.'

'The heat –'

'The skirt of her dress was tucked back, you say?'

'Yes. Yes, right back. To a birthmark.'

'You mentioned her blouse. Do you mean the top of her frock?'

'I – They might have been the same. You know? Not a blouse, but part of the dress.'

'Perhaps,' I quipped, 'marital life would have instructed you in such minutiae?'

Gilbey looked across at me stonily.

I straightened my face.

'Could you please tell us the colour of this – possible – dress, Mr Gilbey?'

'The colour?'

'The colour, yes.'

'Yellow.'

'You're sure of that?'

'Yes. Yes, I'm sure. Yellow. The colour of buttercups.'

'You'd been looking at it for several – seconds, at least?'

'Yes. At least.'

'The blue dress?'

'Yellow.'

'Not blue?'

'Yellow. Very definitely.'

'Ah.'

'The fair hair, you see. Fair-ish. It was all of a piece, more or less. That's how it seemed to —'

'I think, Mr Gilbey, I need detain you no longer. I'm very grateful to you for your assistance.'

7

Are you such fools, you Israelites, as to condemn a woman of Israel, without making careful enquiry and finding out the truth?

*

But here is a woman of Judah who would not submit to the ways of villains.

*

Then Joakim gave praise for his wife Susanna, because she was found innocent of a shameful deed.

8

Davies took my hand afterwards with a firm, powerful grip and pumped my arm.

'I knew you could do it, Pendlebury,' he said.

'I thought – perhaps they wouldn't have checked on *all* their details.'

'No. No, they didn't.'

'The smallest ones. Only they weren't so insignificant. They're both, in their way, rather proud men. They came here today *because* they were proud. Maybe they were convinced that no one could dispute it, their memory *couldn't* be at fault.'

'It was, though. Only it wasn't memory at all.'

'No.' My eyes avoided Davies's face and I felt heat on my neck. 'No, of course not.'

'*You* knew it was all ballyhoo.'

'I —' I realised I couldn't tell Davies that the matter wasn't so simple as that: that perhaps each of the two men had allowed himself to believe the story he was telling.

'I suppose,' I said, 'I – I only had to find – whatever it was that they'd overlooked.'

'The dress?'

'Yes. Yes, your wife's dress.'

'Very good.' Davies smiled at the ruse as he led the way outside, into Wool Lane.

'And I dare say,' I said, 'they just picked the first colours that occurred to them. Then they had to stick to them, for – for veracity's sake.'

'Of course.'

'I —' I screwed up courage. 'I'm interested, though —'

'Yes?' Davies didn't look at me; his eyes searched Wool Lane.

'Does your wife have either a sky-blue or a buttercup-yellow dress?'

'Either? Or both?'

'She has a sky-blue dress *and* a yellow one?'

'She has both.'

'Ah.' Wool Lane smudged. 'I see.'

'They must have noticed her wearing them. As they went about the town.'

'It occurred to me – they'd invented the colours.'

'Like the situation?'

'Yes. Yes, like the situation.'

'You haven't seen the dresses?' Davies asked.

'I – I haven't noticed, I'm sorry. Maybe I *have* seen them, I don't know —'

'The impression must have gone deep. With Fishlock and Gilbey.'

'Yes.'

'They associated a dress my wife had worn – its colour, which they must have seen her wearing one day – they associated that with the vision of – of what was beneath it.'

'Yes,' I replied, and I heard the faint din of roundabout bells in my head. 'Yes indeed.'

'I'm not quite sure why,' Davies said, leading the way. 'Perhaps at the time there was a wind and it caught at my wife's dress. Walking down Pack Street. It catches the wind doesn't it? The Abbey Green gets it too. Some time they saw and were disturbed —'

'Yes,' I repeated a second time. 'Yes. "Disturbed".'

We turned the corner into Pack Street, carnival bells clanging.

'I wouldn't have thought it of them.'

'You wouldn't?' I said, looking up and finding Davies's eyes on me.

'Pillars of the community, more or less. Our elders.'

'But – but you didn't —'

'Believe them? Of course not.'

Davies glanced past me, to the activity on the pavement.

'It's a scurrilous lie. Didn't we say?'

'Yes. Yes, we did.'

'We don't know *what* was in their minds.'

'Maybe the colour of the dress too,' I said. 'It was just a wild fancy.'

'I've no doubt.'

'Can you guess *why*, though?'

'Maybe I'd be the last to know. But...'

'Yes?'

'Sitting there,' Davies said, 'didn't you think —?'

'Think what?'

'When they were talking —'

'They'd read it somewhere? Or they were making up?'

'When she was rubbing at something on her leg – they said.'

I smiled, down at the pavement. 'In that case, what's it going to be like at sixty?'

'My wife *does* have a birthmark, though,' Davies said. 'Just under her right hip.'

My smile stuck on my gums. I stared at the pavement.

'They got that right.'

'What?'

'Just under her right hip. Very high. They knew that somehow.'

'*What?*'

'A strawberry mark.'

Davies stopped, stood still.

'I —' I couldn't think.

'Just as they told us.'

'Well – Well, it must've been coincidence,' I said.

I lifted my eyes again, and caught Davies's moving off my face.

'Yes,' he said. 'Yes, it is.'

I shifted uneasily from one foot to the other. I willed myself to put the birthmark out of my mind for the meantime.

'Good men, Pendlebury. Our judges, our verderers. Good men and true.'

'Yes.'

'Our recording angels.'

Davies smiled. He always smiled in a way that put me on my guard, that caused me to distrust him. The gesture was too ready: he made it seem, not affirmative, but a concealment. At the very moments when we ought to have been talking to make full sense, it was then that I felt he was avoiding the vital matters our words professed to be about.

*

A couple of days later I met Davies in the bank. We exchanged a few, very obvious pleasantries but he seemed anxious to be gone.

When we walked out into daylight and Pack Street, I noticed several new bite-marks on his neck. His left ear-lobe seemed to have suffered likewise.

He saw me looking and turned and walked off, with a cavalier 'goodbye' dropped behind him.

*

I couldn't forget about that strawberry blemish, so high on her right hip.

*

One evening afterwards I walked into The Plumes for a drink and it took only twenty seconds, no more, for the voices round about me all to fade away to nothing.

*

Early another afternoon I was standing on the pavement on Pack Street when Davies drove downhill in his car. I walked to the kerb to raise a hand to wave to him, to say something, but he didn't stop, he didn't even slow. It must have been shock that preserved my balance and didn't knock me backwards and send me sprawling.

*

A day or two later.

Eldridge in the office had been to Davies's surgery. He reported back, not about his own complaint but about something else. He had obviously been impressed by the fresh bite he'd spotted on Davies's neck. His right ear had been nicked too.

'His right ear?'

'Yes.'

'Not the left one?'

'The right one.'

It only meant one thing, Eldridge said. Mrs Davies was as randy as —

Something made him stop just in time, or maybe I *would* have done what I knew I should, swung my fist at that pimply jaw and cracked it open for him, given him a hospital visit this time.

*

And then, of course, there was the enduring mystery of the birthmark...

*

Lettice Botterel was generous in her admiration. She sounded a warning too.

'They wonder how you know.'

'Know? About what?'

'Everything to do with it. That she didn't – well, what they said you said, that she was framed —'

'It's my job,' I told her. '*Was* my job. To know.'

'They remember *you* were at the house too. When Davies wasn't there.'

'For quarter of an hour, that's all.'

'It might be long enough.'

'For what?'

'For what was supposed to have happened with *them*. Fishlock and Gilbey.'

127

'They misunderstood. That's all.'

'But *did* they? They claimed – she said things. How could they both have misheard?'

'I've no idea.'

Then an idea *did* occur to me, one I could have made use of at the hearing if I'd thought of it then.

'There might have been music,' I said.

'There might have been any number of things. Did anyone mention music?'

'No. Not that I recall.'

'But they did mention words?'

'I'm sure they didn't even *see* her.'

'*You* saw her.'

'When?'

'When you called at the house.'

'Yes. But we're not talking about that. It's Fishlock and Gilbey this is about.'

'Two against one, William.'

'Yes. Exactly.'

'Were they both mistaken?'

'Obviously.'

'You're quite sure of that?'

'Their stories didn't match. The judgement went against them.'

'Did it, though?'

'Of course it did. The ruling was, there *was* no case.'

Lettice bit her lip.

'We won,' I said. 'We beat the town.'

'How did people know you were there? At the house?'

'I can't say.'

'No?'

'No. Truly. I haven't a clue.'

'You're not – protecting her, by any chance?'

'"Protecting her"? That's absurd, Lettice.'

'Is it?'

'Why in God's name should I want to —'

' – protect your Mrs Davies?'

'Not *my* Mrs Anything.'

The Mrs Charles Allingham-to-be leaned against the door post, laid her head back, and considered me. Her smile was opaque and inscrutable.

*

128

Mrs Davies had been seen in a headscarf, even on a day of broiling heat, and wearing sun-glasses.

She took to high collars, for a week or two. No one could get close enough to speak to her.

From the lane I saw her twice, in the garden, sitting in a deck chair on the top lawn, flanked by the columbines and mignonettes and drifting sweet rocket. Both times she was wearing sun-glasses and a yellow dress (*the* yellow dress?), and had her face turned to the sun. Her arms hung loosely and limply by her sides, her hands trailed on the grass.

Love bites. Dark glasses.

*

Then a neighbour, Miss Murgatroyd who lived directly opposite, heard, with her window open.

Screams, in the middle of one night.

The first scream, and then a second.

Then silence.

*

Mrs Pomfrey spotted the doctor's wife in the Castle grounds, walking quite quickly between the Orangery and the lake.

'How can she *bear* to wear a headscarf? In *this* weather? And those sun-glasses, how odd. Does she think she's in Hollywood?'

*

Eldridge from the office had to go back to see Davies at the surgery.

I overheard him in the other room telling Hoyle that there was a fresh nick on his *left* ear now, the blood couldn't have been dried long.

'Oh, she must be a randy little tart, that one.'

*

In Catto Lane I looked back and saw Davies's car parked by the kerb. Then I realised his face was behind the windscreen.

I tried continuing my conversation with Mr Eustace, but I'd lost my train of thought.

Twice more that day and several times more in the course of that week, I noticed the car within surveillance distance of me, and Davies behind the reflection in the windscreen, behind the dapple pattern of trees and the glare of sky.

*

The case didn't appear in the newspaper as I'd expected. I had good reason to believe that Messrs Fishlock and Gilbey had been able to apply some pressure, via a third party, on the editor.

Years later the journalist did retell his story (in part), as an anecdote in a London evening newspaper, but he had forgotten most of the details and – thankfully – all the names.

9

Oddly, our contacts more or less ceased afterwards. It wasn't what I'd been expecting to happen. But the couple seemed to withdraw into themselves; into the routine of the surgery and the privacy of the house on Laud Street. Fewer invitations of the social sort were issued to them, and they declined most; they didn't reciprocate those invitations they did take up.

Solid wooden fences and gates replaced the iron railings and gates at the back of the house and I wasn't able to glance in any more returning from a walk. Months before, I had occasionally spotted one or both of them walking in the grounds of the Castle proper, where you went only with a permit: but now, keeping an eye open for them, I didn't see them at all.

Clearer to my memory than the hearing was the conversation in my room in Botterel's office the afternoon she called, in the heat. She'd spoken to me with a directness and purpose no one else in the town – even the well-intending Botterels – had used. It might have seemed that we were working towards an understanding. But my convictions concerning – not her 'innocence' – her technical *inculpability*, those had never been wholehearted, especially in the course of the actual hearing. And I didn't include Davies himself in any notional concept of an 'understanding': quite the opposite, my participation – at his request – had apparently resulted in the man's determined indifference to me, if not hostility.

As the town viewed matters (according to Lettice Botterel's hints) I had nailed my colours to the mast and there was no going back to the way things had once been. Perhaps there were stories circulating that I spent some of my time at Laud Street, with or without Davies being there or even knowing. I preferred to think that the Botterels would keep me informed: but they didn't mention any such stories, which only persuaded me they must be doing the rounds but had been neatly diverted about Moat House.

*

I did dream about her, however, in my night sleep.

Either she was lying upstairs of an afternoon in the darkened bedroom, on a rumpled bedspread, one hand idly riffling through the pages of a book: sometimes Flaubert, sometimes Fontane, sometimes Jung or Freud. She never seemed to notice, or else care, that I was standing there in the doorway, watching.

Or she was sitting on the paving beside the sunken pond on the terrace. One foot and ankle were trailing in the water; the other leg was tucked beneath her. Her dress had risen up, baring her thigh. The mound of her buttock was just visible. Every time it would strike me at the same moment, almost as an afterthought, that she wasn't wearing any underwear. The fountain rained lightly on the pond's surface, spreading its own rumour of coolness. I glimpsed, just, the birthmark.

Nothing happens, though. Nothing ever happens in this private palladium, kept – almost – a secret from our little town: in this disabling, paralysing delirium of midsummer madness.

*

The storms didn't come to end the summer. The good weather merely ran down and fizzled out into days of fresher breezes and gentle drizzle.

Or rather, she correctly prophesied in one sense, the doctor's wife: the storms *did* come – but not until the spring of next year, when their fury seemed more random and less rooted in causality, the principle of one set of conditions determining and making necessary another.

*

'But perhaps you never knew?' Mrs Botterel said, with a glint in her eye that might have been mischievous, in an amiable way.

'I'm sorry?'

'About Frederick Gilbey. And Vivien Davies's father.'

'What's that, Mrs Botterel?'

'Years ago. It was Mr Gilbey who made the discovery that Antrobus gambled.'

'He did? How?'

'Friends of friends. Mr Gilbey is holier-than-thou, so it could only have been hearsay. And somehow Mrs Antrobus heard and so that's how she learned, although her husband wouldn't admit to it . He though he was being very discreet, Antrobus, and I think he probably was. Anyway, Adeline Antrobus kept the knowledge to herself, never mind that Gilbey's circle must have known, or known something. And that's when she discovered her husband was a liar, which was the painful part, and so she waited for her moment to confront him. That only drove him into it, worse than ever, so it's said. While she determined that their daughter would be a lady and no mistaking. Which was where all Vivien's problems began.'

'Mrs Davies knows? About Gilbey?'

'Knows and remembers, I'm sure so. From things she's let slip, and her mother before her. Adeline Antrobus got to hate the man, *I* heard; but kept tight as an oyster about it, to *us*. How *could* her daughter have forgotten, though?'

'Why didn't you – if I'd known —'

'But a town is layers deep. Layer on layer. You'll have to learn that. A town is vertigo to look down into.'

'Ivell Abbas?'

'So you have to think what you can do about that.'

'"Do"?' I repeated. '*What* do you do?'

Mrs Botterel had her answer pat and ready.

'Say your good mornings, my dear. Walk past trouble. Keep a civil tongue and your eyes just passing over the outsides of everything. And always,' – she gathered up my teacup and saucer with a splendid little flourish – '— always resist the temptation to drop your eyes and look down beneath your feet.'

*

132

And the books, it occurred to me one evening walking past, lined up on the sitting-room shelves. They were bought as a job-lot in a sale-room, and transported out of someone else's life (who died, who had no more need of them) into theirs.

*

An imaginary conversation.

Fishlock: *A peaceful end, Doctor.*
Davies: *I shall have to think about it.*
Fishlock: *Mother wouldn't know anything, she wouldn't suspect.*
Gilbey: *A humane solution.*
Davies: *But she's got all her marbles, hasn't she?*
Fishlock: *She's got some of them.*
Gilbey: *Mrs Fishlock is a strong woman. Strong-willed. And – well, fairly difficult.*
Fishlock: *I would have to agree with that, Doctor.*
Davies: *She already takes tablets, of course?*
Fishlock: *Of course.*
Gilbey: *Of course.*
Davies: *And what does your sister think, Mr Fishlock?*
Gilbey: *Mrs Wills is an impressionable woman, Doctor.*
Davies: *That could be a danger*
Gilbey: *Another whisky, Doctor?*
Davies: *Thank you. A short one this time, I think.*
Gilbey: *Nonsense! Double or quits!*
Fishlock: *It seems to me – fortuitous, you see – with Goodden handing some of his responsibility over to you.*
Davies: *Admittedly that is – fortuitous.*
Fishlock: *Naturally this would be a compact between us, Doctor. Among the three of us.*
Davies: *'Compact'?*
Fishlock: *Well . . .*
Gilbey: *What my good friend means, Dr Davies, is that it will go no further than ourselves. There will be no risk of any – awkwardness.*
Fishlock: *We shan't refer to the business again, ever.*
Gilbey: *It will seem that Mrs Fishlock has merely – lost her strength.*

Davies:	Her body is a little frailer than her mind certainly. But —
Fishlock:	And my mother is a wealthy woman, Doctor.
Gilbey:	In a word, 'loaded'.
Fishlock:	We would obviously – show you some expression of our gratitude. No little expression.
Gilbey:	That would be the least we —
Fishlock:	She must depart this earthly life sometime, after all —
Gilbey:	Shuffle off the mortal coil.
Fishlock:	And she would wish it to be when she might – exit from the stage with dignity.
Davies:	She's said that?
Fishlock:	Not actually 'said' so, in those exact terms. But I have a blood instinct —
Gilbey:	If you could know her as I know her, Doctor.
Fishlock:	She wouldn't wish to deteriorate and be unable to help herself, Doctor.
Gilbey:	Or be a shadow of the woman she is.
Fishlock:	She knows how sad it is, how laughably sad. She has had her fun at the expense of others. To live so long and be so well-to-do at the end of it, when it's late to do anything with your resources...
Gilbey:	She would be the first to see the folly of that, the futility —
Fishlock:	But we're thinking of her good – her good above all else.
Gilbey:	We should be doing her a favour, I have no doubt: in the final scheme of things.
Fishlock:	You will have nothing to reproach yourself with, Doctor, not at all. No stain of any sort on your conscience. Your soul will be unblemished.
Gilbey:	Like ours —
Fishlock:	And like my mother's, as she prepares to meet her Maker. She has told me that death holds no terrors for her, none whatsoever. She is prepared —
Gilbey:	Ready —
Fishlock:	She is only waiting. Waiting for her moment. Waiting for her deliverer.

As I said, an imaginary conversation.

Davies:	But —
Fishlock:	Yes, Doctor?
Davies:	If I shouldn't —'
Gilbey:	You surely will, Doctor. When you see the good sense in it.
Fishlock:	I am my mother's son, Dr Davies.
Davies:	By which you mean —?
Fishlock:	She is a woman of many wiles.
Davies:	'Wiles'? Yes, indeed.
Fishlock:	I have learned much from her.
Davies:	A vengeful woman too, I have to say I've heard.
Fishlock:	Oh certainly.
Davies:	You have that in you too, the revenge?
Fishlock:	Indeed. If I don't get what I wish.
Davies:	While she thinks you wish something else entirely, which is only the commendation of doing her bidding?
Fishlock:	Her mind runs in its own set grooves.
Davies:	She thinks you're a devoted son who will do her will?
Fishlock:	Yes.
Davies:	Not realising?
Fishlock:	We think we know best, Doctor.
Gilbey:	Having lived here all our lives.
Fishlock:	Whereas you —
Davies:	But my wife was born here —
Fishlock:	She isn't really 'one of us', though. Is she?
Gilbey:	Hardly, Doctor.
Davies:	No?
Fishlock:	No, she's quite different. Not 'one of us' at all.
Davies:	What is she then?
Fishlock:	I wouldn't like to say.
Gilbey:	Nor I.
Fishlock:	Would you like to know? Doctor?
Gilbey:	Or you wouldn't like to know?
Fishlock:	We could tell you. It would only be what everyone in Ivell Abbas has guessed already.
Gilbey:	I've heard them say so. I have heard other things too, Dr Davies.
Davies:	Heard what?
Fishlock:	You really don't know?

Davies:	I...
Gilbey:	I don't believe you do, Doctor.
Fishlock:	An educated man like yourself —
Gilbey:	An education, don't they say, is never finished.
Fishlock:	Yours, Dr Davies, least of all.
Davies:	I think I'm learning. All the time.
Fishlock:	I hope so, Dr Davies. For your sake.
Davies:	My sake?
Fishlock:	There are lessons Ivell Abbas could teach you which you would never forget .
Gilbey:	Never forget.
Fishlock:	Not until the last breath you take.

10

Fishlock suddenly left the town in early October, with the town still sweltering: for a holiday, his sister announced to her surprised neighbours.

He travelled along the coast to more temperate Budleigh Salterton, where his late wife's sister and her husband lived. Their régime was strictly social, and he was dragooned into bridge and pontoon sessions and beetle-drives and charity-group discussions and golf fours and round-the-clock dog-walking.

Perhaps the general pace of life there, living among the retired generals, would have weakened anyone's heart. Fishlock proved a readier victim than most and, in the course of his fourth week in the town, he slumped sideways off his chair after winning his first game of canasta.

He was taken to the cottage-hospital but, in the lingo of the press, was 'found to be dead on arrival'. His hosts and their guests had known only too well that all was over, waiting for the body to twitch on the rug like a landed mackerel – but nothing happened: his eyes stared up at the ceiling, glassier than a mackerel's even, and his flesh started to take a sea-chill.

His sister-in-law was mildly shocked, for an hour or so, but she was the practical kind, who wouldn't have felt pity in the normal course of things for any (another Fleet Street term) 'inconsolable' widow — so it was most unlikely that she would betray her own convictions in similar circumstances. She picked up the receiver on the telephone and called her brother-in-law's sister in Ivell Abbas, giving a brief and un-emotional account which principally detailed her own virtues as the embarrassed hostess of the evening.

Thus occurred the death and passing into glory of Bertram Havergal Fishlock.

*

The second death came in another season, in the wet spring of the next year.

A woman from the town exercising her King Charles spaniel made the discovery. She had dispensation to use the Castle grounds, and at half-past nine of that morning was taking the cinder path between the Orangery and the lake when she noticed the body.

It was afloat, face down, and entangled in an island of water-lilies.

The woman ran to the lodge and returned with help. The lodge-keeper pushed out a boat and rowed them both to the spot. The person in the water was wearing a fishing-jacket which had filled with air. The man leaned out of the boat and tried to take hold of an arm. He needed several attempts.

The head was covered by vegetation, and the man had to tug on the arm to pull it free. Somehow — thinking they would be defeated by the weight of it and almost over-turning the boat in the process — they did both haul the body aboard.

'It — Good God, it's Mr Gilbey!'

The woman had to look away from the face with its bulging eyes and twisted mouth. The skin, she told her friends afterwards, was the queerest colour: Paris green, verd-antique.

*

The speculation started soon enough, in the first hour the news got about the town.

An accident, conceivably: he'd lost his footing and the weight of what he was wearing prevented him from recovering his balance.

Or...

Or just as conceivably – the more sceptical minds started to consider in subsequent hours of reflection – Mr Gilbey's death had *not* been an accident. He was an experienced angler after all and there had been nothing untoward about the circumstances – a quiet lake, no tides and currents. Was it possible, for whatever reason, that the fishing-rod had been a convenient prop, and that the dragging weight of his clothes had been most precisely calculated on?

But why should he have *chosen* to die? Depression, presumably. He'd had no problems with his health, so far as anyone knew; but (no one had forgotten the summer) a troubled mind visits its own afflictions on the body, and perhaps – rather more than had been appreciated at the time – his mind must have been tried beyond the safe limits of reason.

*

One morning in the second week of November Davies drove his wife to the station and unloaded a couple of suitcases, a vanity-case, a shoe portière and a hat-box.

He explained to enquirers that Mrs Davies had gone off 'to visit an old schoolfriend', in Bath.

The weeks passed and there was no further sign of the doctor's wife. Someone did catch a sight of her in Bath, on Pulteney Bridge, riding a man's bicycle with a crossbar.

Later Davies was obliged to announce that his wife had moved on 'to visit another friend' from her schooldays, who lived in Glamorgan. To the town Wales was a land apart, distant and occult, and no one had a clue: the doctor could just as well have told us 'Samarkand' or 'Timbuctoo'.

*

Just before Christmas I put my back out bending down to lift a pile of books. I didn't know what had happened, not there and then, and I went to see Davies.

I was shown into his surgery. He said 'good afternoon', but didn't smile; we might never have met before. I told my story, gave him the details, with rather more formality than I'd planned. He asked me some questions but he seemed chilly and disinclined to be more than minimally civil. I mentioned 'hernia' as a possibility (with a stage grimace).

He asked me to lie down on the couch and to unbutton my trousers. He stood over me, his shoulders itching uncomfortably inside the jacket of his bespoke suit.

I thought I could catch the trace of spirits, the drinking kind, on his breath.

His hands were cold as he inched down the waistband of my underpants. He asked me to describe the pain in my groin, perhaps to draw my attention away from him. I tried to concentrate on the words, on their sense, as he pulled on the waistband to expose my crotch.

His brow furrowed and his eyes grew smaller. I looked away.

His fingers made contact with my genitals. I could feel them contract with his touch and the embarrassment. He handled me quite roughly. He had me lift each of my legs in turn; he bent them at the knee, pulled the calves and ankles this way and that. Whisky, I thought the smell from his mouth might be. He told me to cough: cough again. Then he jerked at the waistband, tugged at the underpants and turned away.

'It's not a hernia,' he said. 'Up on your feet. I'll give you some exercises.'

I aligned myself directly in front of him, with my back to him, and did as I was bid.

He told me I'd 'displaced' a disc in my back. There was nothing I could do except leave it to get better of its own accord. That might take months.

'Many months?'

'Yes. Quite possibly.'

He warned me against lifting heavy weights. A displaced disc could become a slipped one all too easily and then I'd know all about it. I'd have shooting pains from my head to my ankles and I'd be supine.

I nodded at the information, which was imparted quite factually, without any suggestion of sympathy.

'As I said, you'll just have to leave it.'

He stood up as I did and placed his hands on the edge of the desk. Memories of the summer came rushing back. He opened his mouth as if he was going to say something. But then he closed it. His eyes sped over the paperwork in front of him and his brow furrowed again. He lifted his right hand and swept back some hair. Lines appeared at the corners of his eyes, the worrying or laughing sort. That's an expensive tweed suit, I was thinking, and the corduroy waistscoat is a cut above the usual, she wants you to cut the proper dash.

I held out my hand. He hesitated, then took it. There was less strength in the grip than I remembered, than I would have expected from a man of his build. I told him I'd be careful, I wouldn't go lifting any more than I needed to.

'You shouldn't lift at all, anything that's heavy.'

'Very well. Just as you say.'

As I walked to the door, I heard water pouring from the taps in the basin. He bent over the bowl, lathering his hands with soap, to remove the feel of me. I said 'goodbye'. Perhaps I didn't say it loudly enough, because he seemed not to hear, and he didn't reply. I stood for a moment or two with the door open, delaying. I thought his head lifted slightly, but he didn't look round.

He *has* told me what it really is? I wondered.

I walked out into the hall and closed the door behind me. Even that simple action made me feel gravely unsettled, as if I'd lost crucial ballast and was unbalanced, like a listing ship.

*

Mrs Davies stayed away until the new year.

Her famous absence somehow only emphasised her prominent part in the town's recent history. She was discussed, but cautiously: or perhaps the caution was reserved for those occasions when I was on hand to hear. Heads were shaken and corrugated folds appeared on brows. No one had the appropriate knowledge to judge, and prejudice made her its focus instead. Perhaps the purpose of that was revenge, with its origins in fear.

The fundamental fault was not of her own making: she was a woman, and that (in those days) was the cardinal point. There was no neutral middle ground between (dutiful) wife and (rampant) whore. Either way a woman could not determine her own destiny in life: she was defined by the definitions of others. I started to appreciate that the essential mistake perpetrated by this doctor's wife was to create such a mystery of herself. She should have reflected and offered back, instead of which she was a self-contained bubble of transparent matter, so slippery-surfaced that no definition could stick; the watching eyes simply passed right through her to the other side. She confirmed that she was no one except in herself. She had even stopped going to church, when appearances (having a doctor for a husband) depended on it. It was as if she was announcing, I am made in the image of nothing at all, except myself, and that is purely a matter of speculation anyway.

What she'd done was to crack a seam in the otherwise seemly fabric of Ivell Abbas life: an unsightly rent that jogged the topmost surface well out of kilter, out of what was thought to be true. Behind – if one were to stare long enough – there opened up the prospect of a drear place of no perspective, knocking the senses for six and causing, at the least, extreme queasiness. Behind the familiar lurked *everything that was not*, no more than a hand's reach away.

How could the town have forgiven her, for undermining the structure of things as she had? The very temple was quaking, and she could set it rocking again by nothing more than a lazy sideways tilt of her head.

In their troubled, fitful dreams men and women alike were admitted to the garden, and there they encountered those long, sheenless legs under the rucks of skirt – the drooping pendulous breasts immodestly, flauntingly moulding the material of a blouse – the wayward arrangement of her hair, worn as nature had fashioned it (instead of crimped and waved as the rest of the town did) and drawn up from the neck on to the crown of her head and the escaped strands left trailing – the flush of her body's heat on her cheeks and a triangle of semi-circle exposed on her chest, just above the point where her breasts began – the groove, the gulch, the crevasse – those unladylike stripes of tan mapped on the aked offerings of flesh, as if she were an island girl, or the intended victim of some tropical ritual of sacrifice.

*

She returned some time in January, when the season's festivities were over and done with. She appeared in the town wearing some new clothes, and sporting a variety of toque hats and two-tone shoes with peep toes. One day she was to be seen walking a half-grown red setter on a leash. The dog accompanied her for several days, but then she reappeared without it and it was never seen again.

A few invitations were directed to 31 Laud Street and were either declined or brought an apologetic reply from the doctor, accepting on his own behalf but excusing his wife because she had a chest cold or a slight stomach upset or — But she was to be seen several mornings a week in the town, speaking very little to people and yet always, so it seemed, in quite robust health.

The doctor by contrast was beginning to look worn, with shadows under his skin. His staid, stale smiles for politeness's sake didn't connect with the other features on his face. His eyes had a haunted expression, and they restlessly moved among all the details of the room but so quickly that almost nothing must have registered in his memory. His fingers played with the cutlery and rolled the edges of his napkin. Conversation swilled about him like high-tide water and his mind floated off on its own troubled course...

Speculation started in the town that there must have been a *reason* for Mrs Davies's absence, and perhaps the so-called visit to 'old schoolfriends' was really a fabrication, a fiction. It might have been that she had been 'incautious', the meaning and imputation of which everyone understood. But in that case, how could she have been riding a bicycle, and a man's bicycle at that, over Pulteney Bridge?

Of course no one had forgotten the summer – how was it possible? – and the cause of the business in the Old Schoolroom: which *I* had managed to turn into a sort of rout, and a vindication of a woman who wasn't deserving either leniency or forgiveness. Lord Marlott, with another (Tenerife) tan, and Messrs Tremlett and Dolce had suffered no substantial loss of prestige as a result: they were merely to be pitied for having been hoodwinked by the Davies-Pendlebury conspiracy.

I knew very well what was going on inside the deviously calculating, dissenting mind of Ivell Abbas.

And all the time the condition of Davies was becoming more noticeable. He had clearly lost a deal of weight, and his tailored tweeds appeared to have lost some of their former well-bred swank. He seemed to have shrunk an inch or two, except in his arms and hands; and his face had grown longer and thinner. He was seen in the Castle grounds on several occasions, walking unaccompanied. His patients could rely on his turning out whenever he was requested to; his manner, they agreed, had acquired *more* rather than less douceness with living in the town. He knew what was what in his job: he muttered words to himself which only *he* could hear, but didn't stop for any chit-chat of the normal sort, and was on his way again at the very first opportunity

No other information was forthcoming. The maid didn't consort with other residential staff, and the daily help and sometime cook – by no accident? – was hard of hearing in one ear and uniquely forgetful of the ins-and-outs of life in the house. There were no further sightings of Martha in the vicinity of Heyton Woods, on the hillside where the woman who made babies lived. The doctor's car wasn't spotted speeding at sixty miles an hour through a pea-souper fog. No one identified Mrs Davies riding a bicycle, although that was one (apocryphal) image which seemed to take hold of the town in the seasons after the hearing: a hot summer's day again, but in Bath, not Ivell Abbas, the young woman astride a man's bicycle with a crossbar, and the draught tugging at her skirt, blowing the folds back to her knee and further perhaps, peeling back the slip, and not a care for what anyone might be seeing and thinking. Schoolboys must have overheard their parents, and imagined a glimpse of Mrs Davies's thighs, seen to best effect sheathed in fine stockings: the outsides of her hocks and the insides lightly grazing, rubbing against each other, and the stockings swishing. Higher up, where the stockings stopped, were straps and hooks and two round bands of bare flesh, with none spare to wobble. Higher up still, hidden beneath the girdle and a knicker leg was something else that must have been discussed, with voices lowered, in the snugs of pubs and the crannies and inglenooks of adult social life, once the word got out, to be overheard all over again by a younger generation: the birthmark on one hip, the strawberry blemish that told her to be no other woman than this one, the wife of Dr Davies who was turning into such a dour, dark, uncommunicative, guarded man, and close as wax.

11

In the spring Davies's end came about too, in appropriately dramatic fashion.

He was found hanged in the outhouse behind his surgery.

His feet were hovering in mid-air above his doctor's bag and an overturned chair from the waiting-room.

*

He'd seen his last patient of the afternoon at half-past six. It was remembered that he'd been especially sparing of words and patience that day. His notes were studied afterwards, but they proved to be as orderly and to-the-point as always, and made perfectly good sense.

*

His body was taken down and inspected by Dr Goodden, who requested the presence of a colleague from the next town to confirm the circumstances of death and to witness the signing of the death certificate.

*

Mrs Davies, so the maid in Laud Street announced repeatedly, wouldn't be back tonight; she had gone away for the night, to Bournemouth, she didn't know whereabouts in Bournemouth.

Calls were placed, to hotels, and she was traced to one of the best. She answered sleepily, but seemed to take in the information quite clear-headedly, quite calmly. She said she would leave for Ivell Abbas first thing in the morning and, without any evidence of tears, replaced the receiver.

She arrived back at lunchtime the next day. She walked to Laud Street from the station, with her luggage being pushed behind her in a handcart. Back in the house she changed out of her pale resort-wear at the first opportunity, into a slimly elegant black ensemble, which must have been purchased recently to be so up with the fashions – a pleated dress with long lace sleeves and a matching two-thirds-length crêpe de Chine house coat, black silk stockings, four strings of sparkly jet beads, and two black malachite bows in her hair. Her eyes, it got about, had no signs of redness about them.

She had the maid telephone the fishmongers and the licensed grocers and place orders for two dozen oysters and a magnum of champagne. (For the sad obligation of entertaining in the circumstances, it was presumed, but no one was to set eyes on – let alone taste – those two most ostentatiously expensive epicurean luxuries the town purveyors could supply.)

*

The funeral was arranged for the Thursday, not at the Abbey but at Saint Jerome's, the little church which had once served the Castle and the estate workers.

It was too soon for venom; the town was still in a state of intense curiosity concerning the doctor's widow. She wasn't in circulation, which could be of no surprise to anyone. People were left to their imaginings, to picture how she was taking the tragedy. ('Tragedy' in the town's consciousness was a term approximately synonymous with 'shame'.) The maid, Martha, was no help in the matter, true to her form.

*

I feel bound to recount what happened the evening before that of Davies's death, as if some clue might lie there.

About six o'clock the skies had closed and during the next couple of hours the thunder came in, rolling across the county. Walking back home, raindrops the size of silver sixpences were splattering on to the pavements. Risking the disc in my back, I ran back to the house as best I could. I'd just shut the front door behind me when the skies opened again and, in seconds, rain was ricocheting off the roof and windows.

Lightning shot the sky brighter than daylight. Thunder bellowed, almost overhead, and the lightning ripped. Dogs caught out-of-doors howled with terror.

More thunder, and five miles away the thatched roof of a cottage at Heyton was struck by a bolt and went up in flames. In Yelton, even closer, an oak tree which was centuries old was split in two.

The atmosphere must have been singing with the overload of electricity.

Sometime between nine o'clock and ten, sparks fell on to the roof of the Abbey's side-chapel. There were several witnesses. Wild current ran along the guttering, smashed a gargoyle's head to pieces, and slithered down the wall, cracking the stone. A window exploded and spangles of flame and glass flew through the air as the current homed in on some timbers. More sparks flashed. Canon Vintrey saw a silver-blue streak flare and cleave the wood; the timbers caught fire in seconds.

The blaze – against the odds – was confined to the side-chapel. Firemen managed to angle water on to the flames in such a way that they didn't spread into the rest of the building. Water was being pumped until almost midnight, when it was thought that the last embers had been doused.

The walls of the side-chapel were still standing in the morning. Its roof had fallen in, but because that part had been built to a lesser height than the Abbey's, the destruction was at least limited to only one part of the structure. The Canon said they had indeed been very lucky: pale eyes smarting from the smoke, he told all of us who were there to bear in our minds and hearts that God in His wisdom had been generous in sparing us worse distress than this.

Which words having been spoken, another joist crashed down from the bare bones of the ceiling and a fresh cascade of sparks crackled and spluttered.

At the funeral Mrs Davies was fetchingly accoutred, in a long fitted coat and with her veil of speckled tulle drawn back from her face.

Mourning suited her as it suited no one else in the uncomfortable crowd gathered at the graveside: the rich black satin and the three strings of pearls gave a contrasting glow and health to her skin.

She conducted herself with great composure. As if they were only being offered an example, no one among the fifty or sixty persons present wept. The vicar's words floated up into the branches of a budding ash and were lost there. Red clay of the fields was politely strewn on the coffin. The widow continued to scan the other mourners, quite dry-eyed, as if now she was really challenging them, defying them to think certain thoughts.

A buffet luncheon had been prepared in the house on Laud Street. Thirty or so of us were invited to attend. Only one – a Devon cousin – declined.

Mrs Davies reappeared without her hat and veil. Her hair was piled up on her head and fastened on top with a coquettish black velvet butterfly bow. As she matter-of-factly explained what was what on the table and sideboard I stood – back aching – three or four feet behind her, with my eyes fixed on the bony ridge of her neck; the tip of her spine was just visible, beneath the clasp on her strings of pearls.

She wished us 'bon appétit' and smiled at Martha to begin the operation. All through the meal – eaten by us in an oddly party-ish frame of mind, even though we had to do without the oysters and the champagne – I saw her keeping an eye open for the maid, continuing to flash smiles in her direction. The girl kept her face sedately compliant and complaisant, as if she was only being encouraged to do her job, to do it well and without sorrow in a roomful of sober flannel and black crape.

At a certain juncture I also noticed that the material of the widow's dress showed no marks of the hooks or straps on foundation garments. I gingerly moved about the room so that, discreetly distancing myself, I could watch her from the front. Perhaps she understood because at one point I looked up and caught her eyes moving off me as she turned to talk – in profile – to someone, the hunting cousin from Bath with the decibel delivery. I could see that if he had ever held any fascination for her (or she for him), now he was only boring her.

After that I concentrated on the food, and the low-pitched conversation, and the pain in my spine, until it was time for us to take our leave. I was shaking her hand when coincidentally she took an opportunity to thank someone else over her shoulder. I thought it was as if she was wanting me to look, defying me as she had us all at the graveside: smiling bravely, dispensing politesse as if there were nothing remarkable about this day.

So why did I refuse myself and *not* look at her, if that's what she was intending?

Had I looked, then maybe she would have turned her head on her neck much sooner than she did. If I'd looked, I would have been making a victim of myself, to my own guilt. *You are all of you guilty for what has happened, oh this appalling tragedy.* I knew better than that, at the same time that I had difficulty in keeping my eyes off her.

She kept me waiting, my hand held in hers (and the disc in my back forgotten) so that everyone else might see and be troubled by their natural suspiciousness and by the little skewer pricks of conscience. When she did turn round and finally let go my hand I felt my face firing. I'd forgotten what to say and struggled to find the words.

'You're very kind, Mr Pendlebury,' she replied, taming the smile. 'Thank you so much for coming.'

Her eyes were incredulous, laughing as her mouth couldn't; irony shrank them. She stretched out her hand to the next person and her eyes shifted, sliding leftwards, with the mockery untempered.

'Like mother, like daughter' it was remembered in certain quarters. Like mother, like son-in-law even. Life was cruel and heartless in its symmetries.

*

The man must have been more miserable than he had ever let on. He ought to have confided. But then, to whom would he have been able to trust himself in his despondency?

*

The incidents of the long summer were recalled all over again: the brouhaha of the courtroom, and the suffocating heat, and my own much-advertised involvement in the proceedings. 'Wasted effort' was the consensus of opinion. The woman had led the town a pretty dance. Now that it had come to this.

*

Why, I wondered, had there seemed to be such haste in

despatching the certificate of death?

Goodden had signed, and his colleague had witnessed. No bland inference of 'misadventure'. No communal burden of shame to weigh on us.

*

The headstone was delivered from Fishlocks' stonemasons' workshop and raised in Saint Jerome's churchyard.

'*In Eternal Memory of Francis Edmund Meredith Davies 1903 – 1935 R.I.P.*' (No '*loving memory*', no '*dearly beloved husband of*'.)

Once a stranger to the place, the doctor now belonged to it for time in perpetuity.

*

Mrs Davies began to add some colours to her widow's black. It was said that she didn't look as grief-stricken as would have been expected: a woman in her situation might even have been haunted to lunacy by such terrible sadness.

But Mrs Davies was wearing beige and olive with her weeds, and someone – humming the chorus of 'Vilia' – unkindly made the first reference to 'The Merry Widow'.

*

I'm not a professional writer, I'm not a thinker, I can't pretend to talk of ideal if speculative concepts like fate, destiny, predetermination, *in*determination. But coincidence does play a part in the affairs of all of us.

Living here and there in England, I've sometimes felt it's like nothing so much as an overgrown village, where news conspires to travel faster than sound, and to arrive – somehow – before you. In various spots I've been told 'Your reputation goes in front of you', and I've never been sure if there hasn't been a kind of malice in the tone. I don't know how it is that in places which (admittedly) share a certain social identity, there are always – without fail – people who know people who know people...

*

It was the lunch hour.

I'd gone for a walk on the Castle avenue. Holding my breath for my back's sake, I negotiated the fence into the field

149

behind the lodge, and took my time as I climbed up to the iron gate at the top where the bridle-track began.

I didn't hear her approach.

'So...'

I spun round, forgetting the hazard of sudden movements.

'*This* is where you come to do your reflecting?'

'Oh. Hello.' An ache seeped down into the small of my back.

She pulled the gate open. She was wearing suede gloves, a tweed coat, a headscarf, and gumboots.

'Do I look the part?' she asked.

'"The part"?'

'For walking? I'm not one of life's walkers particularly. This is for sentiment's sake.'

I held the gate open for her and she passed through.

'Would you care to accompany me?' she asked, prompting a question I knew *I* should have asked.

'I – Yes, of course. But I'll have to —'

'Just as far as the stile. I need the air.'

I came through the gate behind her.

'No bloody dog-walkers today,' she said.

'No. No, I don't see —'

'Will your shoes get dirty?'

'It doesn't matter.'

We took the bridle-path and followed its descent between the fields. The valley's sides sloped like an amphitheatre's.

As we walked we exchanged pleasantries, about the weather, about the likely state of the harvest.

'D'you think it'll be a summer like last summer?' she asked.

The chances, I said, were probably against it.

'That *was* a summer, wasn't it?' She smiled. 'How they're supposed to be and never were.'

We'd reached the trees on the flat. I was looking all ways for anyone who might see us. Then ahead, but too late, I caught sight of a heifer being mounted by a bull. The path passed within about twenty yards of them. I realised she was watching them.

'I want to tell you something,' she said.

'Oh.' I nodded.

'Before I *regret* telling you. I didn't tell Frank. I haven't told anyone, ever.'

I nodded again, not looking at what was taking place on our right-hand side.

'A girl at school invited me to her house,' she began.

I turned my head and, falling a step behind her, I stared at her, at the groove of bone on her neck.

'I must have been fourteen. For some reason she and her sisters went off one afternoon, with her mother. I stayed in the house, in the drawing-room – as they called it. I was reading when the door opened. Who should come in but her father, mine host. Smiling at me, very nicely. So *I* smiled. And he came over, and sat down at the other end of the sofa.'

We were in line with the grunting bull and panting heifer.

'He found some excuse for coming closer. I kept on reading my book. I didn't – I didn't *know*, in so many words. But in another way, I did: I sort of *felt* I knew.'

She stopped still and looked into the field.

'All that terribly proper furniture, and good rugs, and nice paintings, and silver, and the room smelling of flowers. And Louisa's father sitting with his trousers open and his you-know-what on his lap.'

I coughed, spluttering saliva, and stoppered my mouth with the back of my hand.

'It was so ridiculous. That it was happening, I mean. I didn't know where to look, I'd never even – if I'd had a brother, maybe I would have – I'd never *thought* about it. Well, very little. Maybe he imagined I was more grown up than I was: although I was just Louisa's age.'

She turned away from the coupling and walked forward.

'We just sat there. Me, him, and the thing. The thing wasn't responding properly, even if I didn't know it then, it couldn't decide.'

I stared at the flints under my feet.

'*I* didn't do anything, for it was up to him. And he had to clamber off, and the thing looked much less sure of itself, it shrivelled away. He left the room, very shamefaced, and angry too, I suppose. And that evening his wife came to me, looking very shocked, and she told me I was to leave the house in the morning and she wouldn't invite me back, ever again, but she had no intention of telling my mother. I didn't ask what it was about, I just walked out. And maybe *I did* know then.'

I repeated her, just to have something to say. 'You – you just "walked out"?'

'Louisa didn't understand. Somehow I *did*, inside me, I had a feeling. In a certain bit of my anatomy. And I felt a special kind of sickness, a different sort, I hadn't had it before. But it was the *other* ache – of wanting something —'

I couldn't look at her.

'So I *had* grown up, you see,' she said. 'And Louisa, she didn't. And it was all done in only a few hours.'

She didn't speak again until we'd almost reached the stile further up the hill.

'I think Louisa's mother must have hated me very much. She believed I'd made it happen, whatever it was.'

'What —' I swallowed. 'That – that's all that *did* happen?'

'Oh, I was telling you *my* side of the story.' She spoke with the voluble confidence of an actress playing a favourite scene. While I was suddenly remembering the orchard at Moat House and her dramatic entrance that first Sunday afternoon, so long ago now.

'There's bound to be another one,' she said. 'Or there's an outside and an inside maybe?'

She stretched her neck, turning her head several ways, preparing for the true revelation.

'I'm leaving,' she said, unpinning the grenade she'd kept hidden till last.

'What?'

'I'm leaving here.'

'For a holiday?'

'For good. If you'll pardon the expression.'

'When did —'

'I've made up my mind. I've had it made up for me, really.' She paused. Her eyes swooped on me. 'Are you going to try to persuade me otherwise?'

There was another, longer pause. How much was hanging on that interlude of six or seven seconds?

'No,' I said at last. I looked away. 'I – I don't think I can persuade you.'

'You're not the man for that?'

'I don't —'

I stood shaking my head.

'This isn't the sort of place for me,' she said. She stopped and looked back. Her eyes filled with the view of encircling fields.

'I'm sorry.'

'But you won't stop me?'

'You know your *own* mind,' I heard myself saying.

'In that case —'

She climbed up on to the stile. She perched on the top bar, side-saddle.

I looked at my watch, so as not to be caught looking at her. I suddenly realised. 'I'm afraid – I have to go back now,' I said. 'It's time.'

'The law is a demanding mistress?'

'Yes. Yes, she is. And Mr Botterel is a keen clock-watcher. I wasn't thinking. About the time I mean.'

'So. I shan't detain you then.'

'I —'

'But thank you for your company.'

'I – I've enjoyed it.'

'It'll be our last conversation, I expect. I suppose I knew that.'

'I hope – you enjoy the rest of your walk.'

'I've been here too long, too many years. I don't mind if I never see these fields again. To be honest.'

'"Honest"?' I repeated, but hadn't meant to, only dwelling on her use of the word and what it could mean.

Her eyes tightened; then – a moment later – the skin at the corners relaxed.

'Please, excuse me. I must —'

'Of course.' She smiled. 'Goodbye, Mr Pendlebury.' She offered me her hand, and I took it. 'And "bonne chance".'

I felt her eyes on me as I made my way downhill. After maybe a minute, or a little less, I stopped and looked back.

She held up her hand and, wresting triumph from defeat, she smiled again, waved.

*

The words and pictures stayed in my head: they were locked inside and there they pursued their endless flights of further fancy.

For several nights I dreamed the same dream.

I'm walking about the panelled corridors of a country house, with rolling fields outside the windows and red-jacketed, mustard-waistcoated huntsmen on their mounts jumping hedges.

I turn the handle of a door, it swings back, and I see, sitting on a sofa in the middle of the room, a girl of no more than fourteen.

She doesn't look up, appearing to be preoccupied with her book.

I walk forward on tiptoe.

She's positioned so that one leg is tucked beneath her. Her skirt has risen up, very high, and I see, on her bare right leg, the tell-tale of a birthmark, in a secret place little short of her hip.

I drop on to the cushion beside her and cause a little flurry of feathers.

She's reading a translation of *Le Rouge et Le Noir*.

'Which part have you reached?' I ask her, keeping my voice low.

She doesn't lift her eyes from the print.

'I think,' she says, very quietly, 'Madame de Rênal is about to give herself to Julien for the first time.'

I recognise the voice, from somewhere else, ahead of her in her future.

I lean back in the sofa and close my eyes. I clench my hand, the one by her leg – only inches away from it – and I bunch it into a fist.

*

I didn't know what to do. She had confided in me, for what purpose I couldn't tell. Was it to put the record straight, with one person at least? Or had the intention been a different one? – to incite me? Or had she told me for neither of these reasons: her story wasn't even true, but only so much hocus-pocus spoken off the top of her head in order to confuse the issue no end?

I allowed her a verdict of not proven on the last point.

She had wanted to tell someone before she turned into the eventual version of herself which would be remembered in these parts, the legend; and she had told *me* because she knew I would keep the information to myself and because – because she wanted to see its effect on me? But why should she have cared one way or the other how *I* reacted?

Unless she understood me and my confusions better than I thought?

My enduring memories of Fishlock and Gilbey were of their mystifying composure and the certainty that they had indeed been enticed: even as the adjudication turned against them and unanimously, they both maintained their demeanour of blamelessness. *They* had had the fieriest summer in the last twenty to plead in their defence, if they'd wanted to: but they'd preferred instead to leave the matter as it was, as it had been decided upon, as if the fieriness had consumed the notion of either veracity or its opposite. Standing at my lectern in the stifling heat of the Old Schoolroom it did seem to me that they *believed*: and in the immediate aftermath of the hearing and its ruling and the town's silence I sensed most fully the inviolability of the place, when there was no proper 'evidence' in the case one way or the other – the town had its own methods of rooting out what didn't belong to it, and custom and history would decide the matter, not an upstart of twenty-three years old.

12

She went quite suddenly, in a taxi to the station, with only such luggage as could be carried. ('Without a backward look,' Miss Mallelieu across the street commented.) The faithful maid accompanied her mistress.

The house was emptied by a removal company and immediately afterwards put up for sale by auction. The successful bid was that of the elderly Mrs Fishlock, but she happened to die of a coronary seizure eleven days later, and her distressed daughter submitted the house for auction a second time. After a slow sale that reminded some of what happens to properties with a 'past' or rumours of a ghost, the house was bought – at a lower price than Mrs Fishlock had paid – by the Reverend Canon Vintrey from the Abbey, to (as he put it) 'enjoy his retirement in'.

So, with the prospect in the town's mind of those rooms filled with divinity tomes and bible-reading groups and pure thoughts and favoured brownies from the 'Mab' pack and an institutional smell of carbolic, the day's business at the auctioneer's was concluded.

*

Therefore, eight months after the hearing Mrs Fishlock was also dead.

The executor of her will was the son of a long-retired lawyer to whom Botterel had been apprenticed. The younger man, Outhwaite, came by the office one day, to speak to Botterel. Later I found him waiting for me in my room. He introduced himself: we chatted, quite affably. He had been well briefed on the hearing.

'I was asked by Mrs Fishlock not to divulge the information, but I don't suppose it matters now. I wonder if it has any bearing on what happened.'

'What's that?'

'Old Mrs Fishlock was a woman with – I'll have to call them – strong notions in her head. Thoughts that took hold of her. But she also had the means, the financial means, to indulge herself in whichever – let's say – fanciful conceits she wished to. That made her seem either eccentric to other people, or possibly rather dangerous. She had a long memory too.'

'I see,' I said, puzzling where this might be leading us.

'She was a stickler for secrecy too. That got worse with age, like her fancies. A couple of years ago or so, she told me she wanted to – her words – to get her hands on the house on Laud Street: Mrs Lattimer's house, which she'd just sold to the doctor and his wife.'

'Why was that?'

'She'd wanted it for years apparently.'

'Mrs Lattimer's?'

'It's quite a fine house, isn't it? And unbeknown to most people Mrs Fishlock owned other properties on Laud Street, four or five, which she let out in very secretive ways. She enjoyed the secrecy. I wasn't to tell anyone, *any*one, she was quite insistent.'

'I see.'

'Then she told *me*. It went back to the time when she was a young woman, and so was Mrs Lattimer, and they were still both unmarried. It had to do with a man, someone they'd

156

both taken a shine to. More than a shine. I suppose the two women turned out to be rivals for him. In the end it was the other woman who won him. About the same time someone called Fishlock came into view, who suddenly found a bride for himself and hardly needed to try. Without realising that it was a case of "on the rebound". It happens often enough, I dare say.'

'"The other woman" – ?'

'The man was called Lattimer – of course. He was an accountant, and she became his wife. While the Fishlocks had the solace, so-called, of each other. When they'd been married a few years, the Lattimers, they moved into the house on Laud Street. I think Mrs Fishlock could never forget how they'd been rivals, Mrs Lattimer and herself, and how the husband and the house should really both have been hers. The friendship was a thing of the past, and after that she pretty much steered a path round the couple, the Lattimers, which can't have been very easy in a town this size.'

'No. No, not at all.'

'It wasn't just that she didn't forget what had happened, it preyed on her mind: she couldn't excuse the other woman's obvious happiness. She and Fishlock started buying up some houses on Laud Street, when the prices were low and all you did was take a risk. Done very circumspectly, though. I suppose because she knew enough about herself to realise why she was doing it, to compensate herself in some way, and she couldn't even admit it to her husband, why she wanted to close in like that. As I said, she had the means to finance her little whims, she'd also been left some money of her own. But she had to wait – years and years – until long after Lattimer and her own husband were dead, when Mrs Lattimer finally decided to sell up. She still wanted the house, just as much, but maybe now it was to lay the ghosts to rest, and so she found a way of making an approach, which didn't reveal who the interested party was. Only a *potential* buyer, because – I don't know if Mrs Lattimer guessed what was going on or not – she was quite obstinate and wouldn't be swayed by the money. Mrs Fishlock would have paid, even someone she'd envied most of her adult life. But Mrs Lattimer said she *knew* who she wanted to have the house, the sort of people: a young couple who – she thought – were bound to appreciate

157

it. The doctor and his wife just fitted the bill, to her thinking. And so Mrs Fishlock lost out, and I suppose that turned everything that was in her to bitterness, the envy went rancid. I'm not sure what her son knew: I'd guess he got to know a good deal about it, because latterly she was doing many of her business transactions through him. In which case...'

There was a pause.

'I see,' I said. 'I see.'

'Maybe her fixations switched, from Mrs Lattimer to the couple, the doctor and his wife. Or maybe it was Fishlock himself, he'd inherited the habit from his mother, and *he* was the one who became obsessed by them. Of course, being how she was, it wasn't likely that Mrs Fishlock was going to let it all *not* matter to her at that late stage. After *his* wife's death, Fishlock – the son Fishlock – and his mother became closer anyway. "Like a vine round a trunk", someone once said to me. So, perhaps they hatched something between them. Or Fishlock acted at his own behest.'

'And contrived it?' I said. 'The famous seduction in the garden?'

'Imagined it, you think?'

'Maybe,' I said.

'Hmm.'

I detected an equivalent doubt in Outhwaite's mind.

'She survived him though,' I said, 'his mother?'

'By a few months. I expect she gave him a hard time.'

'But Gilbey killed *himself*.'

Outhwaite paused momentarily before continuing.

'Someone else said – in a sort of *knowing* way – deep, very clever-clever —'

'Yes?'

'Said that they'd always been very "close". Gilbey and Fishlock.'

'I suppose so.'

'Were they? "Close"? Did they seem so to you?'

'I don't know. I didn't think about it. But – how do you mean, "knowing"?'

'This town is all hearsay, no? What you didn't suspect, and *couldn't* have suspected. There must be things going on just now, for instance – at this moment – that we don't have a clue about.'

'But Gilbey,' I said, backtracking.

'Could it have been an accident? The drowning —?'

'I don't think so.'

'He could have been ill. A terminal condition.'

'He could have been,' I said, and nodded. 'No one said so at the time —'

'How close were they, do you think?'

'I noticed people often talked about them together, as a pair. In the same breath, more or less. They were – I suppose they were institutions.'

'Depression then?'

'Why depression?' I asked.

'Take your pick.'

'Guilt?' I suggested. 'If it—'

'Or madness. That vision of female sensuality.'

'Yes.' I agreed about the possibility at least.

'He never married?'

'Gilbey? No.'

'Fishlock did, of course. Perhaps to escape his mother, I used to think.'

'No one mentioned her much,' I said. 'The *young* Mrs Fishlock.'

'It's her fate to be forgotten obviously. I wonder if it's Gilbey's fate.'

'He was rather a pompous man,' I said. 'With an "air" about him.'

'*Can* we really know? The "why" and "wherefore"?'

'Perhaps not.'

'One dodgy grandparent would be sufficient – with a streak of the unpredictable.'

'He was something-or-other at the Abbey,' I said.

'Was he?'

'Warden. Vestry clerk.'

'Good and godly?'

'Unless he just woke up one morning —'

'Yes?'

'And —'

And the sky fell in, I meant: what was left where it had been was a hollow, everything went tumbling into it, the Abbey, his seed shop, his friend Fishlock, a bag of golf clubs, dog-eared volumes of horticultural wisdom, snatches of hymn-tunes, all bobbing about in a sea of darting fish and the blades of paddling oars and a foaming dress of buttercup-yellow and the worst, most shameless, most debasing words that man or woman ever spoke.

13

Mrs Davies didn't come back.

The next year I could take no more of the place, and returned to Bristol.

No so long after that a great war came about and I was spirited away to Surrey, to Guildford, to a tracking and decoding centre.

*

I kept up with Mr and Mrs Botterel, and we exchanged amiable letters containing our news. I also wrote to Lettice Allingham (as she now was), and by return she wrote to me: her scribbled letters, full of non-sequiturs and margin arrows, were more informative about the town than her parents', even though she was now living twenty miles away.

Among the cryptic politesse in one of her letters was an item of local intelligence tagged on as a footnote. '*Is it a piece added to the jigsaw or taken away, do you think?*'

A story was only doing the rounds now, that in the same year of the supposed seduction, the baker's boy had been 'interfered with' one winter's afternoon, under cover of dark-ness. The two men who invaded the lad's privacy had chosen their spot carefully: a cutting behind the golf course which he used as a short-cut on his deliveries. Neither of the adults spoke during the de-bagging, and the victim wasn't able to guess their identity from anything seen or heard.

Learning about the incident brought back that other time, and – in particular – Outhwaite's words about those good friends, Messrs Fishlock and Gilbey. Gilbey was a bachelor; Fishlock's marriage had ended when his wife died in a late labour, and I'd always heard that he'd shown no enthusiasm to tie the knot a second time. For a while I had mulled over the inference Outhwaite seemed to be driving at but I'd rather lost track of it among the other disclosures. One and a quarter pages of Lettice Allingham's letter suddenly transported me all the way back to Ivell Abbas from the air-sealed, static-laden, underground no-man's-land west of Guildford.

Certainly, I considered, the two men had made no inadvertent disclosures about themselves. There had been no twee mannerisms, no fluttering fingers, no liquid looks in cow eyes – which would have been the only clues I could have picked up on. I supposed that I simply hadn't known enough, and that the indicators – if there'd been any – must have been the sort that had wholly eluded me. The town perhaps had known no better: or those who'd had an inkling had kept the secret very well hidden, just as the baker's boy's family had done with their own shame.

It was Lettice Allingham who later sent me a cutting from the social lists of *The Times*, while her father and mother failed to mention the matter at all. I read it in the Operations Executive canteen one lunchtime, with the tittle-tattle of war going on around me.

> **The engagement is announced between Mr Humphrey L.T. Elliott of Chelsea, London, and Vivien, only daughter of the late Mr and Mrs J.C.P. Antrobus, of [name of county].**

I looked again at the letter.
'This caught my eye. Oh, you missed out there all right, but I'd count my blessings if I were you.'

There was no mention of the betrothed man's parents: which meant one of two things to me, either that he didn't have any or, being an *arriviste*, he disclaimed them. The Christian name suggested to me someone more mature in years, and I was inclined to believe that his parents were probably deceased. His fiancée had already been the wife of a man close to her own age and had discovered that something was lacking; maybe she imagined that this way she had nothing to lose, and in fact a great deal to gain.

The address – Chelsea – put me in the picture very well.

*

Davies:	The boy came to see me.
Fishlock:	So?
Davies:	You know quite well. That's why I asked you –
Gilbey:	You'll have to explain.
Davies:	He guessed.
Fishlock:	He couldn't have.
Gilbey:	Who'll listen to a baker's boy?
Davies:	Look, he knows.
Fishlock:	Impossible.
Gilbey:	What've you been saying to him, Doctor?
Davies:	I questioned him, that's all.
Fishlock:	Put ideas into his head, more like.
Gilbey:	You'd better watch yourself, Davies.
Davies:	And why's that?
Fishlock:	Cocky, aren't you?
Gilbey:	Clever dick.
Fishlock:	We can sort you out, no problem.
Davies:	Oh?
Gilbey:	No problem.
Davies:	How?
Gilbey:	We have ways.
Fishlock:	We're not as stupid as you choose to think.
Gilbey:	What can't two minds work out between them?
Davies:	Or two pairs of hands?
Fishlock:	Don't get that way with us, Davies.
Gilbey:	What gives you the moral right?
Fishlock:	Married to a woman like that?
Gilbey:	The whole town's talking about her.
Davies:	Talking about her? About my wife?
Gilbey:	Who else?
Davies:	But why?
Fishlock:	If you don't know, you soon will.
Gilbey:	We'll give them something to talk about all right.
Davies:	I'm seeing the boy's parents.
Gilbey:	If you do—
Fishlock:	If you bloody do, Davies...

*

I found the name and full address in a telephone directory: **Elliott H.L.T., 14 Jocelyn Street, Chelsea.**

I made a point of visiting Chelsea and 'passing by' the

same Jocelyn Street a couple of times, on day trips up to the city from Guildford.

No. 14 was a tall, narrow, Dutch-style house in a terrace. The front door, at the top of a flight of steps, was formidably solid, with an inset oval of sombre stained glass above eye level.

The first time there was no sign of life inside the house.

The second time was late one autumn afternoon. When I got there the windows – as I'd feared – were dark. I walked up and down the street several times until I realised I was being watched from certain houses. I moved off round a corner and decided to do a circuit of the block. As I reached the top of the street again, a taxi swung in off the main road. A woman in the back lurched against the nearside window. Her eyes were trained forward, through the windscreen.

I recognised the face from six years before – the occasionally tight, pinched, private face, not the languid, perspiring, semi-public version suitable for the garden at midsummer heat, nor was it the blithely social mask worn like a talisman at the Laud Street dinner-table, to preserve an illusion of genteel normalcy.

I was lucky, she was too preoccupied with her own thoughts to see *me*. I set off at a sprint, keeping the cab in my sights and with the trees screening me. The cab pulled up; its passenger perched forward on the seat and opened her handbag. I ran as close as I dared and stopped maybe fifteen yards away. I concealed myself behind a tree trunk and watched as the back door opened and a Chelsea wife emerged. She was wearing a royal-blue dress and jacket, broad on the shoulders and nipped in at the waist, with lighter-blue scroll motifs on the sleeves; and a small upturned hat, like a miniature horn of plenty. But I had very little time to see as she hurried across the pavement and up the steps. She was holding the front door key in her hand and she pushed it, rammed it home, into the lock. The door opened, she disappeared from my range of vision, and I could distinctly hear the sound of a bolt being pushed to after she'd slammed the door shut behind her.

The taxi had moved back over on to the left-hand side of the street and was proceeding very slowly. It stopped after twenty or thirty yards.

An idea came to me.

The driver was sitting counting money. I decided in a trice; I crossed the street, dodging between passing cars, and ran at full pelt for the taxi.

When I reached it I tapped on the driver's window and asked – with just enough breath left – was he free?

'Jump in, sir.'

I pulled the door open and climbed in the back.

'With you in a couple of ticks.'

While I found my breath again the driver sat for half a minute or so sorting through change and dropping it into a satchel. Then he set the meter and let off the handbrake. I told him 'the West End', that I was just trying to think where. The engine rumbled, and we started to move.

'Busy day?' I asked.

'So-so.'

'Chelsea, this is your base?'

'Go wherever I'm asked, sir!'

'Ah.'

'The passenger asked me to come to Chelsea, so I came.'

'You – you go anywhere?'

'Usually. Where the punter asks.'

'If the passenger asked you to wait – then you'd go all the way back again?'

'That's his pleasure. Or hers.'

'"Hers"?'

'Just dropped off a lady.'

'And I'm not making you go back on your tracks?'

'Doesn't matter. Where to, sir? Decided?'

'Let's say...' I thought of a destination. 'Marylebone High Street.'

'Marylebone High Street it is, sir.'

'Where – where do ladies come from to get to Chelsea? From Belgravia?'

'Some of them do.'

'You didn't?'

'What's that?'

'You haven't come from Belgravia?'

'Mayfair. Same thing.'

'Nice life for some.'

'Well...'

'Late lunches.'

'Like I said, that's *her* pleasure.'
'Swanky Mayfair friends?'
'Troup Street's not so special.'
'I thought Mayfair was *very* posh. Swish, chi-chi!'
'One of the clubs.'
'I see.'
'Only I'm not supposed to notice.'
'Ah.'
'Police give them a wide berth anyway.'
His eyes watched me in the mirror.
'I'm not police,' I said quickly, remembering the line from some film. 'Some chance.'
'Didn't think you were.'
'Ah.'
'Can tell that right off.'
'So...' I hadn't time to waste, but the mood had to be light, inconsequential. 'What's so special about clubland?'
'Not that kind of club. Eating, drinking. And something else.'
I smiled again.
'Loose women?'
'The other.'
'Ah.' I cottoned on at last. 'Gambling?'
'No one says the word.'
'Right.'
'You see some surprising faces in Troup Street.'
'You've a memory for them?'
'Know them from the papers. Middle of the morning, middle of the afternoon. I cut through, you see, from Curzon Street.'
'Good tips?'
'Depends. How their luck is.'
'Did the lady tip you well?'
I noticed the eyes finding me again in the mirror. I crammed my face with innocence.
'*Some*times a big tip gives them confidence. Makes them feel it wasn't so bad.'
'A *Chelsea* lady?' I said, in mock astonishment.
'Chelsea ladies have friends.'
'In Troup Street?'
'*Any*where.'

The rest of the journey passed with little more said. Every so often I thought I could catch traces of perfume or eau de Cologne. I placed myself where she had been sitting when the taxi swung round the corner into Jocelyn Street.

At Marble Arch I suddenly leaned forward and heard myself asking to be let off please, I'd remembered something I had to do. I paid, got out, and let the taxi drive off before I began steering myself through pedestrians in the direction of Park Lane.

I reached Troup Street by way of Curzon Street. It was narrower than its neighbour and a third of its length; the houses were less grand, but Mayfair after all is Mayfair and the differences of degree are only slight.

I walked along the pavements on both sides. Most of the houses were still residences; a few had professional brass plates beside the doors, naming whose legal or medical practice was conducted within.

Outside one house I spotted a movement out of the corner of my eye, the net curtain at a ground-floor window twitching, and I looked round quickly enough to see a sallow face imprisoned in a wing-collar watching me. I caught the reflex of a sleeve of what might have been a morning coat, and then the curtain fell back.

There was nothing to distinguish that house from any of the others, except a single black, wrought-iron Ionic column, taller than a man and supporting a torch-holder: a naked flame would have burned in it once, in the more gracious days of Edward VII, when such things were done.

Behind me I sensed a car hovering: no less than a dove-grey Bentley, I saw as I walked past. The car slowly edged into the kerb. When I reached the end of the street, on the Curzon Street corner, I glanced back and noticed two men standing outside the house with the torch-holder, on the top step. One of the pair, wearing a camel coat, had turned his head and was looking over his shoulder, the way I'd just come.

I nearly bumped into a policeman on his beat, but he side-stepped me in time. He even smiled, and didn't spare so much as an oblique shift of his eyes for the subterfuge life on Troup Street.

*

I didn't see Troup Street again for many years and by then some of the private householders had moved out and more lawyers and assorted medical consultants had replaced them. The building with the black ironwork torch-sconce flew a brightly striped flag: a plate at the door announced it to be the embassy of a small, newly independent former protectorate in the jungle heart of central Africa. The windscreens of cars parked outside were plastered with notices of parking-fines. Even in that salubrious and expensive street a dustbin had fallen over and its rubbish was spilling out and the office workers were carefully stepping round the mess in their patent court shoes and buckled kid moccasins.

The 'club', if there had ever been such a place, hadn't survived to enjoy profitability and/or legislation. And so it always is, the past is swept away, and those who have the remembrance in any wise are left to trade their conversation, or their clues – as it were – among the ruins.

In the life after Guildford, in the first months of the peace, I was reading a colleague's *Telegraph* one lunchtime in the office I'd joined in Ipswich. I had no more than half a mind on the pages of print when a name in a news item tripped me up. It took a couple of seconds to make the connection. My eyes jumped back to the top of the first paragraph.

> **Sussex police are investigating the circumstances of a motorist's death on a stretch of road near Hastings on Friday evening.**
>
> **It is understood that Mr Humphrey Elliott of Chelsea, London, lost control of the car he was driving. Police believe the car crossed over on to the opposite lane before leaving the road and dropping down an embankment where it collided with trees and burst into flames. Emergency services were called but arrived too late to save Mr Elliott's life. Mr Elliott, aged 63, was a retired member of the diplomatic corps. He had had distinguished service in almost a dozen postings, including Nyasaland, Togoland, Rhodesia, Ethiopia, Liberia and Persia.**
>
> **He is survived by his wife.**

Sussex police have announced that Mr Elliott's death is being treated as 'accidental', but that they are anxious to receive further information from witnesses who may have seen a black Daimler car being driven between Hastings and St Leonards early on Friday evening.

14

I was in Ipswich for two years. I completed my further law exams, and in the ripeness of time I was called to the Bar.

I moved to London, then back to Bristol – before a final return to London.

*

And in this fashion Daniel set out to make of himself a great man.

*

Out of the blue a letter arrived from one of my quartet of great-aunts, the Hove one. (I'm now talking about the heady days of the mid-1950s, in the New Elizabethan Age.)

My Great-Aunt Julia mentioned as a 'PS' to her ramble (on legal affairs, of course – I was the family's unpaid adviser, presumed to be permanently available for consultation) that she'd made a discovery about one of her neighbours. *'She's hardly one of our sort, but I expect she sees us as old dragons in our lairs. Anyway, she has been a neighbour for five years – Mrs Reuben – and it only happened the other day that I was in the room to catch someone saying that she was some-thing to do with a family in that town where you once lived, people called Antrobus. It is quite an unusual name, I re-membered you mentioning it several times to me, and I thought I must make a point of telling you, in case you have knowledge of such a person. Do you?'*

*

Before very long I contrived a visit to Great-Aunt Julia in Hove.

Back among the gloomily overgrown gardens with their cedars of Lebanon and monkey-puzzle trees, it struck me on reacquaintance that my Aunt Julia was settling very contentedly into premature Old Age (she wasn't more than sixty-three or sixty-four), playing a rôle she felt Hove expected of her – a spinster *grande dame* – and crossing that rôle with another: the stoically suffering, constitutional invalid.

And it was *here* of all places that she was living, this 'Mrs Reuben' who saw her neighbours as lair-lazy dragons.

The town – with its prissy manners and *belle époque* formality and sanctimonious mien of well-being – oppressed me: it was a sensation — the mental equivalent of breathlessness — which I hadn't experienced since my time in Ivell Abbas twenty years before.

I couldn't spare much time and I tackled the subject as soon as I felt I could do so with any degree of seemliness.

I told my great-aunt there *had* been a brewing family called Antrobus in the town.

'I could invite her here,' she offered.

'No, no.' I shook my head. Not at all, too much trouble.

I asked her to explain, please, about this person I might or might not know something about.

'Oh, they were very quiet. I hardly knew they were there. The house is called "Holdenhurst". They're not truly neighbours, but I know someone who knows a couple nearby. She's not at all suitable for us, she's very young and rather smart too.'

My great-aunt smiled.

'I see,' I said, focusing, zooming in.

'Quite attractive, in a sort of – unpredictable way.'

'She's fair-haired?' I asked.

'Yes. Yes, I believe so. But she doesn't have the pale skin.'

'No?'

'Looks more like her husband for colouring. Of course his was – what's the word? – "gen–", "gener–". "Generic", that's it! She enjoys the sun, I'd say. Which was never quite "done" here.'

'Ah."

'Her husband wasn't like —'

I took the liberty of interrupting.

'"*Wasn't*"?'

'What's that, dear?'

'*Past* tense?'

'Oh, yes. She was widowed quite recently. Which was maybe how it came out, about her name, because someone was discussing her history, you see.'

'Her husband —?' I prompted.

'He was a Jewish gentleman. But *I* am quite open-minded myself about such things.'

'Ah.'

I narrowed my eyes, to concentrate completely on the subject.

'He was ill, her husband?'

'Well, he was quite elderly. Sixty-five, seventy. He came here to have the advantage of the sea air. Sometimes, though, when people are unused to it —'

'He didn't *come* from Hove?'

'Oh no. From London, I heard.'

'What – what did he do?'

'He wasn't a *professional*. All my neighbours used to be, once.'

'Ah.'

'No. Trade.' My great-aunt's pared eyebrows arched and Hove expressed a judgement. 'I'm not certain *which* line of business exactly. Construction? Something of that sort. Building.'

'I see.'

'I heard he'd made a lot of money, but I dare say I could have guessed that. They lived in a very big house, with a maid and a cook, and you know how very difficult it is nowadays —'

My great-aunt then spoke at considerable length on the topic of staff and the difficulty of finding and engaging same. But at last I was able to bring her back to the Reubens.

'It was a late marriage. In fact they weren't married to each other for longer than – what? – two years, it must have been. It has left *her* very well provided for, I don't doubt. Notwithstanding his being a Jew and having umpteen dependants, so that none of *them* could go short. But she is – I dare say – quite a "catch" now.'

My great-aunt offered again to invite her here to the house, or to try to solicit *me* an invitation to the house of a mutual –

For a couple of seconds her face took on an expression that was in equal parts baffled and sly – perhaps she suspected me of dowry-hunting?

I hurriedly informed her that I could only stay one night, and that we had *other* business, of the legal sort, to discuss in the time.

'Needless to say, I have – picked up things. On the grapevine.'

'You have?'

'What is the word? – it may be that she's rather – yes – rather "fast".'

'Why – why is that?'

'Some young man – I don't call him a gent – in much the same line of business as her husband, he seems to have quite an eye for her, by all accounts. One of those new fellows: no background, and I guess she doesn't care too much. And there's this "black market", isn't there, which everyone talks about. The country's supposed to be on rations, *supposed* to be, but it strikes me that if you've got the money you can have anything you want. Aren't I right, William?'

'Yes.' I said, impressed by her knowledge of the world. 'Yes. I think you *are* right.'

'Speculation' was another term being bandied about at that time: I imagined it meant being just one step ahead of your competitors, having eyes in the back of your head. There was also another life, an underworld which seemed to have nothing to do with a town like Hove. The business had begun, simply enough, with coupons, and with life's modest little luxuries: that was the level at which most black marketeers had been operating. But soon enough that grey-shaded middle-ground of illegality had darkened into the properly criminal: at the extreme point, such heinous activities as counterfeiting and now (so I'd read) – putting adventure back into lives sated with the tedium of the peace – gun-running.

'She can do as she likes now, our Mrs Reuben. With her

wherewithal. Although brewing – didn't you say? – that's a decent enough occupation, and there *is* money in it.'

I agreed.

'I did hear he's younger than *she* is, this – this friend. He's called – what? He's called —'

She tapped her finger on the side of her head.

'Partridge? No. Parfitt? Parton? Part– Pard– Pardge– Yes, Pargiter! That's it. Pargiter. He's from Bournemouth way.'

'Ah.'

'He has a fancy car. He probably thinks she's the most stylish woman he's ever seen, and she is a bit like that, true enough. Her husband bought her good things, but the Jews have an eye, don't they?'

'Pargiter isn't, though? Jewish?'

'No, I don't think so. He's from London. But no one knows anything much about him. That is probably no accident.'

My Great-Aunt Julia laughed, in a worldly, quite sprightly way that told the lie about the age she pretended by her habits and dress and posture to be.

'And –' I elected to risk the question. ' – and what do they say about *her*?'

Fortunately my intentions weren't suspected and the reply had no astringent 'point' to it.

'I heard the "Antrobus" name, but no one knows very much about her either. She doesn't speak about herself, not if she can help it. She's supposed to have had another husband in London. But that's just talk, I dare say.'

I nodded.

'She's – she's – what do I mean? She's "on edge" all the time you're speaking to her. Although she doesn't *seem* to be: but she is. I'm not sure *how* to describe it. She's not nervous, not that. But it's as if there are two conversations going on at the same time. What you're saying to her and what she's trying to *get* you to say.'

'Such as?'

'Oh . . . That she doesn't fit, or you don't understand her. I've only been to their house once, and it was all very – tasteful. Very right. But – not *quite* right, because the house was empty when they bought it and they'd had to furnish it from scratch. But the things looked as if they'd been in the place for years.'

172

'Maybe they went to house-sales?' I suggested.

'It could have been her parents' house. You might have thought.'

I nodded, knowing she must be one and the same person after all, it could only be her.

'There were grandfather clocks. A china-cabinet. Oriental things. A great gong, too. Even some needlework in a frame. Bowls of pot-pourri everywhere: as if there must be a bad smell to hide. Even *I* don't have pot-pourri. My *mother* did, though. Anyway, the stuff makes me sneeze.'

I smiled, rather mechanically.

'I don't know, that's how it seemed to me. Maybe I'm being unfair. But anyway, that's all about the Reubens I can tell you, I think. And now, William, enough of this woman, now you have to tell me *everything* about yourself.'

*

I went out in the evening, after an early supper, for a breather.

The Reuben residence was large, and rather ugly to my eyes. It was grey-brick, high-church Victorian Gothic; someone had had the good sense to deck most of it in red Virginia creeper, which softened the original stark effect. There was a glass and ironwork conservatory on one side. The garden was formal, and linear, with rectangles of mown lawn and intersecting straight gravel paths, and (for the most part) shrubbery rather than plants and flowers. Weeping spruces and hemlock provided too much shade. It looked a very unhomely sort of house, more appropriate to a boarding-school. Remembering the charms of the Laud Street property, I could believe that the Jew's money had been cursed after all.

Some lights were on, at opposite ends of the building. I saw a head that must have been hers in a room which seemed to be a bedroom, with a three-panelled dressing-table mirror like a triptych just visible. She came to the bay window and pulled each of the three pairs of curtains shut.

It was too far for me to see properly. As I was making my way back down the cul-de-sac, I noticed through the hedge what I hadn't before. Set in the middle of one of the expanses of lawn and just visible in the twilight was a round pond. It wasn't out of place there, like a pond in a public park, with a rim, and a clumsy arrangement of wrought-iron fountain paraphernalia at the centre (as a Victorian benefactor, a poor-boy-made-good, might have willed for the public's edification). I imagined the column and bowl dripping rusty winter icicles. Surely even the birds of Hove would have been too respectful and awed to think of using such a vainglorious and forbidding water receptacle.

*

Thus far had we all travelled since.

*

The next morning I saw her.

She was walking along the sea-front, being led by a dalmatian on a leash. She was dressed quite differently from how I remembered her, in a three-quarter-length musquash coat, with high-heeled navy court shoes and an ivory-coloured satin turban, and carrying a large, very solid-looking handbag of beige crocodile or alligator skin.

She made light of those intervening years, which had included a war. I could tell she was wearing a full complement of make-up, but she appeared to me very much as before: her physical proportions were the same and she walked with that recognisable roll of her hips, unstiffened by time and seaside winters. She might have been a model, in fact, one of the fashionably *comme il faut* occupations open to women of a certain background in these new times.

And was *she* a 'new woman'? – that was the question. Too difficult to answer, I thought, watching her independent progress behind the dog along Kingsway and sensing that every step was precisely worked out (on heels which – I guessed – were a little too high for her comfort).

She was looking to neither left nor right as she took those long, effortless antelope strides I remembered from the cooler sorts of day on Pack Street. She followed an exactly straight line. Dalmatians had become the epitome of canine style, and predictably heads turned (as they used to on Pack Street's hill), but she determinedly kept hers fixed in the direction of the West Pier.

The sceptical fancies I used to have – which had troubled me on and off in my professional life in the years since – they returned this morning with renewed vengeance. Was she as she appeared to be? — matter-of-fact but unnoticing and merely out-of-doors for the exercising of her dog? Or was she too carefully dressed even for dalmatian-walking? Was the effect of insouciance the result of previous calculation? Was she no better than a tease, who barbed and riled the women and set the slow, inactive male loins of Hove tingling again?

Some people looked over their shoulders, but others managed to find alternative occupation for their eyes, hands, feet. Mrs Reuben's heels rang out as she went compass-stepping along the Brunswick Lawns in the wake of the dalmatian, and no one could have been ignorant of the consipracy this woman was creating all around herself.

But acknowledge what, or whom?

Just who the hell *was* Mrs Reuben?

'Mr Pendlebury?'

She didn't seem surprised.

'Am I right?'

At least she offered no confusion on the name.

'H-hello.'

'It is Mr Pendlebury?'

'Yes,' I said. *'Yes, And — it's Mrs Reuben now, isn't it?'*

'Yes.' She leaned forward and pulled on the dog's chain. 'You've heard about that?'

'A little.'

She straightened herself to her full height and hitched her handbag on her arm.

'But I don't look so different?'

'I — I recognised you at once. Even with —'

She nodded at the dalmatian.

'With Prince?'

'Yes. He's splendid.'

'I've never had a dog before.'

'No?'

'No.'

'Ah.'

'We have two. I have two, I should say.'

'I'm sorry —'

175

'A dog and a bitch. I didn't bring her this morning, I think she must be carrying.'

'I see.'

'I'm glad you thought to stop us, though.'

'Yes. I hope —'

'It's easy for walking the dalmatians, on the flat here. It keeps me fit.'

'Yes.'

She drew just a little apart.

'Do you care for Hove then?' she asked.

'I'm obliged to come. Family.'

'Everyone's "obliged", Mr Pendlebury. What distinguishes us is our attitude.'

I nodded. The words, I thought, came tantalisingly close to a self-revelation. Once she had come to Botterel's office to talk, as if she'd meant to speak not about her Laud Street self but about another person. However, it was the heat that had defeated her in the end. And what she had told me on the last day, on the bridle-path to Hang Wood, had seemed like clues to another mystery inside the mystery that I found was still confronting me, somewhere I'd thought too far away on the map for it to matter.

'It's quiet here,' she said. 'Calm.'

'You seem — you seem to create quite an impression. Walking.'

She continued to smile, but the gesture had a distinct suggestion of the glacial about it.

'It's not really a young person's town,' she said, then corrected herself. 'Young-er person's town.'

'You don't mind that?'

She pulled on the leash, weaving the leather strap between the leather fingers of her gloves.

'It doesn't seem,' I said, 'much like anywhere else.'

'No?'

'It's discreet.' Circumspect and clandestine too, I meant. I had my own thoughts about genteel Hove. Money bought the silence of all those cedar gardens, and gardeners worked to pacify a jungle of vegetation and weeds you felt was only waiting to run riot.

(I heard the chiming of carousel bells in my head . . .)

'Discreet?' She smiled at the choice of word. 'I suppose it is.'

'Is it – is it like Ivell Abbas at all?' I asked.

The smile fixed. I felt the air cooling around us.

'That was a long time ago,' she said. 'I don't —'

I decided to allow myself the risk of a reference.

'They both seem still and deep to me.'

'Really?'

She pulled at the collar of Mrs Reuben's musquash coat.

'I think this must be the proper England,' I said.

'Do you?'

'All those secrets buried away in wills and codicils —'

'Prince!'

She tugged hard at the leash.

'I was wondering,' I said. 'I'm staying with my Great-Aunt Julia.' I pointed in the general direction. 'Miss Gamage. I'm leaving at lunchtime.'

'I'm having lunch with some people,' she said. She adjusted the weight of the handbag on her arm. 'But thank you for thinking to ask.'

I stood in front of her, accepting more of the same punishment as before.

'I'll have to come back,' I said. 'Sometime.'

'To see your great-aunt?'

'Yes.'

The dalmatian pulled on its leash and she yanked at the choke-chain, quite fiercely.

I caught her eye. I felt that this time, for the first time, I *was* looking at her: *that after so long – so much time – the moment had come, to say what had to be said.*

But that isn't what happened.

The encounter didn't take place; no words were spoken.

I followed her instead: to Lansdowne Place and the pavement outside the Dudley Hotel, where she stopped and stood with the dalmatian straining on its leash. The crocodile handbag functioned as a counterweight, a balance.

A couple of minutes passed, then a white Lagonda coupé drew up at the kerb. The driver's door opened and a man, in his mid-thirties perhaps and with a lean anonymous face, got out. He was dressed in a dark navy-blue blazer and flannels, the very image of a dapper young blade about town. The pair smiled at one another and the dog's tail wagged. The man opened the passenger door and took hold of the leash. The woman who was Mrs Reuben tossed her handbag into the back of the car and lowered herself into the white leather tub seat in the front, protecting her turban with one hand. Her companion chivalrously closed the door after her. The dog knew the routine and bounded on to the road ahead of the man; it waited for the back of the front seat to be lowered, then jumped in. The driver let go the leash and laughed.

I stood watching as the car moved off from the pavement. Several heads turned to look. The couple had been quite conscious of what they were doing and how conspicuous they were, in the blatant, flagrant full light of day: Mrs Reuben in her Bond Street finery and the enterprising johnny-come-lately, her classless companion with no history, Mr Pargiter, all the way from Bournemouth.

Perhaps what I was feeling was more than a pang of envy for them both, my stomach shrinking to know the loss of something irreplaceable: but it may have been that that feeling belonged with the other spectres and surmises and imagined truths secreted and kept purdah among the dense Himalayan rhododendrons and vespertine Lebanon cedars and hemlocks arboreous and hedged, on a brisk May morning on the front at Hove in the year of our grace and long-overdue bounty, 1954.

15

SS *Naxos*   *Somewhere after Malta.*
                              7th August, '64.

Dear W'm,

Nothing would normally induce *me* to put pen to paper on my hols, least of all when we're paying through the nose to 'enjoy' (that's the brochure's word, not mine) life on the jolly old ocean wave. Frankly, I think we made the wrong choice, but I'd better change that before Joyce comes back into our palatial stateroom and glances over my shoulder (there's hardly room in here to swing Buckley's old ginger tom:

that office in Bristol's going to follow me to the end of my days).

Guess what? Remember the face from the past you used to tell me about, the woman in Hove you saw one time you went down? Didn't you say her old dad was a brewer?

On the first night there was a ghastly captain's party (quite gruesome), and I was talking to someone. She was very knowledgeable about what everyone was drinking, and I asked her how. Maybe she was embarrassed and that's why she told me about her father's business, brewing. I asked where, she said the county, and maybe a bell did ding-dong in this thick skull, away in the distance, the far yonder. Then for some reason someone else in the group mentioned Brighton later, and the Sussex coast, and I saw her turn her head, and something made me ask her, did she know that part? (I *must* have remembered.) Maybe she would have said 'no' if I hadn't been watching her so closely, but I *was* – so she smiled, and she was quite vague in her reply, about 'knowing some of the coast there'. And later still, some old bat was waffling on about her 'doggies' and not having them with her, which got us on to the subject and I overheard her mention – quite definitely – 'dalmatian' and repeat it (or plural was it, 'dalmatians'?) Then after that it got changed to 'borzois', I noticed. I asked her, 'Didn't you say "dalmatians"?' 'No, "borzois".' 'Are you sure?' 'Are you doubting me?' But I *was* remembering, you see, and it didn't all go in one ear etcetera. I must have been standing grinning, because she moved off. She's stayed clear of me since (surprise surprise) and she's kept it up for five days, which takes some doing cooped up like this.

(Is all this boring you? But didn't it all fascinate you a bit at the time? When you thought I wasn't even listening...)

She's Mrs Landis now. Mr Landis is 75 or so, not quite old enough to be her father. Late November and early September, let's say. And he's *American*.

He's rich too, quite obviously, but she doesn't seem to me the type of woman who'd be wasting her time with anyone who wasn't. (Does this tally? Or am I putting my foot – squelch – right in it?) Maybe she just wants protection, I don't know, and money and age and experience all come into it together. She acts like someone who doesn't want to *think* too much. ('Are you with me, Mr Pendlebury?') She plays whist and bridge, and one night I saw her in the ship's casino. (I've sunk to this!) She smiles like someone who's had her face lifted but I'd say she's one of the few women on board this good ship who hasn't. She just smiles into crowds of people, and she could be throwing coins, like an old-fashioned 'scramble'. (I heard about one woman who had her fact lifted so often she was perpetually smiling – she grinned like a Cheshire cat all the way through her husband's funeral!)

Like her, *he* looks the thoroughbred, 'pur sang' and all that. And definitely 'the quiet American' But I wonder...He told someone he had 'business interests', which is about as non-committal as you can get, isn't it? He also doesn't seem to pay too much attention to anything, and I wonder about that too. A few times I've seen him looking at her when she doesn't seem to notice *him*. (She has an eye, and some eye it is, for the dago waiters.) In company she plays up the English-ness, of course: as if she's selling the stuff, flogging it off.

But maybe in Mr Landis she's met her match?

Or am I only seeing what I'm *meant* to see?

Is this all more interesting to me now than it is to you? It helps to pass the time at any rate: *some* of the time. Next stop is Athens. We're all keenly Cultural, of course (which, if you could see us, you would appreciate *is a joke* – the blind following the blind into the lumber room of history).

Joyce sends her best, like me.

À bientôt,

Derek.

16

And then, another decade later, two decades after Hove, in the mid-1970s, in the cocktail bar of one of London's new American-owned hotels.

I was walking through from the lobby to meet my daughter and her new husband. In an inner room a pianist was playing, another age's music. 'I won't dance', 'Glad to be unhappy'.

I recognised her immediately.

She was manoeuvring herself on to a bar stool. She threw off the weight of lynx fur and it fell on to the next stool.

The young barman smiled, as if she was no stranger in the place. She said something to him and he replied.

She was wearing toning beige woollens: across the room a gold bracelet dazzled on her wrist, also a cluster of stones on her left hand. There was another exchange of words, smiles, and she laughed, although the laughter quickly disappeared beneath the happy-hour music.

The barman poured a pink concoction into a long glass and garnished it with a slice of orange and one of lime, a yellow paper parasol and a swizzle stick with a cherry on its tip.

Her hands floated over her nest of grey hair.

A few more words followed, then the barman moved off to serve another customer.

The medley continued: snatches of 'Deep in a Dream' and 'Dancing on the Ceiling'.

Her fingers played with the little parasol. She took it out of the tumbler. I sat down against the back wall and watched as she folded it, pushed the spokes up, folded it again. Then something seemed to go wrong, she couldn't make the spokes rise. She took both hands, applied pressure from a different angle, but the parasol still wouldn't open.

She laid it down on the counter-top. For a few seconds the fingers of one hand fidgeted with the swizzle stick. Then she inched herself forward on the stool, lifted the glass and sipped. One ankle and foot wrapped round the leg of the stool. She sipped again. She caught sight of her reflection in the panel of mirror behind a row of bottles. She looked away. Her left hand – with the brilliant stones – fussed inattentively with the meringue of hair, and then it dropped on to the counter-top. She tilted her head slightly on her neck and sipped a third time. Her head turned leftwards again, to the mirror behind the spirits and liqueurs. She looked away again. She put down the glass. She placed both arms on the counter-top and crossed her hands, with the ring glinting on top.

The pianist cut from 'I got plenty o' nuttin'' into 'Oh! Look at me now'. *I'm not the guy who cared about fortunes and such, I never cared much. Oh! Look at me now.*

She'd kept herself trim, in good shape: her pride had seen to that. From the other side of the room I could make out that her face had altered, but only a little: the skin was slacker, and her eyebrows had been plucked to actressy arcs, and she wore a high collar on her jumper with a silk scarf knotted at her neck. But, as such things go, she had won out over the years. In a manner of speaking, I took off my hat to her.

Meanwhile the pianist moved into another song, a more recent one. Stupidly I couldn't identify it from the first bars, although I knew I knew the tune, and very well. I closed my eyes. Then it came back to me. *Love, who knows about love? And even those who do know won't repeat it.* The song had been one of my favourites ten or fifteen years before, whistled over and over. *You can try to play at love, even be blasé about love. But although you doubt it you can't live without it. That's pretty strange.*

She turned round on the stool. Her eyes swept the room, speedily, advertising what was really her indifference. Or conceivably her sight wasn't so good, at long distance, and all she could see were blurs.

While she continued to look – and not look – her left hand with the ring found the glass. Her other arm lifted, as if she were about to wave, and her hand settled on the combed chrysalis of evenly grey hair. The gold bracelet glittered its newness.

She turned back round to the counter. The tumbler was back at her lips and she sipped with a professional's accomplished backwards tilt of the head.

The barman had finished attending to an order and was managing to keep himself busy at the far end of the bar. The other stools were unoccupied; there were only a handful of customers, and they sat at the low marble-top tables in the soft coral glow from the shaded side-lamps. She had just the other woman's face for company, eyeing her warily from the mirror behind the shelves of bottles.

The pianist started to swing: clutches of notes in the treble slammed down on a wandering, vibrato bass. 'Nobody's Heart'. Her left foot was tapping on one of the stool's cross-spars; her shoulders twitched, first one and then the other, alternating, and they continued like that, in time to the pianist's beat.

After half a minute or so the tempo changed, it slowed, and the jerkiness turned to a calm, reflective treatment of the tune, almost in the style of a nocturne. Her shoulders stopped twitching and she sat still. She was looking straight ahead, at the panel of mirror: at the watching woman in the luxurious woollens, at such details of the background as came into her line of vision – tables, lamps, the slubbed-silk walls, the faces of the strangers who chanced to be sharing the same niche of time with her, this time out of all time.

Then my daughter grabbed my arm, laughing, and drew me to my feet, planting two kisses on my cheeks. Her new husband stood at her shoulder, grinning broadly.

Lindsey pulled me out to the foyer.

'But I can't *see* you, Daddy —'

I blinked at so much sunlight from the street, blazing through the windows. I stared at my hands, at the veins like blue wires: suddenly I was the age that I was. And when I turned with the inevitable twinge of stiffness in my neck and looked over my shoulder, my eyes couldn't adjust to the discreetly subdued lamplight in that inner sanctum, like a place of covert rendezvous.

Lindsey led the way.

'Isn't this wonderful, Daddy? Being able to see each other?'

I might not have been in this country at all, with so many American voices round about me. Lindsey's new Australian husband took my other arm.

Had she been waiting for someone? For *any*one? But not for an American, surely? What would have been the point of repeating herself?

Images came into my head, quite vividly: a sequence of time, many days rolled into one, memories of an ambience. The doctor's house, the cool dark rooms in shade and the heat roaring along Laud Street, the dribbling fountain in the garden, the underclothes hanging motionless on the washing-line, the circular tracks in the park field, the bride's hand reaching out to lure the butterfly, a silver mist of thistledown and the fallen straw where the horse-drawn haycarts had passed, rubbing against the top storeys of buildings.

'We've found a place for us to eat.'

'Ah.'

'I'm sure you'll love it. Won't he, Bill?'

Lindsey pulled me away, to the automatic doors, and then walking outside it occurred to me...

Here I am with a daughter and a history and a life apparently accounted for, and I wonder if that is quite so, if just as much and more hasn't escaped me. The memories we will talk about are of holidays, and her mother and my wife, and this house or that, and a show we once went to see, and *their* own first-born, and not at all about those still and windless days and about the part of the past – the greater – that will always be unresolved. The absences grow more insistent with the years and define the present time, but they were always there: a penumbra of uncertainties.

Sitting under Pomfrey's roof on hot evenings, fingers prodding at the typewriter keys, I could imagine I was – what? – a little god: because I was young and I had a conceit of myself and I thought I had a novel in me. But my confidence was chipped away at, and how could I have foreseen that the novel would become impossible and I should long after turn into the person I am or seem to be, elderly, dressed in a bespoke three-piece flannel suit with polished doeskin shoes, supported by my daughter and her obliging husband, who both presume I have a modest kind of fame but the most respectable kind, because my name and official designation sometimes appear in newspapers when a trial catches the press's attention and they need an informed opinion on the legal niceties. They don't know that there were things I did not do, and situations which I chose not to know any more about because the laws of the land had been side-stepped rather than contravened and because I half-believed I was already her accomplice in thought, in my imagination.

17

I married eventually, because – I knew – I didn't want to become wholly possessed by my guilt.

They say it's surgeons who are the authentic gods of our

times – with the power of giving and taking life – but judges are credited with something of the modernly divine too, at a lesser level of veneration.

In subsequent years I became by turns a South Eastern Circuit judge, then a Queen's Bench judge, then a Lord Justice of Appeal. A knighthood led to a second appendage – 'Honourable' – and then a third – 'Right Honourable'.

Lives and experiences have passed before me, hundreds of them. I remember some, a few; most of them I've forgotten.

I have always slept soundly, seven or eight hours every night without fail. Some mornings a case would be the first thing to come into my head; or it might be the weather outside, or a social occasion in store, or a job to be done in the garden.

I live now in a small country town in Berkshire, about the same size as the one I was living in fifty years ago. I've lived there alone since Margaret's death.

Sometimes I think I had no *right* to be doing the job that I was. At school once I sat an exam with the dates of Henry VIII's accomplishments inked on my cuffs. There was a Welsh classics master with a red dragon's temper and once I – quite calculatedly – sent him into a rage like no other, which had him tossing books on to the floor and crumbling sticks of chalk between his fingers and splitting a wooden pointer; I believed that I had a sort of innocence in the situation which put me beyond the considerations of wrong and right, whereas Griffiths was incriminating himself deeper second by second, reeling under the load of reproach, losing his footing in the sinking sands. At Cambridge I smuggled reference books out of the Law Library, stashed inside the waistband of a pair of baggy trousers, so that no one else might write a better essay on Intestacy or Probate than my own. I didn't return to England for my father's funeral and claimed that the telegram had failed to reach me in Brittany. I dismissed a maid from our service, not because she'd helped herself on several occasions to some of Margaret's vegetables (a root or two of leeks and handfuls of pea pods now and then, and strawberries from under the nets), but because she had an outline in profile like Sylvana Mangano's in the days when she played peasant girls in the films. I told Michael, who called me his best friend, that I couldn't get away when he called one midnight, and he was crying tears into the phone because his marriage was on the rocks and he had to see me please, to speak to me, he knew I was busy, but not on the phone, please; the next afternoon he opened the door of an express train on a stretch between stations and a far finer legal mind than mine was extinguished thirty years prematurely.

Somehow, though, I could sleep the sleep of the just at nights, with Margaret's shape and mass beside me on the mattress, in her adjacent hollow. I would wake up in the morning thinking, not of my own history, but of a case, or the weather, or dinner somewhere, or that task to be attended to in the garden. I could forget that I'd dissuaded a mutual acquaintance from buying James's second house when James and I were bidding against each other for the quayside holiday cottage at Rock: so that James hadn't the assurance to offer when the price went up, so that in time it was Margaret and I who became summer residents of the village on the estuary James had introduced us to. Or that I'd pruned an elderly, nearly blind neighbour's walnut tree she'd always been so proud of because the twigs scratched on our windows in squalls, like the fingers of a drowned man. Or that I once turned a blind eye myself to a shoplifter because I was double-parked at the kerb outside the shop. Or that I told my invalid aunt, my mother's only sister, that the journey to and from her house took forty minutes longer than it did, so that I could make my getaway forty minutes sooner every time. Or that I used to be customarily imprecise – in competition – when I retrieved my ball from the long grass on the golf course. Or that – in that strangest interlude of all our lives – I conspired in plotting the deaths of young German pilots on radar, from the primus-heated safety of an underground bunker in far-away Guildford.

I slept soundly, and eventually I became prominent among my own legal kind. That is no braggart's boast; I did not seek to be so, but the situation came about, that after several decades I found myself respected as the legal equivalent of a Lord Spiritual.

Ivell Abbas (as I've called the town) receded. I didn't mean to remember: it faded from my active recollection, I might have been looking through the wrong end of a telescope. It was a subject I skirted my way around. Once or twice the old tracks had re-crossed the new, but that (I fancied) had not been of my own first seeking.

I've referred myself to the very letter of the law in every case I've sat to judge, and applied myself to the matter exactly and scrupulously. I've seen heinous deeds written on villainous faces, but had to dismiss the case for the lack of any substantial evidence; I've been obliged to convict because the prosecution has produced incontrovertible evidence, and yet I've believed myself not wholly in possession of *all* the facts which might help to make an incomprehensible act understandable. The law is not a neat game of the psychological jigsaw sort: it is most precisely determined by the book. If I'm a tightrope walker, allowing myself to look neither to left nor right, I perform this routine with the confidence of a safety-net. Like most other things in life, that's just what the business became: merely methodical, systematic, the drill.

I might have chosen to use my life to write novels but it seemed that there was really *no* choice about that: novels would have entailed *no* safety-net, and I would have been left with the full mystery of people's elusive personalities. My characters would have taken me over, haunting me for years because I had failed them in some respect. I wasn't so smugly clever and all-seeing as I thought, because how could I have known . . . something so insignificant that I'd overlooked it, when so often it's the smallest detail which betrays the whole of a life. . . . Every morning a conundrum of motives and impulses would have confronted me, and I couldn't have handled that, with no final points of reference beyond my own idiosyncratic conjectures of judgement. I hadn't the nerve for that, the assumption of the godlike in the melancholy modern vacuum prospected by the psychologists.

By contrast, the Law was ancient but regularly mapped by signposts, so clearly routed that I should have no excuse for losing my way.

*

We fall in love with the possibility of love, or sometimes the *im*possibility. We fall in love with what we know we cannot have.

*

Twenty random questions that come to mind:
[1]Why should one long afternoon in the surgery have seemed so irredeemably worse than any other? [2]How had someone who repaired bodies – by the book – developed such a fear and despair of the mind? [3]Are the body and mind not immutably wed to each other? [4]Why was there no more formal enquiry into the circumstances of the suicide's death?

[5]Why should a practised angler have suffered such an ignominious accident as stumbling and falling into less than his own height of water?

Lightning, some would have it, is an act of God. [6]But what if there is no God?

Black for negation: nothingness, and the witch's art. Red for blood, the emotions, love and hate; the colour of martyrdom.

[7]Why did the police authorities choose *not* to raid a certain address in Troup Street, Mayfair? [8]Can adrenalin levels adjust to normality after the exhilaration of a war?

[9]Why should a man who had driven for decades make the fatal error of crossing both carriageways of a road and be unable to stop the car before it reached the drop with the copse at the bottom? [10]Did his eyelids close? [11]Did he suffer a deadly heart attack? [12]Was the riddle of sunless oblivion easier to plumb than the deceits of his wife, which were like multiple moons about their cold star?

[13]Why should Mr Reuben the Jew have deserted his kind, unless a secret sign pronounced his wife to be another of Jehovah's chosen ones?

[14]Whatever happened to the sleek fellow who drove his white Lagonda to Hove and dealt in such mysterious commodities?

[15]Why did the American and his wife want to watch an Aegean dawn's rosy-fingered whatsit from the windows of the casino on a cruise ship, with snake-hipped waiters ever in attendance, day and night? [16]Did Zeiss sun-lenses flatter or distort the cradle of civilised thought when the ship finally reached it, across the wine-dark sea? [17]And why should she have allowed herself to be caught out remembering a time thirty years before?

[18]How many happy-hours were spent in the cocktail bar of that gleaming hotel built of Yankee money in one of the age-

old streets of London Towne? [19]Was some one stranger in particular awaited in the panel of mirror behind the upturned vodka and whisky bottles? [20]Did he ever come to claim her?

*

We were all her reflecting surfaces.

She lived in a hall of mirrors.

She had lived there so long that she couldn't remember how to enter or leave.

Long ago the hoodoo of the narcissist had fallen on her, till she finally came to be bewitched and mesmerised past sense by that image she saw in front of her, every way she turned.

*

And then, of course, there was the birthmark.

18

The conservatory where we were sitting had settled into an early evening twilight by the end of his story. I presumed the story had ended: the words just trailed away....

After a deferential silence I made gathering-myself-together movements, and he pulled himself out of his chair.

He accompanied me back through the house. The house-keeper had switched on a light in the hall before leaving. The rooms that led off were in darkness. Furniture inhabited them like a dream, in outline, only suggesting at their bulk.

At the front door we shook hands. He offered his rather abstractedly. I thanked him for everything. And for the partridge and port; but he seemed to have forgotten that.

Outside I could sniff frost in the air. Lemon and violet streaks ran across the sky. The skeletal trees stood out, like stage silhouettes.

Driving off I watched the house in my side mirror. The front door closed slowly, and the angle of light on the gravel driveway thinned to nothing.

I slowed after a few more yards, then stopped. Eventually a light appeared in one of the downstairs windows, the study's, where we'd sat before lunch. I spotted a shape passing across the room.

As we'd waited to eat he'd stood looking from that window, even when he knew that I'd found the house after all, I'd arrived, I was there. While we talked he continued to watch.

From the car I saw him take up his position again, in front of the same window, with the light behind him.

What could he have been seeing as he stood at his post, like a man with a vigil?

His own reflection, floating in the glass? The desk-top with its sweep of papers? The shelves of books?

The car's tail lights? I switched them off, with a flick of the wrist, hoping he hadn't noticed: eliminating myself, before the old man had a chance to invent me.

For Felicity and Michael

Sundowners
Fruits de Mer
Schwimmbad Mitternachts
The Second Marriage

Sundowners

But this is England too, she thought, turning from the television screen with its burning ghetto barricades and looking away, towards the balcony windows and the view of the town.

The sea rolled in and walkers pitched themselves into the wind. The awnings would be flapping along the High Street and the loose drain-pipes rattling against walls.

She stood up, whisky tumbler in hand. She was tired by the television pictures, by the sight of other people's rage. She rolled back one of the plate-glass windows and stepped out on to the balcony.

Soon she would have to be getting herself ready for the evening. They were playing at Edie's this time.

She'd never told anyone that she'd had to teach herself bridge from a library book, that she'd instructed herself here in this very town. They all presumed she'd become such a wily hand abroad, on her 'travels' as they referred to her past life. But she'd resisted learning, for as long as she could: playing bridge would have been like giving in, to everything that was expected of her. That would have been one sure way of turning into The Foreign and Commonwealth Service Wife, like every one that ever was.

But *she*'d had other notions of how to live her life.

Back inside, in the bedroom, she opened a drawer in the tallboy and found the framed photograph of her wedding day. The glass was still broken.

She looked behind the figures, to the church's tracery windows and the clipped yew trees and the lych gate and the fluttering pennants. It looked like the England you could only read about now in Agatha Christie novels: pretty calendar villages with, here and there, a murdered body awaiting discovery.

She remembered the determined joy of that day. Her parents putting on a brave show, making the best of it, even though they'd had their own plans for their daughter: she knowing they would have been happier with a dim and silly husband if at least he'd had the personal connections and the wherewithal that went with them. Malcolm was clever, a brain-box (virtually), and his superiors at the Foreign Office had high hopes for him, he was a man with 'bright prospects': but unfortunately, so far as her parents were concerned, he was lacking both the personal connections and the wherewithal. She'd never believed he married her just for the social lift it gave him, but all along she realised that her background – Home Counties, the farm, boarding school, the titled cousins – was giving her her allure, and at the same time it was excusing certain other things: the English angularity of her features, for instance, that and her lack of an education. And *she*'d chosen *him* because – because of some perverse streak inside, because sometimes she'd felt that her so-called 'advantages' in life were causing her neither to think for herself nor to *be* herself. Everyone expected her to be this or that. They didn't expect her to take up her time with a brainy young man of prospects and looks but the vaguest background and a BBC accent which didn't seem to belong to anywhere.

She blinked at the photograph, sipping from the lip of the tumbler. She remembered the musty smell of the church when you unstuck the door and walked in, an odour of dampness and old bibles and blown pollen from the vases of flowers. So much of the past seemed to have that same smell. Was that the reason why she never went into church nowadays, why she experimented with the perfume testers in the chemists on the High Street every time she popped in, and why she kept another of the tallboy drawers so amply stocked with fragrant soaps?

*

That reminded her, and she put down the whisky tumbler and made her way through to the bathroom.

She ran some water into the basin and lathered it; then she

washed her face and, with a fresh towel, dabbed her brow and cheeks and chin dry. She pulled at the rubber plug on the chain and looked straight ahead at her reflection in the cabinet mirror.

She might have been taken for older than sixty-six, even with her trim, disciplined – and, yes, svelte – figure. She pretended to people that the sun on their postings had not been kind to her: meaning *it* had prematurely lined her like this, made the skin sag, pulled down the corners of her mouth.

The 'sun' theory sounded plausible, or fairly so. Everything she chose to say to her friends was meant to sound plausible, or fairly so.

She decided she would wear her green jersey wool dress, with – as ever – a scarf at her throat to conceal the slackness in her neck. She hated stringy necks, she always had; they made her think of aged maiden aunts of the family, and now here she was doing history's echoing work.

She sprayed some Madame Rochas on her ear-lobes, found her good shoes and returned – noiselessly – to the sitting-room. The advantage of a modern flat was its built-in conveniences – reliable plumbing, storage space, double-glazing; there were positive pleasures too, like the luxury of fitted pile carpets, deadening even the sounds of her own movements.

For all her married life she'd had no choice as to where she lived and how. They'd been obliged to put up with the location and the dwelling and to be gracious about it because that was how Whitehall in its wisdom had decided to post and accommodate them: mostly in Africa and the Far East, in fan-ventilated flats with balconies the monkeys could climb, or in great profligate houses they rattled about in like peas in a tin and which gave her the shivers even in tropical heat, or – later – in warrens of cramped cupboard rooms wherever there was an obligatory compound for foreigners and you had no option but to shake down, with views through the windows of modern breezeblock concrete and scrub gardens no one had got round to landscaping.

Here she didn't have any complaints, none at all, notwithstanding the fact that now she also had the sort of responsibilities that befell anyone when they became an owner-occupier. The flat was perfectly comfortable; her neighbours in the block were very decent (to a fault) and, for the most part, kept at a polite distance. Certainly it was just the sort of town she'd always had in her mind when other people used to talk of 'returning', 'going home', with a promenade and tea shops and blue and pink hydrangeas blooming in the sandy gardens. *Then* she'd thought she was above such obvious ambitions. But she was grateful for the place now, very: she'd even come looking for it, if only to be able to pass herself off as unexceptional, as quite normal.

*

She looked at her watch. Matty was picking her up at quarter-past-seven. Just time for another refill from the Johnnie Walker bottle.

She sipped the soda mixture quickly. Her eyes alighted on Malcolm's photograph, on the sideboard. All her friends in the town liked to have photographs around them, and they'd been very surprised on their first visit to the flat to discover she had none. 'Oh, I just haven't got round to unpacking them yet,' she'd announced, telling a little white one.

She'd picked out the blandest of the likenesses to have framed. That particular Malcolm looked every part the itinerant government official: unostentatious, neither solemn nor smiling, a fellow of sound good sense with a reassuring hands-crossed-on-the-table attitude – here was a man who would be prepared to listen to you, to consider, to second and sustain, to understand. After all, wasn't he the personified conscience of Great Britain, Sovereign and Realm?

But consciences, she knew, often come into play too late, too late to do any good. She used to wonder how people *really* viewed them, Malcolm and herself, if they weren't being laughed at behind their backs for Blighty Britain's sake, because of all they'd lost as a country and were now trying, punctiliously, to do the decent thing by. She'd felt Malcolm was aware of it too, just as he was aware of his own professional stagnation. Somehow it had seemed apt, germane, that they should find themselves in one geographical cul-de-sac after another after another.

If he'd taken to drink, say – like so many of the others they met – she might have been able to accept such a thing, at least to comprehend it. But his nature had been more complicated than that. Perhaps he'd been too conscious of the essential *in*dignity of his job, that his function was keeping up appearances for a country in circumstances where it had forfeited its authority, where the Western European wasn't admired and looked up to any longer, but pitied and taken advantage of.

There were two ways of accounting for What Happened Afterwards.

Either he'd decided to take the collective national blame and shame on his shoulders – or instead he'd switched to the other side's cause with a convert's zeal, sold them all down the river.

Whichever was the case, could it matter to her now?

Or was she just trying to find reasons to explain why he'd done what he had, regularly and unrepentantly over the subsequent years: betraying her for his other women?

*

At this stage in the mental proceedings she always required another topping up, and this evening she liberally helped herself, compliments of J. Walker Esq. Not that it made her see any straighter: but it did give her courage to marshal her thoughts and fix on them, hold them.

Without exception they were black or yellow, the women, and always local. (Discreetly local: perhaps he'd drive a dozen miles or so for the rendezvous, to reach the current woman of his choice. No more than one at a time, though, that was a rule.) They were usually in some kind of domestic employment, or they were shop assistants: he knew his level. She would hear about them through word of mouth, by bush telegraph, and each time she'd affect to have no knowledge of any such thing, she would laugh it off or (preferably) feign total, manic concentration on whatever she was doing – sewing or writing a letter or paring her finger nails with an emery board – to the exclusion of all else. She'd presumed they were clean, the women, and could be slipped the occasional minding of legal tender to ensure they said nothing about the 'arrangement'. He'd had his diplomatic experience to keep him right about that.

Maybe – so she thought now – maybe his life had otherwise disappointed him, and he'd enjoyed courting danger?

Maybe she hadn't properly solaced him for the non-appearance of those rewards they'd both been counting on? Maybe if they'd been able to conceive a child between them? Maybe...?

But she wasn't counsel for the defence. She was still Mrs Malcolm Shawe. Now the burden of his guilt was hers, the onus of betrayal and failure, it was she who had the memory of it to cope with. While he...

*

Somehow she would always have the will-power to forbid herself a last drink if she sensed it was going to incapacitate her.

Had Malcolm been drinking on the evening of the accident?

He was never back before seven o'clock at the earliest, and it was only when nine o'clock had come and gone that night, chiming on the mantelpiece clock in the jerry-built house assigned to them on the periphery of the bushland, that she'd tarted to have any anxieties.

Someone phoned her about ten, then came to collect her and drove her out.

His car was lying upside down in a ditch beside the road.

The passenger, she was told by someone else, had died, but the driver was alive.

She tried to forget that there shouldn't have been a passenger, and – with no tree trunk or signpost to lean on for support – she heaved a very theatrical sigh of relief.

But matters proved to be somewhat more ravelled, as was soon explained to her.

Her husband, for some reason, hadn't been driving, not this particular evening. A young native girl had been behind the wheel.

'Oh. Oh, I see.'

Still unsupported, she stood at the road side in lantern light while the moths swooped. She dully nodded at this new, vital information, as if there could be no disputing the awesome, final truth of it.

'I see. Yes. Yes, I see.'

*

'Joy-ride' was the expression introduced to her in the course of her long, unnerving night. She'd never heard of such a thing before. (The words cut her; they'd lodged in her mind for all the years since.)

While she remained an accredited foreigner in that fledgling country like a dustbowl, the other person (the driver of the car) was never openly referred to in public company, at least in her hearing, and she was thankful. She did discover, through her own enquiries, that the girl – a dusky, of course – had worked in someone's kitchen somewhere and been considered quite attractive, by local standards.

For many weeks she wore sombre colours that reminded her of War-time, to signify her new condition as the widowed Mrs Shawe. She sat reading the property advertisements in months-old copies of *The Field* and *Country Life*. She developed a taste for Scotch whisky – she liked the pheasants and stags on the labels – but it was hardly so much as a taste, because she preferred that the amber just slide down her throat, to do what it would all the sooner, make its fire in her chest and pump fortitude into her veins. She was also a bit accident-prone and aloof under these new circumstances, but it was the price of imagining she could cope: if it *really* was coping, because eventually, by the third tumbler, things both near and far receded and she was somewhere else entirely, in the land of double-glazing and tracery windows, of central heating and waste disposal units, clipped yew trees and lych gates.

*

Now, when she saw black women on television, an instinct made her straighten her spine. If she ever chanced to see a half-caste child, that was the very moment to turn channels.

One advantage of the town was that she could restrict her contacts to those (apparently) of her own kind. Maybe her friends and her neighbours in the block thought she was snobbish on that score: sometimes it happened with those who came back, the vocabulary of their plain-speaking was misunderstood as too bluntly racist. But she wasn't *quite* the same as those other people, even them: she had her own reasons for seeing things as she did, in a harsh light like a savannah glare.

*

More than anything else, she resented Malcolm this: that he'd died how he must have wanted to, in transit between two homes and unclaimed by either, heading for his wife but accompanied by the woman he spent his favourite two or three hours of every day with.

*

The brand new motor hotel just outside the town reduced the prices of drinks between five o'clock and seven: stretching the term, it called that interval between afternoon and evening 'The Happy Hour'.

She'd received a leaflet through the letterbox, all about it. Her neighbours in the block had received the same, so it wasn't – as she'd panicked at first – a message from Malcolm from beyond the grave, spirited to her with some super-natural *ju-ju* assistance.

But that would have been untypical. For good or bad, she and Malcolm had never 'had words' with each other, nor – even once – had there been any recourse to the Raising Of Voices: life had been conducted with great civility, on the most adroitly balanced of keels. They couldn't have discussed the women anyway, because neither of them laid claim to the least item of knowledge that anything was 'wrong'. He'd seemed to think that such care and decorum were only what someone of her background deserved: and for her part she was too afraid to dispel his romantic's illusions of her, for fear of discovering how little affection might actually be left without them.

*

Matty had arrived, the car was down on the driveway, she heard her sounding the horn.

She drove her little Jap Triumph like a demon, and the journey was no pleasure. But it wasn't far to Edie's, and traffic on the top streets was slow and cautious. There might be dangers, on some of the corners, but at least there were no ditches.

202

She put on her coat, turned down the bedroom and sitting-room thermostats, then eyed the state of her lipstick in the hall mirror. The horn sounded again. She should have been on the track at Brand's Hatch, Matty. Never trust a woman driver.

Looking in the mirror, she saw over her shoulder into the sitting-room. On top of the sideboard, Malcolm – elevated in his sterling silver frame to the company of her parents and brother and sisters and a brace of very removed, titled cousins – was watching her with all a diplomat's guile. Not *so* subtle in his guile, of course: in some ways she was subtler, flavouring her breath with humbug mints before bridge so that no one should twig to the liquid nature of her diet. And not such a very good diplomat after all – or was that just history's doing, deciding to (as the young vicar on *Thought for the Day* had said the other week) 'bowl' the pair of them 'a googly'.

She let the front door of the flat bang shut behind her, then she turned and hurried downstairs.

Thinking, all the time thinking...

Thinking how most of her friends were widows, like her: or else spinsters. Some had spent time overseas. They lived now surrounded by their knick-knacks, their mementoes. Not everything can sit on a bookshelf or a table-top, however. The past isn't solid and weighted like that, regular and dependable and controlled.

In her dreams, her whisky dreams, she sometimes saw a child, sexless and neither light-skinned nor dark. Running along a dusty road with scrubland behind. It was the time of day when the sun started to slip down the sky. The child kept running, and the dust kept lifting from the road, and nothing else ever happened. Whether the child was running *from* or running *to*, she didn't know. Just running, on and on and on.

*

Matty was smiling from behind the steering wheel of the Jap Triumph, and she smiled back at her.

She'd guessed that Matty must also have her secrets, and with *her* too not everything belonged to the surface.

They were all living their days out with valour, with well-rehearsed dignity: or as near as.

203

Sometimes she thought Matty saw what Edie and Constance didn't, how it was she fuelled her long evenings till *A Book at Bedtime* on the radio. Maybe Matty had the personal experience to judge by, to *recognise*, but she never said.

'Hello, Bea.'

'Hello there.'

She pulled the door shut, hitched the seat belt across her front and fastened it.

'Thought I was going to be late getting here.'

'You're not late, are you?'

'I was watching the news,' Matty said as explanation, and turned the ignition key. 'Did you see it?'

'On television? No, I didn't. I was having a little snooze. Before the brain-work.'

Matty repeated her. 'The brain-work!' She laughed.

Really, playing bridge was playing with chance, but they all pretended otherwise and put on grave faces at the crucial moments.

'I got a card from young Peter today,' Matty said as they drove off. 'From Jersey. Or Guernsey, was it?'

The famous, or infamous, Peter had never had any time for his grandmother, even though *she* wouldn't admit as much. For months past he'd been planning to set up a catering business with a man friend. No guesses where he was looking to find the funds, the 'ready' for their little venture.

'It was nice to hear from him,' his grandmother said.

Her passenger nodded, as if she believed her; then she changed the subject, away from 'family'.

'What's the weather forecast for tomorrow, have you any idea? I missed the news.'

'Oh, quite good, I think,' Matty said.

But she knew better. Between tumblers of Johnnie Walker's peat-water tonic she'd caught the weather chart on the screen. A fuzzy-felt raincloud was destined to hang over them for the next twenty-four hours, throwing down showers.

Then she noticed that the sheet of paper lying on top of the dashboard was the hand-out from the new motor hotel. She was confronted with the words 'Happy Hour' in bulbous, exuberant 1930s lettering.

Matty must have seen her looking.

'We ought to go some time, Bea. En route for Edie's.'

'Oh, I don't,' she lied, brazenly. 'Tipple. Not so early of an evening.'

'Anyway,' Matty said, with the same wry smile hidden in her voice, 'I'd be driving, wouldn't I?' She leaned over from her driver's seat and scrunched the paper into a ball. She held it inside her fist while steering with the other hand. 'I had an Advanced Driver's badge on my last car, did I tell you? The Allegro. But when I sold the car it got left on the radiator grille by mistake.'

Her friend with the sun lines on her face thought that most unlikely, if not impossible.

'What a pity!'

She held her hand out open, to receive. Matty unbunched her fist and dropped the crumpled piece of paper on to the waiting palm.

'Thanking you, Bea.'

It was pushed into the ashtray on the door and the lid was rammed shut with a bold attempt at finality, or what was meant to pass as such.

Fruits de Mer

The restaurant is ageless, which is part of its appeal. The room's proportions are high, generous, and not of this epoch. The painted seascapes on the walls have the patina of time, cigar smoke, decades of intimate conversation: the scenes themselves belong to no period, the constants of rock and sand and froth-capped waves and blue horizons are outside history. The only boundaries to the vistas and distances are the outsized gilt frames, carved with clam shells and trailing seaweed. Between the panels thin oblongs of misty mirror hold uncertain images of the room: the old glass crinkles in antediluvian folds, it's as if no one, no grouping at any of the tables, is to be taken quite on trust.

Fish and seafood, quite obviously, are the speciality here: all edible life that the brine has to offer crowds the narrow-spaced columns of the menu. The menu is another work of art, with a list of dishes flanked by exactly drawn, ornamental combinations of scallops, urchins, flat skate, pink salmon, oysters, Dublin Bay prawns, brill, whelks in their whorls, shelled and unshelled mussels, langoustes, and the waving, dark green ribbons of 'asperge de mer': tendrils, tentacles, tails, pincers, fronds entwined as if to suggest that the creatures of the deep live life as one long riotous party.

*

Which is patently not the case with the terrigenous, land-lubbing habitués of this highly-esteemed restaurant, who — on the whole — behave decorously, soberly, and speak with their voices pitched considerably low.

The businessmen, for some reason, are the least reticent. A quartet of them, seated at a round table with its pale pink cloth and gleaming cutlery, quite unashamedly discuss the losses recently inflicted on one of their clients, a shipping magnate. One of his tankers has been sabotaged and another has been holed in an accident and abandoned to sink. It looks like a double-loss to the insurance concern the men represent. They discuss the tragedy quite animatedly over the entrée of smoked Tay salmon, and figures are mentioned, first single numerals and then double, which represent multiples of millions of pounds sterling. The plates are removed and others set down in their place: lobster in sherry sauce and turbot poached with sorrel are brought to the table, creatures wholly out of their element as the conversation is taken up again in full hearing of the waiters, about similar losses suffered in the Gulf over the past three or four years. More short-hand figures are aired. A few heads turn at tables close to the pin-striped group. Then, quite suddenly, as the waiters withdraw, the talk becomes blithely social and continues so for the next few minutes: Hurlingham, eventing, a hunt down in Kent. At the end of which the signal for a third bottle of Sauvignon is given and the conversation reverts, in firmer tones, to the matter of the scuppered shipping baron – while the crayfish in the illuminated tank to one side of the table continue their slow, sandy probings, quite regardless.

*

Next to the party on the other side, and equally oblivious, sit a couple in respectable middle-age. They are very polite, each listening diligently when the other speaks and taking care not to interrupt. They act in a kind of choreographed synchronization, which must – can only be – the result of two experiences shared for many years.

They might be husband and wife: but in that case why should there seem to be a certain degree of tension in their mutual interest for the other? Surely they're *too* animated, *too* well-behaved, for this to be a simple re-run of all the other restaurant conversations they've ever engaged in together? Perhaps today is an anniversary, a birthday, and they're celebrating: she is in a collarless Coco Chanel suit, he is in grey flannel and a white shirt with a stiff stud-collar. They've paid particular attention to the food presented on their plates – a matching choice of salmon mousse followed by Dover Sole – and their surroundings have called for comment several times.

As they pass from the second course to the third, the situation seems to become more complicated. The first mildly enquiring mentions are made: of 'her' by the woman, of 'him' by the man. (A glance at their hands shows that they don't wear rings – is it from what is now force of habit, or for discretion's sake on this one day?) The replies are hesitant, spare, and accompanied by harmless smiles. The menus go unread, the alternating nods that each gives to the other are perfectly agreeable, reasonable, understanding. The woman explains a little about how 'his' business affairs are going, he explains a little about 'her' artistic activities. More nods, just to confirm that each is enlightened enough to harbour no stirrings of jealousy for the other's new partner and spouse.

The orders for the third course are given to the waiter – they differ this time, cheese and a sorbet – and a silence follows. The man picks at a thread on his lapel; the woman takes advantage of this staged distraction (once upon a time she might have removed the thread herself) to look at him and consider, to remember what it was that persuaded them both they would be happier apart. Perhaps she doesn't have to think very hard about it; the memories may still be all too clear to her.

The man catches the thread. The woman suddenly pushes back her chair and rises to her feet. She picks up her bag, nods towards the back of the room, and starts weaving her way between the tables in the direction of the Mesdames'.

The man sits watching her, his first wife, and he doesn't lower his eyes again until she reappears and begins the return journey. Her face has been repaired, she's taking steps with a new confidence and purpose.

The woman sits down. The waiter brings the couple their orders. They tackle the sorbet and cheese enthusiastically. When they've finished, coffee arrives – before they have to do more to infill an untimely little gap in the conversation than mention one of the features of the décor, the cornice frieze of sculpted plaster shells, which has been painted in a different colour from the one they remember.

Clearly they know this room. They give away the fact to anyone listening that they came here on the same afternoon last year, and the year before that. Perhaps this is the anniversary of the day on which the divorce was finally settled: or – if that seems too callous a deed for a couple who appear so eminently decent-living and well-balanced, un-vengeful – they've picked a date in the calendar with happier, more pleasant associations for them both, which reminds them of all the other visits in those earlier years, leading them back into the past: which is like a long tunnel to look into, a deep dark well, after all the reflections of the light and space above them in the room, overhead, in this more positive here and now they each know they wouldn't exchange in the wisdom of their quiet second marriages, which they wouldn't be tempted to give up – not at any price.

*

At the next table sit a quite different pairing.

The woman is forty-ish and wears a youthful suede blouson. The teenage girl opposite her is rather lumpish and wears an unflattering flower-patterned dress and a matronly padded chintz jacket.

A mother and daughter: or so the situation might appear. Except that, on a second look, the two do not seem to belong wholly to each other. They have few physical similarities: neither facially, nor in the colouring of their hair, nor in their types of complexion. They even sit in their chairs in contrary ways; their attitudes to the situation don't coincide.

The woman, tanned and as thin as a rake, does a lot of smiling, lifts her eyebrows, passes things about the table, nods her head, sympathizes, confides, suddenly makes light, laughs, calls for the waiter, reads aloud from the menu.

'Quenelles of Haddock Monte Carlo. Goodness! Would you like that, Emma?'

The words have to be pulled from the girl. Her eyes consider the crockery a good deal; she seems increasingly embarrassed to find herself where she is, having lunch with such a slimly elegant woman, being humoured by her.

'Or smoked sturgeon? Sounds a very grumpy fish, doesn't it? What about – let's see – monkfish and ginger?'

At intervals Emma's whey face fires, her fingers pull at the toggles on her rose-garden jacket. Her eyes rise dismally to the woman's, and the brave, plucky, hockey-sticks smile she manages every so often is forgotten again, stranded on a part of her face where she can have no control of it.

The situation is a sort of pastiche. Circumstances declare themselves, through what is said and what is not said. The woman isn't a mother, but a step-mother: the girl is the child of the woman's second husband, by a previous wife who is being slowly but surely and determinedly exorcized from the scenario of this current marriage. Lunch together is an attempt, by the step-mother, to turn them into one another's friend: the trim woman with the high cheek-bones and disguising, over-sized jewellery at her lean, stretched throat, and the stocky girl who's still at school, with her unformed face and unruly breasts and those chubby hands that are the bane of her life, which she looks at with desperation whenever she has to wield her cutlery. These two persons have to make allies of one another and all because of a third person – the husband and father – who calmly and invisibly occupies the middle-ground between them.

They do it for *him*, and also to ensure their own survival in this arrangement that is even more complex and perilous than a marriage. They both move with the awkwardness of puppets: one hyperactively jerky and uncoordinated, the other woodenly clumsy and slow. Each is pushing the other into being a caricature of herself, and each knows the falseness and inevitability of it, that they don't understand enough about one another to think how they can admit what's happening. With time their performances have become more involuntary and the pair draw further and further from each other, even though – now – their hands (the chubby/the long-fingered) are almost touching on the table-top, on the carnation-pink cloth.

The woman laughs (a social, party laugh), and the gold bracelet of her watch catches the light and glints as she raises her hand to her coiffure. The girl nods but doesn't smile, her eyes look down at her breasts, burgeoning even as she sits, and maybe she mentally undresses them both and compares the rolling, fecund landscape of her own body with the arid obliquities and hollows and depressions of *hers*, and for a moment a kind of justice is restored to this bleakly incomprehensible world.

*

While, two tables away, sit a pair of lovers.

Only the expense of the food compels them to eat. Otherwise they would be content, more than content, to feed on air, the bliss of the other's presence. The rest of the room, everything that they exclude, is of an inferior reality, and exists in (at least) one dimension less.

'I didn't know *that*!'

'You certainly do now!'

'Darling, I want to know every single thing about you —'

They may be given the benefit of the doubt: love is love, and they are natural as they've never been in their lives before nor will be again.

'You *have* to tell me. Every *single* thing, remember.'

Or ... Or is it possible that, in their subconsciousness, they're each remembering scenes from films they've watched, which replay on a private mental screen for one? Are they only behaving as others in their condition have the happy obligation of behaving: with the room distanced, their eyes fixed on the other's or moving over the face's features, reading the indicators, identifying the mirror-image of joy that is inside each of them?

'Everything?'

'*Every*thing.'

'You're sure?'

'Positive.'

'Every weeny thing?'

'*Teeny*-weeny —'

Perhaps the pair are as much in love with love as they are with each other, and they can't tell the difference: that is their delicious confusion? But what do the pronouns – 'they', 'their' – *mean* in these extraordinary circumstances? He and she have now entered into the experience of centuries and aeons of time, of all lovers in all ages, and their identities are submerged, disowned. Almost totally so: except, of course, that this is the Modern Age, the second half of the 1980s, and in the mind's eye an imaginary, metaphorical camera lens trails us everywhere, spies over our shoulder, to possess every intimate exchange. So – that is to say, to be quite accurate – the two of them are *nearly* but never wholly alone together.

'Everyone's looking at you, you know.'

'No, they're not.'

'Yes, they are. Cross my heart. Would I tell a lie?'

'You're imagining it.'

'They're thinking, who's *he* with her? Wouldn't mind being in his shoes. Or whatever. Some chaps have *all* the luck —'

A pretty girl, a handsome boy: they might be made for each other, islanded in this room, on their own sea-bound domain. They have the confidence of their youth and their looks. People recognize in them images of themselves, only more perfect, more favoured; the couple exist as extensions of whoever see them – perhaps, it might be said, perhaps without the confirmation of those watching eyes they wouldn't be believed, they would fade into impossible abstractions?

They're laughing at something: the sight of a lobster being carried past, en route for the boiling pot in the kitchen. Such is only the way of the world, and the cruelty of its death can't offend them, it isn't conceivable in their rapturous condition.

'D'you think they'd let me eat this off your arm?'

'My *arm*?'

'Or anywhere else —'

'What?'

'I'd start on your arm —'

'You're mad!'

'I don't think so. Everything's quite clear in my head.'

'I don't care if you're mad or not, not really.'

'You'll take me as I am?'

'If you promise me you'll never change —'

They long to be everything to each other, to turn themselves inside out, to work towards the magic numeral, ONE, to lose themselves and also to be claimed. That, so they've read in magazine articles, is the goal. Once upon a time they might have suffered a terrible solitude, not knowing what was expected of them, how they should behave. But hearts operate nearer the surface nowadays: hearts aren't cardboard and padded velvet bibelots, Valentine-style, they are a physical function of the organism. This Romeo and Juliet eat courtesy of American Express, they already know each other intimately; gently jogging in the park they plug two sets of speakers into one Walkman set and get healthy and wise to their favourite Philadelphian blue-eyed soul music, Hall and Oates' 'Method of Modern Love'.

*

Failing to observe them, an elderly woman and a child sit at the next table. They're more interested in the seascapes on the walls, and the tank of fish, and the counter at the door laid with boxes of oysters in ice, garnished with wedges of lemon and loops of ribbon weed.

The location is probably a mistake. They ought not to be here: instead they should be in the din and hurly-burly of one of the superior hamburger restaurants that draw the crowds, or sitting on stools at a soda counter, if they'd known where to find one. The spectacle of fish was what had appealed, as a distraction: from the real business, the fact that they have no choice but to be lunching together, a boy of seven years old and his grandmother.

They've been dumped on each other, that is the hard truth of the matter. The knowledge shows in the woman's face: her mouth is drawn down, her expression is close to hopeless. She concentrates on the child picking at the crab leavings on his plate with the skewer. When the boy looks up from the debris of claws and broken shell she manages to smile: a tired smile, ready to proclaim defeat. The boy's eyes drop again and she loses the smile, slowly, and sits twisting the stem of her water glass as she protects the child with her gaze.

They protect one another: from total defencelessness. They construct the artifice of companionship from fifty-four years apart, from 'circumstances'.

What's to be construed of those 'circumstances'? – what would anyone sitting at another table make of them?

Let's take an inspired guess.

The boy's mother is the woman's daughter-in-law. She, the grandmother, shares their home, at her son's request, but it is presumed that the money she's saved from selling her own home will help to guarantee a fund of school fees until her grandson is eighteen. She'll manage notwithstanding, and even have enough left over for treats like this: that's what her daughter-in-law understands.

But it's not clear to the woman how much else the boy's mother understands, of her own reading of the situation for instance. She knows that all is not as it might be in the house. Now there seem to be too many business trips for the boy's father, and there are too many unexplained mysteries in the day, when the morning mail is being rapidly sifted or when the phone rings and a stranger's voice speaks (a man's voice, so it always happens) or when a taxi rolls up to collect the boy's mother and she's taken out for the evening, to 'dinner somewhere', with unspecified company.

At the age of sixty-one 'Granny' isn't meant to notice, she's supposed to have had too little experience of the world to be able to spot the give-aways for herself. Her daughter-in-law makes rather tart jokes about her forgetfulness, her old-fashioned ways, but she knows that she's a protection as well, for all of them.

Perhaps it isn't her business. But she feels it's her duty to do what she can for the child, for him at least. Eventually he'll make a discovery, push the wrong door open, pick up the telephone receiver. His life is as fraught as a novel, the kind they seem to have no end of room for on the library shelves: suburban possibilities await like tripwires, and sometimes she wishes she'd gone to live by the sea, in a modern flat with an uninterrupted view, and then she couldn't have given her son and daughter-in-law the excuse. Somehow, her presence in their home is meant to be a blind: it can't be happening with *her* there, such a worthy and thoroughly ignorant woman of the old school as she is.

That's just the cleverness of it.

A live lobster is carried past and the boy looks up.

'What's *that*?'

'It's a lobster, Robin.'

They both watch as a favoured customer is allowed to inspect. The man nods and grins with the relish of a character in a television cartoon, in his eager anticipation of the first taste.

They both continue to watch as the doomed creature is whisked away, to the pot of boiling water behind the kitchen doors.

Robin's grandmother smiles: a more forthright smile than the earlier one, which was ready to acknowledge her defeat: more forthright, but also committed to a deceit. That all is better than it is, when they are truly powerless to prevent what will happen, what must be the outcome, in spite of themselves and their wishes: even with the best and purest intentions they have become accomplices, accessories to the deed – to an event that is simultaneously taking place in another restaurant, where an overdressed woman is being entertained to lunch and champagne from an ice bucket by a man who isn't her husband.

At the very same moment – is it by some awful telepathy that bridges the years? – the boy and his grandmother shift in their chairs. *Her* eyes contract, a nervous reaction; *his* eyes blink quite matter-of-factly at the crab's fate, where the thing lies smashed to its components on his plate.

*

On one of the plush banquettes sits a hefty man in a business suit, squiring a woman young enough to be his daughter. But daughters are not inclined to cling limpet-like to their fathers, except emotionally, and not to link an arm through his in public *quite* so showily, or to try the finger-weaving-into-a-basket technique, which – at long last – he tells her (through a side-of-the-mouth smile) to stop.

They might be in a film. That is precisely her aim for herself, even if this man is not her dream of an ideal romantic lead: *she* is an actress, frizzy-haired and bony-chinned with Cleopatra eyes, and *he* catches all her references and improves on them to remind her that films are his living and in his blood and that *he* calls the tune, he 'makes' her or he drops her. But that's only half the story, let's say. She's more intelligent than she appears to be, and maybe she's a little ashamed of her calling, that she's never grown out of her need to hold a room's attention by singing a pretty song in a little girl voice. She chooses to demean herself, and a gay man friend has quoted so many lines from Jean Harlow films to her that she feels as comfortable with that vocabulary as she does with her shoes off under the table, wriggling her toes inside her French silk stockings.

If the man on the banquette is embarrassed in turn he doesn't show it, but he tries to keep the conversation trained on her future, exploring the myth of her talent.

'I'm seeing Green on Thursday.'

'Better than seeing red!'

'I sent him your stuff, he knows all about you.'

'He does?'

'Of course he does.'

Apart from that she adds a frisson of excitement to his life, especially with her obviousness, which she has now grown into so that there is virtually no distinction to be made between what she pretends to be and what she *is*: every so often she seems (literally) to be shrugging the performance aside, to be casting that skin – only for a few seconds, though, until it's as if the line pulls tight again, she's called back into character for the occasion, which may or may not be her but in which she is by now fully implicated.

For his part, his face clouds from time to time, he seems to be elsewhere: with his wife maybe, or with his daughter, of whom his companion is a mere caricature. (His only child, Leonie, went to a convent, and is now working in a Vigo Street art gallery.)

'I used to think I must've been made in a cinema.'

'*Made?*'

'Well ... *you* know —'

'Oh. Conceived?'

'And that's why I was called Louise.'

'How d'you mean?'

'Louise, in *Gypsy*. With Rosalind Russell. Louise was her child. You know – "Sing out, Louise!" She didn't let her grow up, but then she did, and she became Gypsy Rose Lee. The stripper. You know?'

'Oh.'

He isn't sure if this is a business lunch or not, if they really mean any of the things they're saying to each other: about his putting in a word for her when he meets Green, about how stage-talk is mother's milk to her, and she can't *not* make it big. Of late he's started to lose his delicate touch in such matters, these strictly extra-marital tête-à-têtes that may well take them off in a taxi afterwards, to an impersonal hotel behind Piccadilly where he's not a stranger. It used to be that the man always decided and set the pace, but it's not necessarily the case in these enlightened and liberated days.

She's talking about a friend of hers, called Sara Peploe – it's a crazy story – who went out to Hollywood and got 'involved' with some director who confused life and fiction and, when the movie went over-budget, he tried to kill her, for the insurance money and the publicity. Sara Peploe discovered and the man was burned to death when his house went up in flames, probably – but not positively – because his attempt to fire the building got out of hand and he hadn't time to get out. Now Sara Peploe has a different name and she's working in a Hollywood super-soap, playing an English Rose character.

'Which is the last thing he wanted for her, but too bad. Hey, what d'you think of all that?'

The man smiles, as if she's made it all up and, really, she'd better not start telling those kinds of moral tale to *him*, Hollywood has its own 'modus operandi' but so does Frith Street and Wardour Street. This lunch is expenses but it's costing money all the same: everything *costs*, and no one – him or her – gets anything for free. So it always was: only now perhaps he's a little less able to anticipate all the moves in the game.

He likes the food here (he has to live with a duodenal ulcer), the ambience is muted, there's something comforting and consoling about the décor. He's sure *she* has failed to notice, but in that respect he underestimates her. If he only knew it, she's an actress because she never feels at home anywhere, and she's very sensitive, like litmus, to her surroundings: she takes them in almost subliminally, but she has excellent recall of all the restaurants she's eaten in and the food she was 'advised' to choose from the menu. They're both conscious of the décor: he is restored by it, he's in warm womb-like waters, while she feels helpless to understand it, a geography of shore and sea and swimming things that refuses to include her. Were the lunch going less well, she might feel hostile towards the room, threatened: as it is, her host has said enough flattering things about her abilities almost to convince her they're true and so she's in a frame of mind to forgive such ridiculous surroundings, knowing for the nonce that the plaster won't crack and the walls crumble and fall in and drown them with the weight of rushing flood water. She doesn't fancy the prospect of seaweed in her hair, or a silver fish slithering in the gully between her breasts, which pert appendages she's had to take an out-and-out market view on and rate as her top assets.

*

And then, somewhere else in the room, there's myself.

What is there to say? I can believe myself to be so sure about those who are round about me, filling a space and making an atmosphere, but what certain knowledge do I have about myself?

Principally, that I eat alone: that I choose to eat alone. There must be reasons why, but these are lost to me, they belong in the dim, nethermost recesses of personal history, where – if I were to look – I should only err and stray and never find my way back. So, it's enough to know that I prefer to eat alone, and not to feel I'm obliged to share the occasion of a meal with another person. Maybe I would only make them uncomfortable, they would imagine I wasn't concentrating on my seafood platter 'St Malo' but I was looking through them with X-ray eyes, and then they would start to fidget in their chair. I don't want the embarrassment of their reactions: I don't want the obligation of having to play through a performance with them. I prefer solitude to that.

I *can* tell you this, that I travel a lot: that the pleasure for me consists every time in the last seconds before the journey's end (wherever it is), in climbing the staircase with the key in my hand to open the door of a room I've never set eyes on before. The rooms that come closest to perfection are the barest and simplest, those with the minimum of personality and the fewest clues of prior possession. My mind expands to fill those, to furnish them and people them. To me, the view from the window is very nearly beside the point: very nearly.

I don't mean that I'm not receptive to my surroundings – most often I am – or that I only live with my recollections, or cocooned in a kind of fantasy. I mean that I'm the happiest, the most free, when I give my imagination and sympathies their loosest rein.

You've read this because you've wanted to read it: so I presume that you can understand the impulse in me, as it exists in *you*, to extend the limits of yourself, to travel in experience, to see into other people's lives so that – perhaps – you can appreciate better what is worth appreciating in your own: or – perhaps, more simply – the purpose is merely to enable you to feel less lonely in yourself.

But I don't subsist by theories. The particular is always more interesting to me. On that score nothing is not important.

A hand's gesture, the tic of a mouth, an eye turning, it tells an undue portion of the story. My 'story' is about being on the fringes of other people's stories. *You* are currently a character in, maybe, two dozen unfinished tales; you endure all the hazards – chance, coincidence, non-sequiturs, what isn't explained, overstatement, a trite little moral at the end. You deserve half of them (half at least, and let me tell you that's way above the average) to have happy endings.

In one of the mirrors between the painted panels I watch myself watching. The room is recreated in front of my eyes, then a second time in an approximate pattern of words that comes into my head. The room repeats itself, just as the sea repeats and returns and re-makes a scene that never seems any different.

I am to be pitied perhaps: I'm the crazy one who always returns to the same rock, to stare out at the same unchanging stretch of breakers and foam.

The room's voices are the mesmeric song of the surf. The sea is casting up its edible offerings, the fruits of a different element from our own. For this moment it seems to me that we've come here to eat – like Picasso's lolling ancients, like temporary gods – on the harvest of a very deep and lightless, maybe fathomless, place.

Schwimmbad Mitternachts
A Hollywood Adventure

I can make happen whatever I want to happen.
Tomorrow I'm having lunch at The Vineyard with
Catherine Deneuve. I've decided so late in my long life that
it's French beauty I admire the most, and my good friend
Catherine has deep-frozen it to perfection.

Three days ago I had lunch at Le Saint Germain with
Paloma Picasso. We discussed CD, then our friend in common, Yves Saint-Laurent. I told PP that I'd stayed with Yves
briefly, at his elegant holiday home in Marrakesh, Morocco
they showed in *Town and Country*. We discussed elegance,
Paloma and I, and I let her know how highly I reckoned it
among the civilised virtues.

I've watched them pass through Hollywood, the elegant
women of this half-century: Garbo, Greer, Ava, Nelly Nyad,
Grace, Audrey, Claudia Cardinale, Anita Ekberg, Linda E. As
I said to Catherine Deneuve in La Petite Chaya only the other
day, after her 'Today' spot, there is no true equality in this
life, thank God, there *are* superior beings. I told her I was
seeing Paloma P (Tuesday), and I said that superiority can be
passed from generation to generation, and wasn't that a relief
to know?

'I can make happen whatever I want to happen,' I tell my
lady lunch friends, in all the best restaurants in Hollywood
and Beverly Hills. They smile and tip their heads because they
want to discover, they want to hear all about it.

Unfortunately I can't entertain here, on the premises (as it
were), but that is no loss. People in our trade eat to be seen,
and all my life I've dined out: cafés in Switzerland, fifty cent
diners on the Lower East or Fulton Street, now – because
there's an urgency about getting all the things in life attended

to I want to attend to – in the very best restaurants in north-west LA.

I tell my lunch ladies, oh what I could have done for you, the scripts you could have had from me! *You* would have read between the lines, seen all the affection I put into the character. As it is, you won't remember...

They say they *do* (hand resting on my wrist), and I wonder. I haven't worked in the studios since 1954, and my tv work only gets shown now in the afternoons, when the shades are drawn and my girls are asleep in their rooms, cool in their satin lingerie: re-runs of sixties cowboy shows, and a fifties comedy series I once wrote with a team. These days it's camp, the series: it's called 'Yodels in Yonkers', about an Austrian family (Germans weren't thought 'publicly credible') who settle in New York City. Who remembers, who doesn't have the evidence of their eyes?

'Ah, "Yodels in Yonkers"...'

Catherine's hand touches my wrist, she smiles. She smiles – that's enough.

But comedy wasn't my *métier*, I explain: even though someone did suggest me to the producers of 'Hiram Holliday' and, later, 'Get Smart!'. Maybe I look too Teutonic to be convincing. I can make Carol Channing laugh when I call her up, and I think I can see my influence in Lily Tomlin's act. Long ago, before the War, Aryan was a swell thing to be in this place; later the studio bosses just didn't want to know you.

My mother was half a Jew, and I was born in Berne, but I had a name that sounded German and that was that. So maybe even my famous friends just pretend to have heard of me? What I'm lunching with is their *legend*, maybe: as people perhaps they don't exist. As a person perhaps *I* don't exist either?

I reckon I'm only worth my memories, and the offerings of my imagination. No one should be interested in how I live, where, what I eat when I'm not out lunching, what I eat just to survive, how I get my laundry done, how many pairs of slacks I have in my closet. That's too dull, it's nothing, it's beside the point. Anyway, who's ever one person? You go through this life, and the border of *your* personality, so-called, that's shifting all the time, like duneland; or you pick up habits and tricks, thoughts and opinions, from this friend, that acquaintance. People flow in and out of each other and sometimes you can't tell where 'I' stop and 'you' begin. That's fine, that's just how it should be.

Thank the good Lord.

I said it already – who wants to know how I fill the rest of my day when I've got my clean laundry back and I'm not lunching or calling from the pay-phone, to all my friends in the Hills, too many to tell you. I watch tv a lot, old films, those programs, cowboy shows shot in four days. The cowboy actors were all gay, but you got used to that, and the queen acts between shots: all you see in Mr Reagan's America is the frontier spirit, and men with square jaws and flat stomachs, and grateful women.

I voted for Mr Reagan both times but I never listen when the radio next door comes through the wall at me, all about Congress and those terrible gun-crazy places all over the world. I'm old Hollywood, you see – I remember people telling me the great sign west of Griffith Park used to read 'Hollywoodland Realty', until the 'land' fell off – I never stopped loving the stars, the unchangeable, women in the fullness of their grace, such beautiful women, born in Heaven.

*

That's what *she* might have been.

It was in Switzerland, in Zurich, that our paths crossed first. I had an appointment at a fancy café to meet someone who knew someone in films, and *she* was at another table waiting to meet an agent who was working for another agent in New York City.

She was an actress, I recognised her. She called herself 'Sophie Niederhauser'. I'd started out in the theater, and had a good memory for faces and names. She *looked* better than she acted. She looked great, chic-kultiviert: classy, as the English say. And some. And mysterious too, as if no one was going to get to know all there was to know about her: *if* there was so much, of course . . .

That afternoon at The Glockenspiel she kept glancing over at me. Eventually she came across. She thought *I* was the man from the agency. I said 'no'. She laughed, she was so

222

embarrassed. A bit on edge, I guessed. She asked me my name and *I* was so nervous I told her my real name, not the one I was using to write under. Then I corrected myself. 'Peter Keller,' I said. It vaguely registered with her, I could see.

I stayed on in Zurich, just to have a chance to talk to her again. We met another day on the Bahnhofstrasse, by accident (more or less), and she told me she was being taken over to America. I still remember how she sounded, so excited and amused and incredulous and proud, breathless too. She said, all her photographs had been sent out without her knowing anything about it, and they'd caught the eye of an agent who knew one of the senior European directors working in Hollywood. Gunther Volkhardt-Prinz he was called, an Austrian. She was smiling right across her face as she gave me the name. I shook my head, meaning I was impressed.

'America's a world in itself,' she said. 'A whole world.'

I repeated her.

'They've got a "Little Italy" in New York,' she told me.

'There's a "Chinatown" too,' I said. 'Somewhere.'

'In California there's a place called Venice.' She laughed. 'With real gondolas.'

She was on a cloud, and when I took her for lunch afterwards she didn't seem to know where she was, or who with.

Later, though – in another place, in the City of the Angels, the New Palestine – *then*, I guess, she did remember.

*

Later was the next year, 1934.

A number of accidents – or 'colluding events', let's say – had taken me out to the West Coast. I found I had the same professional name as another German writer working for the movies, and somehow they confused our agents in New York. It was like a film plot when they told me, but by then it was too late: I was out there, it felt like no place on earth, and I'd decided I might as well stay.

Somewhere, in someone's office, I met the secretary to Gunther Volkhardt-Prinz. I'd heard his name a lot: he'd worked with some European actresses, turning them into stars. It must have been a difficult business for him, so I reckoned: they didn't have American temperaments, they didn't speak the language too well (if at all), and they didn't like the heat.

I knew about the last film he'd made, called *The Sultana*. It had come out about thirteen or fourteen months before: it was his first, and very successful, vehicle for his newest protégé, a Danish version of Garbo. Through most of the movie she was in veils, which added to her allure. The publicity posters put it, 'Who *is* Verena Karel?' In those days that was all you needed to do to pull people in: that, and using the sassy-sounding Continental name and those cool grey Skagerrak eyes peering over the yashmak. (People say we lived innocent and naïve lives then, but I wonder.)

The woman secretary was in her forties, tall, austere, European in the icy way Hollywood understood it. I introduced myself. At first she confused me for the other Peter Keller. Then, when I (politely) put her right, she was suddenly less interested. That is, until I mentioned another name, 'Sophie Niederhauser'.

I watched her face set. Her mouth shrank to a straight line, her eyes drilled into me. She shook her head. 'No,' she said, 'I've no idea who you're talking about.'

At the time I was working on a script from a short story called *The Tired Old Detective*, which the studios (the same studios that had Volkhardt-Prinz under contract) had bought rights on. The story was about a private investigator who's becoming over-sensitive because he's stale in his job, whose wife calls him a 'tired old detective' to his face, and who begins to suspect – with just how much justification? – that *she*'s involved with another man in a plot to murder him for an insurance pay-out. Maybe I was too much influenced by that, and saw the world as my tired old detective might have done, over-reacting, reading too much into a situation. Or maybe not.

Any time in future I had to pass the secretary in a corridor, she pretended to pay me no attention: but I knew – I had goosebumps – that she saw me very well, and she was keeping me close in her sights. Meanwhile I asked everyone I met about Volkhardt-Prinz, and they gave me so many versions of him I didn't know what to believe.

On studio telephones I called New York late at night and rang round the film and theater agencies. I spoke to all those the studios had dealings with, but none of them could tell me anything about an actress called 'Sophie Niederhauser'. One of them did have a record of a Swiss actress entering their books the year before, but her name was 'Maria Linsenmeyer': she'd subsequently gone out of circulation, and no one had been able — or had bothered — to trace her. 'That's the business, mister,' I was told.

I found the posters for *The Sultana* where they hadn't been covered over by others. They were starting to peel and tear. I stared at those grey eyes, and puzzled — I didn't know why I should be thinking it — remembering those other, azurine blue eyes I'd been looking into on the Bahnhofstrasse.

*

An automobile knocked me down when I was walking out of the studios one day, and I came to in hospital.

I was there for eleven weeks. Most of the time I could, I spent reading: whatever trash was going around. Next to me in the ward was a Polack who made riding boots for a living, a real craftsman. He told me the studio bosses and directors and the stars were his godsend: he didn't care where they'd all come from, if they'd crawled up from the gutter, now everyone belonged to Hollywood. 'Even you, young man, although you may not think it.' I shook my head. 'You'll never get away,' he said.

He told me about the legs he'd fitted, the beautiful calves. 'Not that they're all like that.' I asked if he'd ever made boots for Mr Volkhardt-Prinz. He nodded. 'And for Verena Karel,' he added. 'Funny thing, though: I went back maybe nine months, a year ago, and her feet weren't the same. She told me they'd grown.'

'*Do* they grow?' I asked.

'Maybe she's a whole lot younger than anyone thinks.'

'She's got knowing eyes,' I said.

'I didn't see her eyes. She was wearing a hat with a little veil. Little, but long enough. In the house.'

'Volkhardt-Prinz's house?'

The man nodded.

'I heard,' he said, 'she's crazy about those looks of hers. She's scared they don't stay, they vanish. She's a real strange lady. Maybe flaky, like they say.'

*

Now people don't remember the name 'Verena Karel' when I mention it to them. Not Bette, not Doug. Sometimes I ask people in the deli, in Schwab's, in the street, no one knows. No one remembers.

Once she was going to be another Garbo.

*

After the accident I was left with a scar on my face.

An actor might have welcomed such an act of providence, but I didn't care for it, and I decided to have some minor plastic surgery done on my cheek. I'd just been paid for something I'd written seven or eight months before, and so I could afford to go into a clinic for a few days.

On the last day, as I was preparing to leave, I was standing at the window and (for some reason) I was thinking of Volkhardt-Prinz and his secretary when I noticed a car like the one the great man was driven around in making its way down the drive. Cadillacs were common enough in Hollywood, of course.

Maybe, I convinced myself, it's something to do with the treatment: you're letting your imagination take over.

*

Maybe.

But I was like a bear round a hive. I searched out Volkhardt-Prinz's house, on Summit Drive. I used to watch the long black Cadillac drive in and out, and the blue Bugatti roadster with the open top. Volkhardt-Prinz always sat beside his handsome chauffeur. Twice I saw him with his arm resting along the back of the driver's seat and his hand on the boy's shoulder. The boy was young enough to be his son.

For weeks on end I'd been asking around about Verena Karel. I'd been told her address was a secret. The secretary had got to hear I was enquiring and had sent me a curt note, certain information was off-limits. A couple of weeks later I had my accident with the automobile, and it was as I was lying in the hospital bed that I wondered if Volkhardt-Prinz had her staying with him in the house. Then what the Polack boot-maker told me, about the fitting, seemed to confirm it.

When I came out, like I said, I spent a lot of time up on Summit Drive, near Breakaway House and Pickfair. There were high walls and dogs in the garden, and I didn't dare to go in. In the early hours, on the other side of midnight, lights would go on and off in the house. A few times I heard noises – shouts, screams. One night – or morning – when I'd stayed on, intrigued by the activity, the gates opened and the Cadillac drove out. The blinds were drawn in the back, but as the car passed down the street a hand pulled one of the blinds back and a woman's face appeared. It was white, terrified. A hand clawed at the glass, till the blind was wrenched back into place.

The gates opened again. The Cadillac was followed by the blue Bugatti, being driven by a woman in a headsquare. For a moment I thought, the driver's face...

I didn't see them come back. I returned on the next few evenings, and walked round the walls and stationed myself in the shrubbery opposite. The dogs barked, but I heard no more sounds from the house.

*

Maybe half-a-dozen times, or eight or ten, I saw Verena Karel's photograph in the newspapers. She was always being escorted by Volkhardt-Prinz, his hand was always on her arm. She wore hats and veils, so you couldn't see her eyes, and coats with their collars turned up, even in the heat.

I discovered she was due to attend a gala première, and on the evening I joined the spectators outside the theater. I pushed forward to the front of the crowd. As she walked towards where I was standing, I called out something in German.

Not Danish – German.

Her head turned, she looked at me, seemed to hesitate. Then Volkhardt-Prinz tightened his grip on her arm, she shook. She reeled a little as he led her forward, guiding her steps.

A trick like that proved nothing really, even the tired old detective would have realised. So, maybe she wasn't from Denmark; maybe hearing German distracted her only because it wasn't American English? It was possible she'd picked up some words from her famous German mentor, like shorthand code between them. But nonetheless I was compelled, drawn to find out more.

*

It was difficult to learn more. Verena Karel's public appearances became rarer and rarer, and she never again met her audience at such close range.

But I persevered. I did: let that be said of me.

*

At the studios production started – in great secrecy – on a new movie starring Verena Karel. Entrance to the set was restricted, by Volkhardt-Prinz's express instructions, but I persuaded one of the extras (at a cost of twenty dollars) to let me take his place as a milling, muttering French peasant among what used to be called the 'atmosphere people' in the background.

On the set she was never let out of the sight of at least one of four persons: Volkhardt-Prinz, who was directing, the secretary, a white-coated woman nurse, and the uniformed chauffeur in riding boots. Around her was gathered an outer group: the costumier and his assistant, the hairdresser, the make-up hand, script supervisor, personal maid, a diction coach. They were constantly encouraging her. Dressed as Catharine de Medici and in smoked glasses ('Don't let the light hurt your eyes, lieblinge!'), she sat there, just nodding.

Once between takes I heard her raise her voice and declare petulantly, 'I'll do it if I wanna do it!' (The remark told me she'd picked up some American English, what she required; on the set, however – even as the high-living, libertine Catharine de Medici ruining sixteenth-century France – she spoke her lines with a decided Scandinavian inflection.)

In the course of time – that same afternoon – I was discovered to be an impostor and instructed, in no uncertain fashion, to leave. I saw the secretary watching me as I was escorted from the building. Behind her stood the chauffeur, in pugilistic pose, eyeing me as if I had a face he didn't mean to forget.

*

I had an instinct I should lie low for a while.

I moved into new rooms. I started a novel, about a young Swiss playwright trying very hard to make it in Hollywood. I called my story *Swimming Pool at Midnight* because I thought it sounded good: in fact it sounds better in German,

Schwimmbad Mitternachts, but the title never got used one way or the other, because the book never got published, it wasn't even finished.

I gave it up after a few weeks, and went back to scripting, for another studio on Melrose. I had a couple of breaks. I managed to put down half on a car. I rented an apartment out in Santa Monica, near the pier.

I hadn't forgotten Verena Karel – like a story I couldn't get right in my head, that eluded me, which I couldn't believe in enough to be able to focus on it properly. It struck me, it was better – safer – not to get involved anyway. A coward's way, okay, but Hollywood was filling up with cowards then, or at any rate with those who wanted to avoid having to make decisions of a moral sort: hence the German–Austrian influx, and all the hopeful young actors – Hollywood fodder – wanting other people to make decisions *for* them.

I heard from an old contact at the studios that the Catharine de Medici movie was in trouble, Verena Karel had been taken sick. At least, that was the official reason. My informer told me, no one on the set felt they knew where they were with the star. One day she'd nod her head, do everything she was told, the next she could remember nothing, the third she was throwing a tantrum and talking German so only the director could understand, the fourth she'd be as quiet as she could be, like she was in a dream. '*You* work it out,' he said, 'if you can.'

*

Years afterwards, in 1947 (or 1948), I got word there was a crazy lady in a private home up in San Luis Obispo, she kept saying the name 'Verena Karel' and talking in a language no one could make out.

I went to see her. After so long she was nothing like the face on the poster for *The Sultana*, although she had the grey eyes. She wasn't speaking, she just glared at me. To test her out, I said another name, 'Sophie Niederhauser'. It meant nothing to her. But I knew it wouldn't. By that stage of the story – with all my tacky credits for lousy B-pictures no one remembered after the last frame – I had the truth. If that word 'truth' ever meant anything in this mixed-up, loopy, jigsaw land.

*

But back to then.

It spread like a bush fire round the studios where Volkhardt-Prinz was shooting that no one knew where Verena Karel was. He'd tried to discover himself, but when he couldn't he'd had to bring in the police. They were saying he should have told them earlier, then they could have done more.

When I got back to my apartment one evening, I saw a black Cadillac – *the* black Cadillac – parked outside. The chauffeur in his maroon uniform and tan boots got out and we 'talked' – which is one word for it. He said, very sweetly, he would give me five hundred dollars for 'information'. A thousand dollars.

Two thousand.

Then the sweetness disappeared as he told me I'd get my pretty face busted, split open, if they found proof I was involved in it.

Luckily for me a police siren started wailing on the next block and he took that as his prompt and climbed back into the Cadillac.

I stood looking after it as it rolled down the road. Still a bit dazed, I had the conceit to think that, if I'd been writing his lines for him, I could have managed something more neatly turned, not sounding as if it had been memorised from a movie.

The car vanished. Like Scott Fitzgerald put it, night had come down on day like a curtain. (There are no moody, thoughtful twilights in this place.)

The road was empty. The police siren faded. I might only have imagined that it had happened: except that I smelled something in the heat of that dark evening, the trace of eau de Cologne, fleeting evidence that – for all the conceivable arguments to the contrary – I hadn't been alone.

*

Soon after that I moved out of the apartment, and went down the coast, to faded Venice-by-the-Sea, to a place on Ocean Front Walk.

The ocean kept me awake, but I didn't mind insomnia. In the evenings, when I was working on a script, I used to come back from the studios, have a drink, then I'd go out walking.

Sometimes, under cover of darkness, I'd head for the Pavilion with its minarets, sometimes in the opposite direction, towards the ghostly ferris wheel or, beyond it, to the Temple of Birth.

Sitting in a diner one night, looking out at a broken-backed gondola abandoned in one of the silting canals, I remembered she'd mentioned it to me – 'There's a Venice in California' – way back in Zurich, she'd said it on the Bahnhofstrasse.

Occasionally I'd feel uneasy, I'd think there were movements among the shadows behind me. Once I was sure I was being tracked home, by headlights: not by a Cadillac or a Bugatti but by a taxi cab – I couldn't make sense of that.

Another night I came back and I knew someone had been in the living-room. There was no mess, nothing missing that I could see, but a box of paper clips lay scattered on the floor under the desk – and, at that period of my life, I was still famously Swiss in the cleanliness and order of my domestic habits. Then I opened the desk drawer and saw that the manuscript of the novel had gone.

I shook my head with disbelief: not at first for the novel's loss, but in total puzzlement for a motive. I started looking for clues, but simply (or not so simply) I couldn't find any.

I'd told so few people about the novel. I tried to remember just who I *had* told.

Or could it have been *his* doing – the chauffeur's? And somehow that accounted for his interest in me, because of the novel he'd heard about, what I might have written in it?

But there was no after-trail of eau de Cologne in the room.

Anyone who'd wanted into the apartment could have got in. I entered from an open balcony, and a kid could have twisted the lock. I had nothing to steal, the furniture wasn't mine, so I'd never thought about it, my 'security'.

*

The police called me in the middle of one of those hot, empty, dogday mornings when I was working – *trying* to work – in the apartment and I felt instead I was becalmed, tossed high and dry by circumstances. They were sending a car to bring me down to Playa del Rey, they said, to the Alpenhorn Hotel.

It didn't seem I had the privilege to refuse.

The hotel was like any other of those frail, spindly structures on stilts with flat roofs and balconies along that stretch of coast, erected from what seem to be common composite parts and put up on scrubby lots with no apparent thought for their future. What distinguished it (in a manner of speaking) were the name, and pine shutters at the windows perforated with the carved outlines of hearts, and a dusty Alpine horn hanging on one cracked plaster wall in the front hall.

And the owner, a diminutive Swiss Jew with a moustache and a yellow-and-white polka-dot bow-tie. He stood in the darkened lobby – the blinds had been lowered, because of the heat or out of respect – and (I'd been searching for years for the sight of someone doing such a thing) wringing his hands.

I was led outside by the officer in charge, out past a kidney-shaped pool. The heat made me think I must be in a witch's kitchen. I could smell melting tar from the roadway on the other side of the hotel building.

I looked about me, as my trade demands. Probably the hotel and pool weren't more than four or five years old: they'd been meant as material feats of bravery and optimism in the throes of the Depression. But already grass grew up between the chipped paving stones; paint had flaked from the rail by the pool steps and rust showed through. Dead flies specked the greasy surface of the water.

The body had been taken back upstairs to the bedroom, which had been signed for with the name 'Linsenmeyer'. She'd been found dead in the pool, sometime in the early hours of the morning: the time just after I'd got back for the three hours of sleep I seemed to be able to survive on now. She'd been lying face-down, afloat on the surface.

What did I know about it? they asked. 'Nothing,' I replied. 'Absolutely nothing.'

They showed me the manuscript of the novel, which had been discovered in the room. I shook my head.

They showed me the victim. I shook my head again. They lowered the sheet over the body.

It *was* her, I couldn't doubt it. They'd changed her nose a bit, it was a little shorter, bobbed. Her eyes were wide open, they wouldn't close: not grey like the Sultana's in the movie, but blue, the colour of a proper, bona fide Beverly Hills pool, or – better – a Swiss lake, like the Zurichsee, on a fine-weather day. Her hair had been dyed fairer, to the

Scandinavian, and the colour was coming out at the roots. But it *was* her: Sophie Niederhauser, a name and a face I still hadn't forgotten, however hard they'd tried to turn her into someone else.

I just stood shaking my head, and when they asked – very particularly – I told them I hadn't a clue who she was.

*

The questions went on for days. Elsewhere they were pumping out the corpse.

They found needle marks on her arms, and traces of tranquilizers, anti-depressants, sleeping tablets, boosters. Some people might have taken to the life better, I was told quite coolly and unsympathetically; but it had all 'gone to her head'. That seemed to me the whole point, but I didn't say: the police on this job didn't look the most understanding in all of God's chosen land of manna, Amerika.

'Accidental Drowning' was the official verdict. I'm not sure they were caring much, until Volkhardt-Prinz showed up for the body. She was buried not as herself but as 'Verena Karel', in a fancy ceremony at Forest Lawn. One newspaper I read said Miss Karel drowned in sassier Malibu, in Paradise Cove, and nicely got around the issue: that newspaper had studio interest in it, and some of the other press notices told different stories, although none of them matched. Volkhardt-Prinz or his advisors invented a myth, that Verena Karel was such a star she liked to get incognito occasionally and hide out. It seemed to confirm that she'd been destined to become too big even for Hollywood.

'She' died young, and so she was spared all that sweating and toiling having to prove it, that she was an extraordinary talent. But 'she' would never have survived; she didn't, so the possibility doesn't arise, and the notion's just an empty hypothesis.

*

I can't help thinking, naturally – what would she have been like as Sophie Niederhauser, why did they want to turn her into Verena Karel – but I try *not* to think about it. Then sometimes, when I least expect I will, I remember that face in the car as the blind was wrenched back, and the person I went to see years later in the Gethsemane Home for the mentally disturbed, and I tell myself, at least – twice – I saw the 'real' Verena Karel.

But was there ever such a person – one person – who was Verena Karel? Or, before the role fell to Sophie Niederhauser, maybe there were others? – Verena Karels plural? In Hollywood does it even matter?

*

I had a funny feeling afterwards. It was as if, I thought, as if she'd been trying to become a character in my novel, my Sophie Niederhauser from Zurich. Certainly I'd left spaces for her, gaps in the story where she was free to come and go, if she'd wanted to.

Can it happen, an author comes to be haunted by his characters?

But I'm not a proper author, so how should I know, of what concern should it be to me anyway?

Volkhardt-Prinz was cleverer than any of us. He was the auteur-director *par excellence*, he had his own scenario written; he was only waiting, as the 'other' Verena Karel went into a sudden, unforeseen decline, spinning on her axis. From photographs he'd already cast the Swiss understudy, shortly before our chance encounter in Zurich, on the terrace of the Café Glockenspiel. To a man of his long experience in Hollywoodland we must have seemed like two orphaned innocents, hopelessly and helplessly adrift: about to be swept away beyond the reach of saving.

*

All the infinite possibilities in this adult, X-rated world – maybe the police really did think I was mixed up in it? – they could drive you crazy, clean out of your box.

*

When it came out I went to see *Sunset Boulevard* five nights running.

I thought it was trying to tell the truth of my life but couldn't get it right, not quite. Some one thing escaped it, kept dodging away every time.

After the movie I used to walk the streets a lot, Sunset,

Macy, Alameda, Temple, long past midnight. I drank a lot of coffee to keep awake. Suddenly, somewhere in the LA night before dawn came in, still in the desert heat and glare of headlamps, under tousle-topped palms, on sodium-pale sidewalks, I would remember the bells ringing on the tramcars on the cobbled Bahnhofstrasse and the two of us standing talking, in the crowd, in the bright sunshine of day, our words flying from us and it didn't matter.

I've never really told the tale before, not properly, I've only hinted, suggested. The problem is, Catherine Deneuve is another generation. I've written to Audrey Hepburn, but her reply – and her reply to the letter I wrote after that – they must have got lost in the mail. Audrey has such tender eyes, so very *simpaticci*, it's like they're looking into your soul. They say Barbra Streisand sometimes shows up to eat at L'Orangerie on North La Cienega Boulevard, but they also tell you her time's very taken up now she's a businesswoman: she's got the intelligence to understand, but maybe I'll make that a drink date, not lunch.

Did I say, on Tuesday it's Paloma Picasso and me, just the two of us, tête à tête.

The Second Marriage

The 'little summer', it's called: St Luke's Summer. With a touch of the 'Indian' this year, to make up for the below-average June and July.

The garden smells of cut grass, and the lawnmower's busy whirring nicely fills the customary hollow space in her mid-afternoons. The new boy is quick about his work, which means he's sooner finished and costs them less: obviously there's a lot he still has to learn, and Mrs Morris takes advantage of his industry and cheapness in the interim.

Beneath the mechanical whine the tennis courts at the top of the lane are silent, no plung-plung and distant whoops of delight as a point is won. Somewhere there's a house-painter or a roof-tiler playing – she supposes – a transistor radio, but it's too far away to intrude on her privacy.

Mrs Morris stands at the sitting-room window drinking Keemun tea from a fine bone cup. The view through the lozenges of leaded glass really could not be bettered.

*

By now most of their friends have forgotten to remember that this is a second marriage.

The evidence is there, however, it persists – if they would only care to look. Why else are they – she and he – so polite with each other, not forcedly so but as if from resolute habit? Why do they not publicly trade stories about the past, or vie with each other when describing the details? Why do they seem to have visited different places and known different people in their lives before?

*

236

His first wife, called Helen, died in a car crash.

It had been an easy, happy marriage, without strains or introspection. He lived on without her, in the same house, for six years. He immersed himself in his work; he took up sailing in his spare time and became competitive in races. He turned into another decade, on the big Four-O.

Meeting Greta – a comely divorcée only a few years his junior – was looked upon as a blessing and an act of God by his friends, the best thing that could have happened, but it wasn't – at least once he'd got over the shock to his widower's system – regarded as such by him. She was always at whoever's house he was invited to, or so it seemed to him: she smiled at him across tables, sitting-rooms, tennis nets. She even chanced to appear at the marina one day in a party of mutual acquaintances. Twice or three times she told him that she came up to town occasionally, and he felt obliged to invite her to lunch. Then, after that first occasion, he believed himself bound to repeat the invitation for another time. She had much going for her, as all his friends (who were probably *her* friends too) kept telling him, but he became oddly impervious to her charms after a while: he wasn't especially given to his widower's ways in the house but he did have a very particular routine which he'd perfected where his work and also his sailing were concerned. Greta, to be blunt, was an unlooked-for diversion: he felt he couldn't *not*, for chivalry's sake, entertain such a striking-looking, pleasant-mannered woman when she said she would be up in town on this day or that, and he thought it would be discourteous to leave her behind at the marina when he had room on the boat going spare. But it was incidental, a distraction from the business of his proper life, a side-show.

And he married her in the end so that he wouldn't have to be thinking about her constantly, so that she would just be woven into the woof of things, so that – perhaps – *he would just be able to forget about her.*

*

She had her own unhappy marriage behind her to remind her of all she didn't want to find in a man.

George had been a mistake. That was understating, of course, but it was far behind her now and she didn't dwell on it: the drinking sessions in City watering-holes and the late arrivals home, the first blonde hairs on his lapel (as if she'd been reading about herself in a short story in a magazine), the first trace of a woman's smell grafted on to his own.

Then it was that she'd begun to spend his money, on clothes and shoes she had no occasion to wear, and on expensive foodstuffs she hadn't the heart to prepare. She'd sat in the 'Maids of Honour' tea-rooms down the road in Richmond, eating cream cakes – or taking aimless bites out of them, leaving the remains on her plate – and drinking enough cups of tea to send her floating home on a cloud of theine.

For a while she'd thought it must be her fault. Then she'd become angry. Then she'd tried to ignore that it was happening.

Somewhere along the way she'd lost one of her skins, and coming out of it – the skin and the situation – she had seen in the mirrors that she was recognisably herself (still slim and tidy, thank God) although she was feeling quite different inside: as if she'd somehow bubbled up nearer the surface, and was making contact all the time with the outsides of objects, the cold shine of windows, the touch of hot or damp or icy air. She had come to fear heights and looking down, even thinking too far back: a kind of vertigo of memory. Where there was one to hold, she had now made a point of reaching out for banister rails and handrails and grab handles, as if she might be about to lose her balance; she had worn heavy shoes when she went for afternoon walks, as if she might be in danger of blowing away. She'd only properly *believed* something if she could touch it.

She had also – sadly – believed the physical knocks and bruises that came later with George. She'd really had no option. At least that had made the business of a divorce easier. But she'd felt so far removed from the legal ins-and-outs-and-roundabouts, as if she might have been in a different room from where the lawyer's conversation was taking place, she couldn't concentrate. She couldn't focus until almost a year later when she was launched back into the social swim and it occurred to her that Michael Morris's was a face she was re-encountering. She suddenly started paying attention. He proved himself so courteous, so – so regardful, in his solid way; he was successful in his work (so she was told, quite often), usually he had a gravity in his demeanour which impressed her and reassured her.

Of course other men subsequently intruded themselves into her field of vision. They were more insistent: and she allowed them to entertain her. By comparison, Michael was much quieter, but she appreciated that in him, she felt herself in safe hands. More and more he came to seem to her – quite simply – like 'base': a harbour, her own marina. She began to dread the thought of his not continuing to be there.

She half-proposed to him – or did he half-propose to her? – and she said 'Yes', without having to think, because she knew *she didn't want to be without him, she always wanted to have him around.*

*

This is just as they always wanted things to be: they have the sort of garden which other people, seeing them on the social rounds, expect them to have, and the sort of house (a new one to them both, in a small town they moved to because neither of them had had previous experience of it), furnished in innocuous chintz and generally cautious good taste. The couple look as they're supposed to look: for local appearances he wears brogues and neatly-cut flannels and checked woollen shirt and (except at the golf course) a mossy tweed jacket, and he might pass for a little older than his forty-five years or a few years younger. She is starting, here and there, to show grey in her hair, but bravely accepts the fact (the grey adds 'character', doesn't it?); for the locale she favours mid-calf woollen prints and quilted mandarin jackets. He wears expensively anonymous suits for the City, and she dresses as youthfully as she dares for her own days up in London, black sheer stockings (rather than tights) and court shoes with the fashionably thin heels. They drive a sensible Swedish make of car. They don't smoke, they drink in moderation, they have an account in the 'Three Worlds' wholefood shop in the town.

They are, singly and apart, wholly predictable. They are on the right and proper side of cliché – just. This way – which is to say, in their most confident and accepting frame of mind – they feel they have achieved their purpose and end in life.

*

But...

Later in the month the winds blow up. The leaves turn, the branches shake and – in time – the lawn shrinks beneath the soft golden mush. The geraniums and chrysanthemums lose their petals. The lily pads close over the surface of the pool and a musty, rather unpleasant smell rises when the wind is carrying in a certain direction.

The clock goes back an hour. Birds lose their summer independence and come closer to the house, looking for scraps, while the blue tits desert their box under the eaves. The washing has to be tumble-dried indoors. Her skin starts to roughen, to flake; she has to use hand-creams and glycerine soaps.

At this time of year she gets a little on edge. More than a little. The rustling leaves seem to be fidgeting on the trees, and when the leaves have fallen the branches creak and tap like fingers against the windows. She thinks of all she had to suffer in her other marriage, with George, and that's why she shivers, that's why she has a generous peg of scotch at four o'clock of an afternoon and puts on a record with a fast beat and turns up the volume knob.

Also ... There's a voice inside herself, she doesn't want to hear it: it's trying to speak, something about change, everything changing, in the garden and her life, nothing being retained, all being a falling away. Oh, God. When she's in one of these moods, the simplest objects will have the capacity to hold her, to absorb her, like a spell – the spatula in the kitchen drawer, the plastic toothmug on the bathroom wall – and she'll know that somewhere else, behind the beech hedges and the soft conifers, darkness is gathering.

Her comfort in the house is, as it were, only one side of the coin.

She sees quite clearly, unmuddled by the whisky. This, God help her, is when she suspects the very worst. That she gave away her best years before she could realise that's what they were. She did it because – because she was too frightened of being alone. Of having too many choices, of not knowing how to decide.

Oh God, Jesus God.

And now she knows inside what she wishes she didn't,

that she only took for herself the way that was easiest after all.

*

After work her husband sits in a Smithfield sherry bar with a number of his colleagues. They talk about the weather, gardens, cricket, a public flotation, holidays. Every so often they glance at their watches. Around them the room fills with voices and tobacco smoke.

They perch on stools at the bar counter, away from the mirrors. If any of them ever chances by accident to catch his reflection (they know better than to try), the unlucky man finds himself looking at the startled victim in a photograph: he's suddenly exposed and vulnerable and he feels cheated, as if he's been caught – impossibly – with his mortality written on his face.

*

She gets herself ready; checks the windows are snibbed, locks the doors; then she brings the sensible Swedish car out of the garage and sets off for the station.

Burglars and intruders are never far from her thoughts. She's heard about the suspicious-looking cars that patrol these quiet back-roads; their beady-eyed drivers are called 'sharks', and she can't understand for the life of her why something can't be done about them. Her serenity is forever on the point of being denied her like this: she feels – she feels the door is about to be blown off this security safe she lives inside, it'll be ripped off its hinges and dynamited through the roof.

She presses the button on the cassette-player in the fascia, listens to a snatch of the re-recorded *South Pacific* before switching it off and turning on the radio. Voices: just voices. She doesn't hear their sense, watching the road ahead of her through the windscreen.

Dipping her headlamps, she follows the broken white line.

*

He settles into his customary seat in the second front carriage. First class: he feels he's worked for it, for years, that it's one thing he owes himself.

241

The routine is seldom disturbed. Sometimes an unknown face joins them in the compartment, an accidental traveller who doesn't understand.

He checks his watch against the platform clock. A whistle blows. There's a shudder beneath them, then the beginnings of movement. The whistle blows again.

He undoes the zip on his briefcase, removes the newspaper, returns the catch on the zip, lays the case on his lap. He unquarters the newspaper, quickly scans the headlines; then he finds the City and finance pages in the list of contents, and opens the paper with a crack.

*

She changes gear, the inevitable few seconds too late.

Another woman passes her in another car, driving in the opposite direction. Their eyes meet momentarily on the corner.

She has never asked him about the late Helen. She has merely accepted any information he's given her, unquestioningly: but he has volunteered very little. Ghosts, she knows, are unfair competition.

She keeps her eye on the fractured white line in the dead centre of the road and adjusts to main beam.

She doesn't distrust him, she believes there are no beckoning, seductive sirens. Sometimes she catches a whiff of sherry on his breath, but that's nothing.

*

He closes the newspaper, lets it halve along the line of its fold, and places it on top of the briefcase on his lap. He leans his head back. His eyelids drop. He catches the rhythm of rails, wheels, axles.

Charing Cross and the day fall behind him. Commodities, returns, options, invisibles.

Then he can't remember any more and his mind pales, bleaches, turns to a merciful blank.

*

The white line on the road is like a track of feathers leading into a forest.

She doesn't mind the drive. Not at all. She even insists on it, to Michael and herself.

If she spots someone she knows, she hoots. The person will hoot back. She'll make a mental note for her diary, a drink or dinner sometime. Thursdays or Fridays are best, because on Wednesday afternoons she has her hair done, and she likes the night to lie on it, to take the tightness and spring out of the set.

*

And just as suddenly as it has arrived, the little summer will vanish. It will depart with the trees quaking, as if – she always thinks – a wind has reached them from Lapland.

That means the Snow Queen is back in business. The hour goes back, seven o'clock is six o'clock, and she'll be driving the distance in full darkness.

The second summer in this back end of the year has come to matter more to her than the first. She makes the most of it. She has learned to take everything they're given.

The little summer too is in the way of a gift, like treasure, and she stores it up – against the final reckoning, as it were – along with the other worldly sort.

The Chinese Garden

A man walking his dog discovered the body. The woman had been stabbed, repeatedly, in her back and chest.

The newspapers went to town on the story, for several reasons. It was more than a murder for one thing, it was a mystery. The journalists' subject (now object) was an attractive, shapely woman, probably in her thirties. The murder weapon was missing. There was no evidence of sexual abuse: when she was found, the victim was still wearing a bracelet and a watch, both of superior gold, but there was no bag, no money. Robbery may have occurred, or not: either way there weren't any apparent clues to the body's identity. The killing was presumed to have taken place on the site of discovery, namely a staid, five-sided residential square few Parisians knew existed in the XVe *arrondissement* of their city, in gardens behind railings laid out like a grotto. 'The Chinese Garden', the headlines called it.

The place gave me a chill as soon as I walked in, between the heavy, wrought-iron gates with their fancy scroll-work. It was a dark, dank spot, and felt unhealthy. Paths of beaten earth wound between boulders that dripped water; as I followed the serpentine windings, trees casting too much shade shed silent showers of pine needles; shapeless rhododendron and azalea bushes had run riot; there was a pond of stagnant green water edged with stones. Somewhere in the middle of the garden I came upon a wooden pavilion, fashioned as a little Chinese pagoda with three tiers of peaked roofs; shallow steps led up to a narrow verandah, one wall was open to the filtered green daylight and, inside, the other three walls supported a carved chinoiserie bench.

The woman had suddenly appeared in the gardens from nowhere. In the four or five days preceding her murder she had been spotted several times, walking about and sitting by herself in the pagoda. I sent a couple of gendarmes round the apartment blocks on the square to enquire. Another dog-walker (not the one who'd alighted on the dewy corpse on the path) said he'd noticed her, she'd been deep in thought, there might (he'd chanced upon her by moonlight) have been tears in her eyes but he couldn't be sure. An elderly widow told a gendarme she'd caught her eye too, and the woman – the stranger – had smiled back at her from the half-light inside the pagoda, a little sadly certainly, but she'd smiled. Other persons had observed her pacing in different directions on the trodden earth paths, seemingly preoccupied; they all commented on the neatness of her appearance, one man remembered the slenderness of her legs (her calves in particular), a young woman recalled how well she'd kept her balance and poise on her high heels, another woman remarked on her elegant, careful posture. No one could put a name to her, nor could anyone claim to have recognised her, from any previous sighting in the gardens or elsewhere. Also, no one had seen the woman *with* anyone, nor witnessed her comings and goings. The proprietor of the 'Café Souci' told me she'd come in for coffee on a couple of occasions but she'd hardly as much as put her lips to the cup; she hadn't used the telephone, or the Mesdames', or read a magazine, she'd just sat at a window table gazing out at the railed gardens in the centre of the square, towards the rocks and trees and the pagoda. No, like the others, *he* had no recollection of a handbag either.

Back at headquarters I discussed the case with my colleagues, avidly, over and over again. What the woman had been doing there, specifically *there*, interested and intrigued us as much as the identity of the murderer. Was there a direct association between the two? Was she waiting in that spooky spot for someone to appear? And if so, who? A boyfriend? – her lover, a married man perhaps? – a *girl*friend? I put some questions to the XVe prostitutes, but none of them could tell me who the woman was. Had she been waiting for someone she had to do business with? Or she'd been caught up with sharks, in a drugs ring? – but that's a subtler operation, we all knew at our end, blink-and-they're-gone, you've missed them. Just to make sure we searched the pagoda, but we found nothing.

One way and another I became obsessed. A good-looking woman discovered with knife-wounds to her heart; wearing an Ungaro dress, Jourdan shoes, a gold-and-steel Rolex watch that had stopped at the very moment she fell to the ground; no papers and no possessions to give her a history, someone with the last four or five days of her life to spend in a gloomy, over-grown communal garden while the decent folk of the Place Saint-Étienne went about their ordinary, genteel business indoors only fifty yards away, secure in their middle-class comforts. What – or who – had occupied her thoughts in that vital interlude of time? (I puzzled about it so often, *did* she have an appointment? – or was she waiting on an off chance, that a certain person *might* appear?) And what were her final, very last considerations and reflections in the minutes just after midnight, before the murderer – known or unknown to her – struck?

*

It was Grenier who brought me in on the case. He told me, he thought I needed a challenge.

It's true, I did. For the first few days I couldn't help thinking, while *she*'d been there on her vigil, *I*'d been at work, or at home with Sophie, making supper, helping her with her homework, putting her to bed, and I hadn't even suspected that there *was* a so-called Chinese garden like it in the city, and somewhere close to its centre, a lonely, personable woman was standing – as it were – on the edge of the world.

If only I *had* known…

The offer of a coffee in the Armenian's 'Café Souci' might have saved her, or a conversation shared with her in the garden's gloaming, talking about this or that: about anything at all, so long as it might have made a rope of words, between her and me and between life and death.

But I hadn't known, not at the time when it truly mattered: her fate had been nothing to me.

*

The case fascinated me, it involved and absorbed me more and more, *because* we were getting nowhere. There were no leads, and we had no forensic evidence. We couldn't place her against any known missing persons. (But, it occurred to me,

249

how many of those *disparu(e)s* go untraced anyway, then just get forgotten about?)

I stayed on at the office late, working under desk lamps and drinking the machine coffee. Neighbours looked after Sophie.

To make it up to her for my neglect we drove out together to my parents at the weekends. There I'd do as I always did, I'd sit in virtual silence, watching my two begetters in such a way that my mother would become fussed and clumsy and turn red in the face, while my father would strenuously pretend he was quite oblivious of me. That was my customary method of behaviour in their company. I can't be sure of all the reasons 'why': mainly, I suppose, because I realised perfectly well how very easy it was to subvert the formal system of the house, and that caused me some pleasure. By saying so little, almost nothing, by just watching, I could turn our mealtimes at the mahogany table into unending ordeals of endurance: the ritual and politeness became impossibly strained and proceedings ground to a halt more or less, order was turned on its head. My mother would fix my father with a 'look', an expression that was defeated, offended, impatient, and resentful too: it was exhorting him to *do* something for heaven's sake, but he never did (she *knew* he wouldn't really, that he was incapable of the act, for reasons *he* thought of as having to do with social propriety and which *she* understood as his weakness). Each time it happened I saw a kind of hopelessness of communications, a crisis of personality between them: an impasse that the years had brought about, not me, too many years of living together under the one shared roof, a wife harnessed by the conventions to her husband.

When we took our leave for the drive back to Paris there were lots of pitying kisses for Sophie, but none for me. My progenitors both stood at the front door looking at me as if they wished they could have confirmation that *I* was who I passed for being, their own son. 'Any news of Sophie's mother?' it was on their lips to ask me – but they couldn't, and I gave them no encouragement. I had no news anyway, Lorraine and I had finally lost touch and she'd moved away from her last address, and sometimes I felt it would be *my* name and description I'd find first on the Missing Persons files.

*

Once or twice I took Sophie with me to the Chinese garden.

She ran quite happily along the paths and round the still-water pond and hid behind the dripping rocks. When she tired of being energetic she squatted on her heels to collect some of the outsized cones that had fallen to the ground through the layers of sagging branches. She'd call over to me, she'd keep up a long conversation with me, tell me jokes, tell me her secrets.

The dog-walkers saw and heard, and smiled.

From the terrace of the little pagoda I listened, I watched.

My thoughts returned, as always, to 'the deceased', as the newspapers quoted me.

Who could have killed her? Had there been any motive at all? Where was her home? Why had no one reported her missing?

*

After that I got out of my usual round of people and places.

I drove a lot, by myself, through the night streets. I started revisiting some of the spots I'd gone to with Sophie's mother. I drank at the bars in certain cafés, I ate alone in particular restaurants.

Sometimes I followed a walk Lorraine and I used to take in the *XVIe*, from the Quai de Passy, past the Maison de Balzac on the Rue Raynouard, through the gardens beneath the Palais de Chaillot and on to the cool galleries of paintings in the Palais de Tokyo, and finally uphill on the Avenue d'Iéna to the Champs-Élysées.

I spent a night in the first hotel we ever went to, on the Boulevard Malesherbes, in a room that might have been the same one or a different one, I was too tired to remember.

*

I have a theory.

All our emotions have been lived out previously, by other people in other times.

We're incapable of feeling anything that hasn't already been felt by someone else before us.

There's a range of possible human emotions available to us, and that's our limit: and we run the gamut.

*

251

There had been only one untested experience left to the anonymous woman in the end.

And so she'd sat in the garden patiently.

For five days and nights on end.

Waiting for her death.

*

I came across one of Lorraine's last letters to me, in the wardrobe. She was being stifled, she wrote, smothered. She was starting to think too much of her own mother, she didn't want to finish up like that, Jesus Christ help her. Wasn't I always telling her, she still had her looks? Maybe, she said, any relationship with a man is always just surrender, subjugation, giving yourself away. But I've only got one life, she wrote, do you understand? – and now I have to take possession of it, you and Sophie notwithstanding, I'm sorry, I have to take the risk.

*

I began to be haunted by a dream: only it wasn't a dream, it was a nightmare – the same one every time – that had me waking afterwards in a frozen sweat, panicking.

The woman always spoke with Lorraine's voice, although I couldn't see her face. She was wearing an Ungaro dress and Jourdan shoes with high, spiked heels.

A man's hands with hair at the wrists are passing over her throat, one moves down into her dress and kneads her left breast, over her heart. She isn't resisting: quite the contrary, she's talking softly, speaking gentle, encouraging, arousing words. Then at some point the words lose their owner's voice, they drop on to the earth path like the scattered pinecones and lie there in the dark, for others to tread upon and crack open.

The other hand returns to her neck, they both gather about her throat, they fasten on it. Smiling, the woman produces from somewhere a knife – a small kitchen knife with a slim wooden handle and a honed blade – and she passes the instrument in front of his eyes.

The man, in a sense, has no choice about what happens next.

*

Sophie found the knife in a kitchen drawer, concealed behind the cutlery tray. The slim wooden handle was stained with red: from the juice of some over-ripe summer fruit, in a different summer from this one.

Sophie reached up to the table, pretending to guillotine. 'Chop, chop!' she said. 'Chop, chop!'

She lifted her eyes and looked at me. I was standing stock-still, listening to the echo of the words in my head. It was one of the expressions Lorraine had used, like a chant – 'Chop, chop! Chop, chop!' – she'd say it sometimes, when she had a busy day and she was in one of her bright, housewifely moods (which didn't happen so often), when she feigned it might all be a perfectly agreeable business after all, even though she had good grounds for suspecting it was a callous, loaded game, like crooked crap. *Look at me, I'm the knife-wielder, ha-ha!*

I held my hand out for the knife and returned it, carefully, to the tray in the drawer. Then I told Sophie to please put on her outdoor clothes, we were taking an afternoon off.

Our first stop was Balzac's house on the Rue Raynouard. When we'd looked it over and examined the two mossy stone sphinxes in the secret garden we walked along the Avenue de New York, beside the river, to the Palais de Tokyo: we went inside, tramped the sedate marble spaces and, like the two ghosts of my receding past, we dutifully took in several rooms of the modern paintings.

We came out and made our way up the slope of the Avenue d'Iéna, not too quickly. With the distant rush of the Champs-Élysées just in our sights, we stopped off at a quiet café neither of us knew; we sat at a table and I asked Sophie to order ice-cream sundaes for us both, whichever flavours she fancied, and I hoped in my heart that one day she might be able to forgive me for this and for everything else.

On cue the sun came out and shone hot into the café through the window glass. And then for the first time in weeks, as I sat with my child daughter, just for a moment I forgot the nameless body in the Chinese garden, just for a moment I forgot that there was a murderer walking these same sunny streets, a hundred murderers or a thousand, ten thousand, actual and potential assassins, and that for every one of them there is a victim waiting.

A murderee.

She's waiting in expectation, with the patient resolve of long years and generations of women past, with a net spread ready to mesh her killer.

Rendezvous

A car was waiting on the airfield.

The chauffeur carried the luggage from the plane while the man, smoking a cheroot, walked a delaying circle on the grass. He continued smoking for a couple of minutes, then remembered the point of his visit, and stubbed out the cheroot with the toe of his shoe.

He stood breathing in the tang of pine, trying to savour it, until the chauffeur had closed the car's boot lid and they were ready to go.

He sank into the ribbed black hide of the seat.

A fine day, sir, the chauffeur said.

Yes, a fine day, the man repeated.

Shortly after,

Do you know the area, sir?

A little, the man replied. *But it was many years ago.*

*

The girl said *Here, please*. They were in the middle of the town. The driver stopped. She opened the door, smiled, swung her legs out. She reached into the back for her travel-case.

Thanks, she said.

She watched as the car drove off. Had to be a queer, the guy. Sometimes it happened, all of a sudden they just wanted a girl beside them. Forbidden pleasures. She'd noticed the toilet bag in the glove compartment when he'd asked for the map: full of toiletries, after-shaves. She'd been able to tell by his eyes anyway, fish-eyes.

She only had to walk a block till she came to a *gasthaus*. She asked the dishevelled man who answered the door if he had a room. Please.

On holiday? he asked her as he showed her the accommodation he had. *For a day or two, yes,* she said.

She had no idea. More and more she lived by her instincts.

She unpacked. She'd brought very little, and yet it was everything. At last, she realised, my ambition achieved: everything I own, that I have to my name, it can be fitted into the space of one carry-all.

It made her happy and sad at the same time to think it.

It struck her, I might be carrying a wired bomb in that case.

*

Two porters took his luggage up.

He tipped them, too much. It was an instinct with him. When he had to look people in the eye, he preferred they should consider him with gratitude. When they had their backs to you, you could do whatever you wanted, the most appalling things. But when you had a business to run, you were God Almighty: someone had to be.

*

She stood in front of the round mirror on the wall. Sometimes people said to her, *How long in a day do you spend doing that? As long as it takes,* she'd say. *For what?* they'd ask her.

She didn't know. She just liked to look and check, that she was (a) still here, of course, and (b) that she seemed okay. Also (c), to see whatever there was to see: the people inside her. Possible people, that she might *still* be – and the ghost of her mother, naturally. And she looked too, she supposed, for anything else she might learn about her history, which her mother had told her so little about.

Half the time, she'd think, I'm looking at someone I don't know, at a stranger.

*

He was as lean as he used to be, when he was thirty or twenty-five. Now, at the age of fifty-one, he kept rigorously to the diet sheets supplied by the clinic, and weighed himself twice a day.

As requested, a pair of scales had been provided in the bathroom. He stepped on to them, watched the needle truth with satisfaction, and stepped off again.

After his shower he dressed: silk socks, American under-wear, Jermyn Street shirt, Hermès tie, Givenchy suit, Gucci moccasins.

He sometimes bought his clothes by telephone. His dimensions were dependable as the fluctuations of the money market were not. Trust in whatever you can.

He inspected the result in the sliding panels of mirror in the wardrobe.

He shifted the knot of his tie just a fraction.

He knew what he'd find; he couldn't be surprised. But that's how he wanted it to be.

He turned his back on himself. He looked down at the discreet, close pattern of snaffle-bits on his tie. That bespoke a tradition, a certain aristocratic tastefulness. Paddocks, stables, *selliers*, Saint Cloud, mares cropping with the in-herited house behind, the crop hand, power.

For every man with power, of course, there have to be a dozen, two dozen, twelve dozen maybe, without any, in subservience. Thus it was, and ever would be.

He had the christian name of the tamer of the untameable black mount, Alexander. At home he drove a red Ferrari with the logo of a speeding black steed. Perhaps the choice of car hadn't been accidental: our affairs, he believed, have an underlying system to them.

I am what I am, he'd quite often tell himself, because I decided to be so – but also because there is a conspiring 'fate' (the neatest word for it), a terrible rightness and appropriate-ness in what otherwise appears haphazard.

Mankind, he knew, lives between these two facts and con-siderations. That's why the force of paradox has its hold on our expressionist culture. (He invested in twentieth-century German art, the approved names; he was seen at the first nights of certain well-hyped modern plays.) Thus the triumph and tragedy of human endeavour.

He had his money on the see-saw keeping him high, clear of the shit.

*

She walked into the centre of the town, keeping her eyes open to everything that was happening and everyone who came into her range of vision.

257

She felt herself primed like a cat. A wild cat, she preferred to think.

She walked an exact line down the middle of the pavement.

Men were playing chess under some trees, with pieces half the height of themselves. They stood with their legs apart to move the pieces, square by square.

She could hear music from somewhere, from a bandstand maybe.

*

He could hear the sort of brassy music that was played on bandstands, being carried across the roofs of the town.

He stopped on the gravel path. He looked about him. Very Marienbad. Figures like statues, repeating repeating, we might as well be stone statues for all that we do differently, spontaneously, independently in our lives. But he knew that it was best so, to allow for as few upsets as possible. The appearance of stability was important, without it governments and currencies would go crashing. The world had edged closer to chaos than it liked to think. Uphold the law, support the police, defy kidnappers and terrorists, give generously to wounded heroes' funds.

The figures started moving again. He heard the music. Everyone could hear the music (except the deaf), it was a web strung between lives, at a particular moment in time. A brass band playing with an authority that reached down the years, to memories of this moment.

Normally he didn't think of himself as a man of memories. Not even grudges. He wasn't an intellectual, but he too had a disciplined mind.

He walked along the gravel path, in a straight line, listening to the stilled, regular breathing in his chest.

*

Her mother used to tell her about the town, till she felt she already knew it, how it looked with its gas lamps and pump room, the stately Grand-Spa Hotel and the golden froth of linden blossom, its Russian church and the little gilt and blue plush theatre, the opulent casino and the open-topped horse-buggies for hire, the chess players on the gigantic squares. She used to come across photographs of the town in

258

magazines: once it had been the setting for a romantic film on television.

It had been one of the background myths of her own life, a persistent one. To her mother the town had mattered in some way. Also, because *she*'d never seen it, the town had a glamour in her imagination that not many towns did: maybe her mother had been a different person then. She'd seen the evidence of that sometimes, a nice smile, or how she was wearing a scarf on her neck and standing with her legs crooked, almost like a model's.

In her teens she'd cut photographs out of fashion magazines. She still remembered one which had shown a woman in a ruched petticoat dress of that time, standing – legs angled – on a bridge with a river beneath her and the skyline of the town (*this* town) behind: two old biddies were looking over their shoulders and smiling at the model's bravura, or at the dress. The dress had seemed to evoke another age, yet it hadn't really belonged to any: the 'mood' was country idyll/ frontier woman, of no time and no place. But you forgot about all that in the effect.

Her mother found the photograph, by no accident. She didn't smile, as she'd imagined her reaction must be. Her lips pursed tightly together, then she crumpled up the photograph, and pretended in the artful confusion afterwards that she was tidying up and had thought the picture was rubbish and to be thrown out.

It doesn't matter, she'd told her mother.

No?

No. Not any more.

And she'd meant it.

*

It had been September then too, twenty-four years ago, there'd been the first hint in the air that the year was turning, the first reminder that all this fruitfulness would soon be on the wane.

He'd waited in the hotel a couple of days more, till he caught the leaves on the linden tree outside his bedroom window showing colour on their undersides. Only a wan flush of lemon-pink, and hard to believe it was the initial evidence of decay, harbinger of loss.

How sombre a mood he'd been in, and unpredictable. He remembered her telling him she was in a *gasthaus* somewhere near the Russian church, and he'd gone walking to that part of town, along the leafy avenues, in the vague hope, eyes watching for the onion dome. Looking for Marianne. It was up to fate, he'd told himself.

So that when they didn't meet again, he'd taken it as the pre-determined conclusion of the incident. The thoughts that had caused little pinpricks of expectation during the past forty-eight hours were put out of his mind: they fell away, like cast leaves. He told himself he was entering a chastened season of rime and forgetfulness.

*

Later she found the postcards, she tracked them down, to a shoe-box in her mother's wardrobe. They showed scenes of the town: the dome of the Russian church visible above rooftops, the casino like a miniature Versailles, linden trees, a sedate walkway of the famous Grand-Spa Hotel, old men playing outsized chess. Her mother didn't answer any of her questions, which only intensified the girl's curiosity and focused it.

She studied the views until she was dreaming of them in her sleep. She read up on all she could find about the spa town in the local library. She knew so much she could have gone on a radio quiz show and answered questions about it. But sometimes she felt she really knew so little, of what must matter to her, almost nothing at all: she had a mother but she'd never had a father, and what could the significance be of a pump room and lamplighters and a bandstand in a park and gravel walkways and a peak-roofed hotel rising above blossom trees?

*

He came the first time, twenty-four years ago, because —

Because —

Because it wasn't in fact the first time, but the second.

Because he'd visited the town in the unsuspecting years of his adolescence.

Because the town was a memorial to a more gracious age, a lost epoch of operetta barons, pedigree and chivalry, and gilding and Venice glass.

260

Because now he needed to get away.

Because time, he sensed, was running out on him, like his freedom.

Because his marriage to Elisabeth was only five weeks away.

Because he'd discovered something in himself, remarkably like shame, to realise that being the husband of this particular woman would make him a much richer, much more powerful man.

Because he believed the spa's waters might truly have magical restorative qualities – as books said – which would cleanse him, abrogate him of responsibility.

Because the intention was already in his mind to deceive his future wife, to make the marriage seem only an official arrangement of sorts, not taking all of him but leaving some part – the vital, energetic, life-asserting sexual part – unclaimed.

Because he had a picture in his head of the town from the teenager's visit years before: because he had an image, a generalised one, of a woman who was waiting for him: and because he pictured the town (as he remembered it) to be an ideally discreet location for his determined infidelity.

Because. Because —

*

She saw what she could of the town, but she felt herself too close to take it in: she needed the physical distance to stand back, adjust her vision, get a fix on it all.

She bought postcards, seven marks' worth, from a stand outside a bookshop. The images weren't quite those of her teenage dreams, the angles and perspectives were different, the actual details no longer fuzzy: for another thing, the colour was truer, nearer to life.

*

He had financial newspapers sent up from the kiosk in the lobby. He put off opening them for several minutes, then – when he did – he found himself instinctively drawn to those columns of figures, base rates, commodities, economic indicators, European options, recent issues, closing prices.

*

She walked back to the *gasthaus*, along streets lined with trees, alder and linden and birch.

The air was soft, but – she thought– uninvigorating. She'd imagined coming and having a sense of déjà vu on every street corner. Instead she couldn't get any impression of the town's layout, none at all, and why on earth should she now be heading back to the *gasthaus* with something like relief?

There were cafés, shops, a park, a casino garden, the chess players, but suddenly it was just a town, another town. Nothing looked quite as it had done on the postcards in her mother's wardrobe: on the buildings, either the plaster was flaking off or she didn't recognise the colour of paint. For the first time she understood properly that what her mother had forbidden her was access to the past: and so it had died with her, a tantalising secret.

Being here wasn't bringing her closer: the opposite, in fact. She listened to her stilettos as she walked along the streets, she heard the staccato stabs and they might have been insisting on her loneliness.

*

I'm his chauffeur, he'd told her.

She'd accepted that lie for truth.

I've got a room of my own, he'd said. *In the hotel, Marianne. Like to have a look?*

It's a lovely hotel.

So-so. I see a lot of them.

Do you?

In my job.

Yes.

She'd asked him so little about the job, the job he claimed to have. If she'd probed more, he might have felt he was further from his actual situation.

But she didn't seem to want the exchange of knowledge. In time he learned that much the same was true for her as for himself: she was involved in a match, of the marital sort, and one that had been decided for her. Her family had urged her: the husband-to-be, Johannes, a commercial traveller (with a suitcase mind?) was considered a desirable catch. But it seemed *she* had her doubts, and didn't want to travel, as her fiancé was asking her to. She suddenly needed roots – so he guessed, her listener – she needed to limit herself and to make ties. Such is the perversity of human behaviour, he knew. What she was doing here was clear enough to him: she was limiting herself to this place, wanting the weight of this here and now on top of her, pinning her – motionless and thoughtless – to the spot.

*

She was carrying a photograph of her mother in her bag, she usually did, it was a superstition with her. The custom had begun just after her mother died, when she'd felt guilty about going back to work (the job before the last before the last), having a life – her own – to continue to think about.

She looked at the photograph with its curling edges as she walked the final stretch of pavement to the *gasthaus*. Upstairs in her room, with the door locked, she fixed it beneath a hinge on the round mirror on the wall.

People had always told her how much she resembled her mother, but she hadn't really seen the similarity herself – apart from the chestnut hair. She'd presumed it was said to make her not think of the man who'd also been responsible for shaping her features: shaped them more than her mother probably. But that was another story, to which she didn't have the clues, the key.

*

So she'd told him about her engagement to Johannes, the commercial traveller: a man who made long journeys overseas, on slow ships. He wanted to become an agent for the firm, which would mean settling in different parts: Tripoli, Montevideo, Osaka. The names (he realised) were purely fictitious to her. She wasn't able to accept that scenario as probable, as her life, she couldn't imagine finding herself in any of those places. The man was fifteen years older than her, he discovered, and she was poorly off, so what chance did she have? *Money*, she said, *keeps this world turning*. (How obvious, he thought, and how true.)

He wasn't offering her anything else, an alternative, only his (expensive) time and whatever physical comfort he was capable of. He couldn't even offer her fantasy – excepting his story about being a rich man's chauffeur: the only thing in his gift was a kind of short-service amnesia.

263

With each other they might be able to convince themselves – temporarily – they were actually forestalling what they both knew was now only inevitable.

*

There was a television in the *gasthaus*'s lounge.

She sat with the Streckers watching bits of whatever they turned channels to: a game show, a documentary (on Canadian elks), a French costume drama, a news round-up. They finally stayed on the news. There was a filmed report on a riot following a demonstration outside a nuclear defence establishment.

Wouldn't happen if they'd been brought up properly, Herr Strecker said. *In a decent family.*

She watched the pictures and said nothing.

Then came an update on the Dow-Jones Index, and brief mention of worries at the Tokyo Stock Exchange. After that the programme moved on to a feature about itinerant young people, gangs of nomads travelling round the country in medieval fashion.

No home life, that's THEIR problem, Herr Strecker said.

Or maybe they don't want it, she thought. Or maybe we've all become a race of stay-at-homes when it's only in our natures to go wandering.

She stood up and took her leave, politely, and told herself as she closed the front door behind her that she would never make the same mistake again. *Gasthäuser* were 'out', *verboten*.

She would blow the building apart with the bomb ticking in her brain.

*

They'd met twice more, he and Marianne, both times here in the town. On his way to the second of those rendezvous, a couple of months after his marriage to Elisabeth, he had a premonition that this would be the last time.

She was looking tired, strained. During a drive in his car she told him the two related pieces of news she'd been saving: that Johannes had called off the marriage, because

Because what?

Because . . .

She couldn't say the word at first.
I – I'm – pregnant.
What?
He's found out.
But he's in Africa.
Maybe – maybe it's Cuba, I don't know.
Africa or Cuba, how can he know?
He does. That's all.
She assured him *he* was the reason, not Johannes. *He* was
the father.
He didn't disbelieve her.
Well then, there's only one way, he told her.
Is there? What's that? She sounded almost hopeful.
The usual.
I don't —
Have an operation.
What?
An operation.
No. Never. I couldn't —
I'll pay, I'll get everything fixed up.
Like a bad play or a film. But what else was there for them
to do? They had to be practical: a man in his position.
An operation. She kept repeating. *An operation —*
Then, he said, *you can tell Johannes it was a mistake.
Everything's all right again.*
No, she said. *No, it couldn't be.*
He'd believe you.
No. It's not that.
What is it, then?
I don't WANT to marry him. Not now.
Pause.
And anyway, she said, *anyway...*
He knew what was coming. The child was hers too, she
couldn't.
It's against your principles? he asked, in a sceptical tone of
voice he sometimes used in the office. *It offends propriety?*
Like more of the bad play or film.
I just couldn't, she said, and started to cry.
He stopped the car somewhere, beside the road in the
middle of a forest. At first the silence sang in his ears: then he
started to distinguish the strata of woodland sounds, an
imbroglio of life they couldn't see.

265

He tried to persuade her, to give her courage, but she wouldn't listen to him. He who was now finding himself able to persuade men of great worth to invest many millions of marks in the company he was effectively managing for his father-in-law.

I'll pay, he said. *The lot. Marianne, do you hear? You won't have to do anything.*

Do? she repeated him. *DO?*

Except lie there, he meant, let *them* attend to you.

He was a practical man: very well, then, a pragmatist. Perhaps – with the advantage of hindsight – the situation could have been handled more *sensitively*, but it had seemed to him then to be a time for firm decisions, a clear-cut programme of action.

Later, when he never heard from her again, he did have cause to regret his manner, but only because it left him uncertain what had happened. The Swiss clinic he'd contacted couldn't get in touch with her. He was nervous on account of what the years ahead might bring. A man in his position ... *und so weiter.*

In the event (but how could he have known at the time? – how much physical wear and tear he could have saved himself), he'd heard nothing. Perhaps she'd decided to lose the child after all but she'd gone to the wrong sort of place and there'd been an accident? Or, she'd had the child but another kind of accident had befallen them both at a later date?

But beyond the baby's birth there were so many possibilities, too many, and he couldn't stretch his mind to take them all in and hold them.

The human brain had its own defences.

*

Why that town?
  Why NOT that town?
  Who was he?
  Who was he, Mother? Tell me, please.
  Why?
  I want to know.
  It couldn't make your life any better.
  And no worse. It would fill in all the gaps.
  I don't understand you.

266

I don't understand why you won't tell me.
Because I am your mother —
— and I am your daughter?

*

He could still do something: make an attempt to find out, where she was. Marianne Kiett, as she'd been. He'd used detective agencies in the past for business purposes.

But it would only have been for the sake of vain prurience, and what good would it have done *her?* She must have seen his photograph in newspapers and on television and realised his influence. No requests had reached him, though, no demands for recognition or money. The mystery persisted, so of course his curiosity was engaged. Why, he wondered, why should he remember *that* affair (if it had even been as much as that)? He'd had a dozen or so in all the years since, and he'd always assumed it was the palest, the vaguest. Perhaps that had to do with her not having known who he was, and his claiming to be someone else – the chauffeur – and his understanding so little about her. The affairs that came after-wards couldn't avoid the crucial matter of 'Who I Am'. That one had taken place almost – almost – in a kind of innocence, a Schwarzwald once-upon-a-time.

*

She heard footsteps behind her as she walked along a path in the casino gardens, past the deserted chess-board, at the other end of the town from the Streckers in their *gasthaus*, so-called.

He caught up with her as she turned to a bench and picked the cleanest spot to sit.

I believe you dropped this.

He opened his hand: inside was a cigarette lighter, showy stainless steel, nothing special.

It's not mine, she said.

Oh.

He looked at it.

But, she said, inventing, *I've lost mine anyway. So I don't mind – if I do.*

He handed it to her. She smiled as she placed it in her bag.

And that's how their conversation began. Painlessly enough.

*

He asked her some questions about the town, and realised she was a visitor here, like him, and that she knew less about it than he did.

He felt safer, that they should both be strangers of a kind.

What's your name? he asked.

She shook her head, looking away. *It doesn't matter.*

No?

No, she said quite definitely, but through a smile.

She was attractive, in a slightly theatrical, self-conscious way: but not *too* striking. He didn't care for women to be *too* obvious. And pretty-prettiness wasn't quite enough: there had to be an element (in moderation) of the archetypal, the clichéd, even.

She wore high heels and a low front to her dress. A charm bracelet rattled on one wrist, a larger-than-life yellow plastic watch told the time on the other. She smelt of some fragrance he occasionally caught in the streets of the city, stepping out of a taxi and crossing a sidewalk; it was common enough, but he couldn't put a name to it.

When she finally turned round to look at him straight in the face he knew that she understood. Her mouth shaped itself into another smile.

He didn't need to ask, she didn't need to respond.

*

Dinner was sent up to the suite. It was served from a trolley by a waiter in a white jacket who pretended to notice nothing.

There were only a couple of courses, and they were both of them hungry, so she didn't have to talk too much. The food was subtle and refined, and she felt that if this was all you ever ate you too must take on something of the same qualities.

He was behaving as if he was quite used to such fare and it was all he ever fortified himself on. Normally she ate quickly, conveniently, standing up sometimes or moving about and always on the camel principle, of putting enough away to keep you on the credit side of hunger. This evening she ate slowly. She didn't pack her mouth too full, she savoured the mingling flavours.

She savoured such excellence, such choiceness, she even wished – absurdly, hope against hope – that it didn't have to end, that somehow she might have been born to it.

*

She was making him think of another dinner 'à deux', another performance of simple pleasure in the taste of the food.

What does Johannes like to eat? he'd asked her.

Her face had turned to a blank.

Don't you know?

No. No, I don't.

You'll discover.

I'll have to remember. Keep it in my mind.

Will you HAVE a mind? Will you, Marianne? Or will you be skivvying —

Her face had taken on a pained, abused expression and immediately he was sorry he'd said what he had.

Well, anyway... He'd wanted them to forget the man, in whichever port of commerce he was, although he was also the reason for their being in the restaurant, in each other's company.

Why here? he'd asked.

Here? she repeated.

This town, Marianne.

Why not? she said. *I wanted some time. I needed – a different space to think in. That's all.*

He'd nodded.

I think I felt the same, he said.

Her face brightened, her voice lifted. *Did you?*

Our situations aren't so apart really, he said.

It's a small world? Like that?

Whoever he was, the husband-to-be, he didn't deserve her.

And she had the sort of looks an expert beautician could have gone to work on. With the correct help, she might have been turning heads on the Kurfurstendamm or the Faubourg-Saint Honoré. Instead of which she would be —

*

But this is something else.

He looked across the table. He smiled, to find himself here, in a different decade, in the same town.

It's like a film. Having a meal served in your room.

A film?

Yes.

How had *she* spoken, how had she sounded, against all the sounds in that restaurant? It was disturbing him that he couldn't remember, quite. Why was this voice talking over the memory of the other one?

Who's your favourite star? she asked.

My favourite star? He shook his head. *I can't think.*

There must be someone.

Well, Mastroianni, he said. *Marcello Mastroianni, I quite like.*

I don't know if I've seen him.

What about you? Who's YOUR favourite?

Oh, that's easy. Marilyn.

Her face brightened as she said the name.

Monroe?

There's only one Marilyn.

Why do you like her?

She's like a sister. You KNOW her. A bit of her is the person you really want to be, and a bit of her is so sad, you want to save her.

And you want to save her?

Oh, yes. She couldn't believe she was beautiful, you know, because every time she looked at herself she saw her neck was just too short. It needed another centimetre and a half.

Really?

I want to save her from that, I suppose. From knowing she can't be perfect.

He sat watching the girl on the other side of the table. He wasn't sure he understood.

There's something about her, she said. *She can't rest. But she didn't die, either. Maybe it's her face, it's still modern. All over the world she lives in people, bits of her. The great kings and queens of history died, but that girl from gimcrack Los Angeles, California, she didn't.*

Oh, he realised, it's death we're talking about, is it? Where else, though, than here, where better: in this town of springs

270

and miracle cures that's survived when the demesnes of tsars and sultans and archdukes haven't.

He ransacked his mind, to steer them both away from the black rocks looming.

*

Sometimes she took money. It was a slender line, between pleasure and commerce. Like an outlaw, she took only from those who could afford to give. That way she was exercising her freedom of choice: to exact payment or not.

He's rich, she knew. There's cashmere woven into his suit, and he wears silk socks, his shoes are fine kid made for carpets, not the city pavements. If he offers...

But she felt a peace with him, this nameless man, in this room where sounds seemed deadened, and it was like therapy, *her* privilege. Until, that is, some of the old images suddenly came back, furtively, the old postcard views which were suddenly supplementing her impressions of today and yesterday. For a while the town she had imagined was more real than the one she was in. The silence in the room was only an echo of her mother's on the subject.

Tell me, please, Mother.

What about?

About the town.

But no. No answer, no attempt. Nothing.

*

Of course she complied. He'd known from the first moment that she would.

She gave herself in a different way, she wasn't coy or modest at all, didn't even pretend to be. She wasn't brazen, far from it, but she was no novice, this intimate and anonymous stranger who wouldn't tell him her name.

Every so often his thoughts would turn back to the past, to Marianne. He puzzled why he should have picked on *this* girl, unless it was because of some physical resemblance? The height, the colouring, the chestnut hair. But as for anything else – the shape of a knee, an elbow, the crook of a leg or arm —

*

He doesn't make the whispered, guilty, fanciful demands of her she normally expects from quiet men.

Instead he seems to be somewhere else. He hardly speaks a word. It's as if he doesn't see her. Maybe he has a young and beautiful wife, waiting for him in an elegant home that's like a magazine spread.

She closes her eyes and pictures herself there, surrounded and cosseted by the man's wealth.

*

Out of the past he remembers what he thought he'd forgotten, the freckles on her shoulders, and the taste of perfume from her wrists.

That quiet woman with the unshowy name – 'Marianne' – had aroused him, in spite of himself, to fever pitch.

At one stage in their love-making he'd been seeing the shadow of a late-blooming blossom tree outside the window, by moonlight – those leaves shaped, he knew, like the hearts on a playing-card – and he'd closed his eyes, he'd imagined to himself a jungle of vegetation and heat and rampant emotions, somewhere very far away, on another continent, in Africa or Cuba.

*

He's careful, considerate, he's steady and sure but doesn't force the point.

She makes herself as comfortable as she can, raising her eyes to the ceiling. It's moonlight outside – she watches the shadow of a tree striping the plaster. She thinks of water in a Venetian canal, its reflection rippling across the ceiling of a bedroom in a grand palazzo.

*

The image of his wife was coming back to him, as it had then, when she'd been his wife-to-be. As he straddled the girl again she was free-floating through his memories, through his perceptions of present time. After twenty-something years Elisabeth had no intention of letting him go.

After twenty-something years he remembers the restrained jungle frenzy with Marianne, but it's only that to him now, a memory. He's a young man inside a middle-aged man's body, and his physical self no longer works as an instinct, a reflex, of the mental.

He does what he can. The girl moans, as if contented, but then this – unlike the first, with the salesman's fiancée – is a financial transaction. She has an obligation to simulate enjoyment, to fake it.

That other time with Marianne there were no moans at all. He remembers the silence suddenly, the realisation of pleasure beyond words, beyond recognisable sound even, on bat sonar.

*

It was a relief, for the moment, not to have to think of anything at all. Most of her life was planning two or three steps ahead. Sometimes it tired her, so much she wanted to get away – to some island in the ocean – and never return. A part of her longed to travel, to cut loose, but another part of her was afraid: and it was that emotion – fear – which always won the day. So she stayed with the familiar, and somehow she muddled by, careering from job to job and man to man (and even, once or twice, to a woman) and imagining she was being modern and taking advantage of all her opportunities, her freedom. But sometimes, in the space inside her mind where she thought she should be aware of her freedom, she seemed to feel nothing, except the space itself: a missing, an absence.

*

He lies on his side, looking at her. She's asleep, with her head turned towards him.

He reaches out his hand and picks the fallen hair back from her face with his fingers. He's seen the gesture done so often in films, to Bardot, Anna Karin, Stroynberg, Adjani.

The girl has a modern face. It's hard to tell why, except that he can't envisage her in the costume of any other age. Elisabeth's face is inbred and rather sharp-angled, he guesses it has done service to generations of women.

She twitches as she sleeps. He listens for sounds, for a word to escape, but she's silent and secretive.

She's told him almost nothing about her life: but neither has he offered her any information about himself. They share that instinct, not to get involved, or merely to forget everything for a while.

She has clean nails, cut to fit the finger and coated with transparent varnish. The veins are blue beneath the thin skin of her hands and her narrow wrists. She has a young woman's breasts, firm and upright, with no signs yet of what must come later, weight and creasing and sagging.

He lays his head on the sheet, with one ear touching her breast. He listens and thinks he can hear what's inside, milk and blood and only the steady contented turning of life.

*

In her dream she's in jungle-patterned silk and wears a florist's orchid tucked into her hair. She's being handed into a low sports car, but suddenly she's in the driver's seat, setting her own pace and direction.

She goes anywhere. The car's grille devours the road. Taped music fills the cabin. (Her mother had a surprising penchant for jazz, so now she listens to that, a sassy modern version, jazz-funk. Miles Davis, 1985, 'Time After Time'.)

She drives and drives and drives.

*

Meanwhile ...

In another room, in a smaller hotel in the town, a third visitor removes a roll of film from his camera. It contains the material he needs, the evidence he has been paid to provide his client with.

There are some shots of the man walking with the girl, and others of the girl at one of the windows in his suite. He also caught the girl leaving in the morning, via the nearest side door, which he'd had a hunch she might exit by. He followed her back to her *gasthaus* (he'll get hold of the name and address she's used), he stood behind a lime tree and photographed her entering: a detail of that sort is of minor importance, may only be glanced at once by his client, but it's all part and parcel of the service.

Just as he never discloses the identity of his patrons, he also prefers (for his own purposes) to think of his subjects as lacking the usual claims on identity and character. When character and causes and motives – of client or quarry – don't intrude, his own job seems impersonal too, and in that way his automaton function overlooks and excuses much he might otherwise suspect in himself: guilt, for example, and a kind of shame. Handled like this, each commission is effected just for money, to the highest bidder, and he has no need to search his soul.

*

In the morning she showered, dressed, made up, came back into the bedroom to collect her things.

He opened his cigarette case and passed it to her. Inside was a banknote rolled up like a smoke. She took her reward and smiled as she uncurled it. Then she helped herself to a cigarette. He offered her a flame from a gold and red lacquer lighter. She drew on it and blew out smoke, a little cloudlet, like Bette Davis.

They talked for a while, rather distantly, about nothing very much. She guessed he didn't want to tell her about himself, and *she* wasn't interesting to *him*. Also, no stories, no come-backs, he'd wised up all right; although the worry must be on his side.

She trusted his eyes, which didn't happen so often. He wasn't bad-looking, but he was probably neglected by his wife and it had ruffled his pride a bit. Was that why he put a staid front on everything: not really smiling properly, holding himself very straight and rigid?

Marriage, she thought, does terrible things. Marriage is a bitch. Let this be a warning, if I needed one.

What do you do?

She started at the question, she hadn't been expecting it.

I work in an office, she replied quite simply, lying.

Like it?

It's a job. It's all right.

He nodded. She didn't need to ask what *he* did. Ruling the roost, making a mint.

It's good to get away, isn't it? he said.

She agreed, yes.

It's not easy, though, he added, qualifying.

I can do overtime, she told him. *Take time off. It's okay.*

If you do overtime, you must be rich.

He was joking: wasn't he?

275

No, not rich, she heard herself telling him. *But I've enough, I guess. To get by.*

And this too, she thought, opening her bag and putting the banknote in her purse.

Going back soon? he asked.

She nodded. *Expect I will.*

Some breakfast?

Before you go.

No. No, I'll get myself something later.

End of story. She nodded again. Best way. Repetitions are always deadly.

*

Best way and not even a name to her, he was thinking.

He lay on the bed in his towelling robe and watched her get ready.

She's used to this, he realised, and she's got the right instincts: sophisticated in the only way that really matters – with a cultivated sixth sense for the appropriate ending.

My wallet's in the top right-hand drawer, he told her. *You'll have to get back to where you're staying.*

I'll walk, she said.

Walk? he repeated, smiling.

What about a buggy then? she said, and smiled too. *The driver can wake the horse for me.*

So you get into someone's photograph?

He felt his smile hanging more slackly on his jaw.

Don't worry, he was relieved to hear her reply the next moment. She continued to smile, keeping up the show of good humour. *If I had any names, 'Discretion' would be the middle one.*

*

Back at the *gasthaus* there were no curiosity-struck faces, no watching eyes – or, if there were, she didn't see them.

She threw herself down on the rumple-less bed. She was hungry, after her walk back. She could have taken the money for a taxi ride, but she felt she owed the walk to her mother. Absurdly, sentimentally. For after all, what would her mother have thought was owing to *her*?

*

Then he decided, yes, he *would* just go after all. He'd meant to stay longer but now he couldn't think what for.

Or perhaps he was troubled, by some inescapable something in the girl. More than the chestnut hair, cut quite differently. Perhaps he'd come closer to the past than he'd meant to.

It was what he'd made the journey for, of course. The source – the alpha, the 'fons et origo' – was *then*, when he'd met the salesman's fiancée, and the memory returned to fill these same days of every year, whatever his other concerns. Why it should have done was an abiding mystery to him.

But now he had seen the linden trees again, in a faded version of their gilded glory. Something else continued to disturb him though.

Any other place at the leaf fall, but not here, not in the same hotel, he shouldn't have ...

It was the girl's independent air that had served to remind him how much people's lives had changed in these past twenty-five years. Twenty-five years ago, it wasn't so long: but *then*, for a woman, it had been like taking your life in your hands.

The girl would have forgotten in a couple of weeks. He was of her parents' generation and they'd never adjusted, not quite. Experiences patterned rings on the brain and you counted back.

He walked across to the telephone. He picked up the receiver, dialled reception, and asked for the chauffeur to be summoned.

He replaced the receiver, then lifted it again and dialled an outside number. He listened to the eerie, empty echoes down the line, then the ringing.

After maybe half a minute – longer than it usually took her – the call was answered at the other end, and with a middle-aged man's indifference and matter-of-factness, with a very lack of joy, he informed his wife that there was a change to his plans, she could now expect him back twenty-four hours earlier.

*

She repacked everything into her case.

She suddenly wanted to get out of the place. It wasn't the

277

place's fault, but her own. Probably. People came here to rest, and convalesce, the air was soft, the water that bubbled up from beneath the ground was supposed to have magical powers, more or less. The guidebook said the town enjoyed a 'rejuvenating ambience': perhaps all the old folk she'd seen, residents and visitors, they weren't as they appeared to be but felt like teenagers at heart?

She'd come to the town, at long last. She'd had to come to realise there was so much she would never understand, not now that her mother was dead. If she'd died at her birth, she couldn't have been very much more in the dark than she was. But maybe that was just what happened anyway: to take life from another person, in a manner of speaking you *kill* them. They'd never really got on; she'd always felt she was interfering with her mother's freedom, causing her to do what she wouldn't have chosen to do otherwise. It might have been better if one of them hadn't lived beyond the first day, her mother or herself.

In the end it was her mother who acceded first to kismet: the woman who'd given her daughter the same name as herself. But surviving and knowing nothing like this, sometimes she thought it was *she* herself who'd drawn the short straw, reading the name they owned in common on the wall plaque in the cemetery.

*

The chauffeur was telling him about his family, his five children.

He shut off.

Elisabeth would be waiting for him at home. His 'business trips' always made her nervous. *More* nervous. (He told her so often she should see someone about her nerves.) It was as if she was afraid he wasn't ever going to come back.

She wouldn't have made much of a mother. They'd always left the matter unexplained, why there were no children. She suspected his sperm count, he suspected it was some innate unwillingness in her organs to conceive. They'd just gone on understanding so little about each other. Somehow, though, they survived on their ignorance. And living together was easier than apart.

The only reason for children would have been to pass

everything on to them. It wouldn't have been to bore other people with your stories about them, as they were always having done to them.

If the childless had a curse on them, the over-fecund damned themselves, out of their own mouths.

He picked up a newspaper. He opened it at the back. Stock prices.

The town endured in aspic. Despite everything the rest of the world had kept turning.

*

She stood beside the main road out of the town. She thought the thumbs-up was demeaning and unnecessary. No one stood at the kerbside, suitcase in hand, for no reason.

If I had the courage for it, she was thinking, I'd have a bomb in this case, I'd be a terrorist.

A red car put on its brakes, stopped twenty or thirty metres away, and reversed.

The driver wound down the window and said the name of a town. She didn't hear but she nodded.

She dropped her case on to the back seat and folded herself in half to fit into the front.

The driver was in his forties, with a wedding ring on his fourth finger. She made her usual instant assessment: state of shirt collar, cuffs, shoes, hair. In her experience the outside was usually a reliable guide to the inner man.

He turned on the cassette player. Jazz-funk. She was going to be all right.

She sank back in the seat, into the cloth, and angled her head against the head-rest for the most comfortable position.

She found it.

Nice.

*

A few minutes later a silver Mercedes swept past the spot where the girl had stood, bound for the airfield.

*

Another tape went into the machine. Californian crossover music, white pop with black soul.

Been on holiday? the driver asked her.

279

She crossed her legs, tucking her knees beneath the dashboard.

Not really, she said. *Just a change.*

Know it here?

No.

A Mercedes roared past them.

Like it?

So-so, she said.

What's your name?

Marianne, she said without thinking, and realised too late.

Later he told her he'd been visiting his wife, two-and-a-half weeks ago she'd walked out, left him.

She didn't want to hear about that, Christ no, and she looked away, out of the side-window.

Worst day of my life it was. Having to be so polite. Interested. You know?

She closed her eyes, just listened to the music. Cars that drove past you and reversed were always a mistake, the driver was too cautious, or his head was too cluttered, or he was just out of sync, or he realised he hadn't spoken to a girl for too long.

Also, I think it's made her greedy. She never used to be. That's what really cut me up.

Bleeding Jesus, tears next?

I just want to get away from here. You know? That's the last time. EVER.

Alimony too, she thought. It wasn't worth it, was it, even for an Audi and Michael McDonald on quadrophonic.

*

A humble milk-chocolate-brown Citroën Visa pulls out on to the autobahn.

Its driver checks in his mirror. He is always careful to look over his shoulder, to keep himself safe from an approach from behind, to cover his tracks.

The camera lies on the passenger seat. It's unlikely that he'll require it again on the drive back, but it pays him to be prudent, at all times vigilant.

Water Boy

The awning's shadow was sliding down the page and his eyes couldn't adjust to the print against the glare.

He put down the book. A felucca passed, its great white sail taut with river wind, slicing the blue air like a shark's fin.

Beyond it, on the far bank, the land shimmered to an uncertain horizon. In no other country had he sensed time's infinitude as he did in this one.

Through a mist of ochre dust he saw the village women slowly pacing themselves against the heat, carrying pitchers on their heads. A man trotted past them on a donkey, whipping it with a switch. Backs bent double in fields. A dromedary teetered under a load of cut straw as high as a two-storey house. Old men sat beneath walls of grey mud. A woman made solitary, flat-footed progress along a track, keeping to the shade of the spiky palm trees; ahead of her a tractor bounced along the wheel ruts, trailing dust like a balloon.

'Take it easy,' he'd been told. 'Relax, enjoy yourself, think of nothing.' On the flight out from London he'd surrendered himself to the hostesses' smiles, the complimentary gins-and-tonics, the lush orchestral music playing over the tannoy. He'd sat close against the window, looking down on the froth of fluffy clouds. Such inexplicable beauty, just there, cradled by the firmament's sunshot blue: and it had been there every day of his life, while *he*'d been living inside his head with only the deafening come-back of his own troubled thoughts.

Up in the plane, five miles high, a kind of proportion was re-established as he considered the grey-brown land mass revealed beneath them. He watched as Egypt flattened and became a two-dimensional geometric tableau of bleached biblical colours: ochre for the vast desert hinterland and pale permutations of yellow and brown and terracotta on the narrow strip where the land was inhabited and tilled, along the banks of the Nile.

He remembered Klee paintings. Then he remembered he wasn't supposed to be remembering, that his mind was to be kept as blank as a clean sheet of paper.

*

The sun dazzled, a thousand suns, on the surface of the river.

Every dawn the goddess Nut was delivered of her child, the sun, and all day it crossed the heavens westwards on its path until, at the particular moment of her choosing, the mother devoured her offspring and digested it.

He'd moved chairs, to the shadier side of the deck. The land was closer from here. He could catch its heat, smell its vegetation, taste its dust like a rough coating on his lips.

In the age of the pharaohs it was held that the Nile had its source beneath the sky: it coursed through the great plain of Egypt and split at the Delta fork as it returned whence it had come, to begin the process again, rising at its source beneath the welkin.

He closed his eyes and when he opened them again, some seconds or minutes later, he saw a pyramid.

It was one of the sort called 'collapsed'. The theory was that the builder had intended to erect two pyramids of different angles, one on top of the other. The guidebook said this 'owed to an arcane principle of dualism': but that 'the architect's daring must have failed him finally'.

It was Heroditus who foisted on the world the notion that slaves were worked to their deaths creating the pyramids. The situation was probably quite otherwise, with the ordinary people volunteering their labour in honour of the divine triumvirate, the gods and the pharaohs and the 'benben', the primordial mound. The pyramid was the knoll on which Egypt's villages perched; the floods rose and receded and then the harvest sprouted in the mud, enticed by the rays of the sun, Nut's child.

The book had said.

Purpose and system. *It was in Egypt that the civil state was first perfected.*

He narrowed his eyes to slits. In front of the fallen

pyramid, trees with trunks like stumps stuck up blue, orange-tipped fingers of branches, like a Hockney illustration. In such a country, he thought, you might also be able to believe in the outlived, disproved myths of childhood: dancing kitchen pots, flying sausages, the fantastic blue-bird.

*

Later he opened his eyes again. The pyramid had disappeared.

Empty desert ran to the glow of sky. Between the wilderness of sand and the river was no more than a few miles of hard-won life: fields of delicately green wheat, the pinpricks of white where the fellahin in their smocks stooped to pick from the earth, the dun walls of a village.

Much closer to, his eye caught sight of something he could focus on. In a field two harnessed oxen were turning a machine, probably – he guessed – an irrigation pump to feed the ditches with river water. The animals were being driven by a boy in a white smock like the gleaners'; he followed them as they trod a wide circle on the baked mud.

One of the tails lifted, fussily, and a turd dropped out. The boy continued, patiently stepping after the oxen, a stick in his hand. The machine creaked and groaned, the boat was near enough for the viewer to hear. He could also distinguish, he thought, a voice singing: an unbroken voice, the boy's, as he followed in the tracks of the oxen: a slow, regular sequence of notes, not words but sounds and a chant rather than a tune.

The boy flicked at the air in front of him with his stick but his charges seemed indifferent, heads lowered, ears twitching, hooves raising dust. The machine strained, it grumbled and protested, as it had been doing most likely for as long as the boy had been alive, and for a generation or two before that, as other pumps had done in much the same fashion for two or three thousand years.

What was going through the boy's mind as he walked the parched mud by the water wheel? Profundities, or nothing at all? Was there anything between the two?

The Nile slapped against its banks. Some ancient, unthinking purpose compelled the boy and the oxen to start another circle and then, when that round was completed, to begin another. The stick caught the animals' rumps; their ears twitched, their hooves lifted, their tails flicked at flies. The driver chanted his rote, the water boy's song, and the shadoof wailed its rusty responses.

*

He was served afternoon tea on deck. It came in a china pot, blossom tea, with a plate of the thin, almost transparent sweet rice biscuits he'd taken a fancy to, like nursery fare.

In another country he had a wife, and a child, and a job where much was expected of him and where much, and many, depended on his clear-thinking and timely acumen in business matters. There he lived in a comfortable house, in a desirable and expensive area, but it was hard for him to conjure them up in his mind now, at this precise moment. In addition to those invariables, his identity also consisted of parents, and a sister and two brothers, and friends, and colleagues, and past acquaintances, and how many forgotten strangers.

'Empty your mind,' the doctor had told him. There was 'not thinking' and there was 'not thinking'. In a way he hadn't really *seen* until the order came to take a rest. He'd been too busy, too preoccupied planning ahead, too myopically close to the business load on his desk. If only he'd lifted his eyes, shifted his field of vision, then his situation now might have been better: but time and gravity's pull is always downwards, so the chances were that things could only have become thus, worse and worse ...

Against all that bears in on you, like a shapeless drifting desert, you do whatever you can in your narrow space, you cultivate and propagate and nurture, you do your best. 'Relax, clear your head,' the doctor had told him. 'Empty your mind.' But what happens *then*, when the channels are drained and the sluice gates open?

*

Tides and currents and the flow of the day carried the boat miles.

He remembered reading that the Nile was perfectly drinkable: that it was more refreshing to taste than refrigerated soft drinks, its temperature was kinder to the stomach.

Meanwhile tints of flame had appeared in the canopy of sky. He sat attending to each of the insects that landed on his arms, his shirt, his trouser legs: spotted and striped sorts, and multi-coloured, and those of no recognisable colour at all. There must be a book to help him identify them, and he wondered if he should start, but the thousands of varieties there must be would take a lifetime to become familiar with and anyway, perhaps after these two weeks in Egypt were done he would never find himself back here again . . .

*

He closed his eyes. In the background, over the running of water beneath them, he heard the tea things being carried away.

What woke him afterwards was the creaking: those mechanical groans.

For a moment he thought he'd gone backwards in time, to an hour ago. But it must have been another water pump, he realised as he looked, although there were two oxen and a boy in a white burnouse following in their tracks. The boy hadn't yet formed into a man; he carried a stick, and the oxen's ears twitched.

How did he keep his mind on the job, or off it, from dwelling on the numbing tedium? Did he ever think what else his life might offer – or *did* it offer anything else?

From the deck he listened for the chant but the song he was hearing wasn't the water boy's but the waiter's as he inspected the other tables, making them tidy before the first spirits and cocktails of the evening were served.

*

Perhaps, he thought later over a gin-and-tonic, I just shouldn't go back. There doesn't need to be a return after all. Someone else could take my place, another toiler. Cassie will adjust to a different father, Jane may come to prefer her new husband. While *I* shall – follow the river to its source. Sink. Then rise. And begin again. In this land of transmigrating souls.

There's a city of men like the man I was, cities of them, all across the world. Point Number One. And the Counter-Argument: there's one particular past that's mine, and one particular residue of circumstances that's mine, and one particular set of modern neuroses that's mine.

Mine, me, myself, I.

*

He took a second gin-and-tonic.

Or instead of here ... He could have gone off to Paris, Nice, Rome, met someone, had a fling, let the deceit propel him back to Jane and Cassie with the relief of knowing he had a home and a family to return to and the vague hope of another meeting with the other woman, sometime.

No one here answered to the description of such a woman.

Joining the boat there had been some confusion, about his name. It was down on the list as Mitchell, not Hitchen. It had occurred to him, he could swap identities and become Mitchell. 'I am expecting to meet someone,' he could have explained to the other passengers on board. 'A Mr Hitchen. He doesn't seem to be here – not yet. I shall wait, though, he will come. Mitchell's *my* name.'

But, after all, he was Hitchen looking for this shadowman, Mitchell. Mitchell had news for *him*, you could bet your money on it: a message of forbearance from home, or else an invitation: to trade one life, his present one, for another.

*

This evening he had a vast, unquenchable thirst and, standing at the deck rail, he started sipping at a third gin-and tonic.

He'd once read in a book, the places we travel to aren't random, we are drawn to those that answer to some quality, some bias, in ourselves.

Why, then, this crowding emptiness, and the fragility of life along the river's course: the chants of boys not yet men, and the howling of water pumps?

*

The steward knocked three times on his cabin door in the morning before summoning help.

About midday the boat received word, through the company headquarters in Cairo.

The body had been washed ashore at a village ten miles downstream from where they'd moored for the night; it was found by fellahnin, among bulrushes. He'd swallowed a lot of water and was floating on his swollen belly, arms spread out as if – queerly – he was imitating a bird.

'Misadventure' and 'Drowning' appeared on the formal certificate presented to his wife at the embassy. She could only think of Giles distended like an inflated yak's skin on a television documentary she'd seen, ferrying people across Himalayan torrents. And those arms spread-eagled – ludicrously – like wings, a bird wanting to swim or a fish trying to fly.

The noises of Cairo had shocked her; they kept pulling and pulling at her nerves' ends, fraying them. She accepted a glass of mineral water from a very minor embassy official, and wished – *wished* – he would close all the shutters against the din and the heat. Please, *please*.

In chilly London efficient friends were organising lunch at the Dorchester, for after the funeral on Monday. They'd told her that flying out with William and Sarah to attend to the formalities would be the best thing, really: she had to keep herself busy and not let her thoughts wander. Always best to concentrate your thoughts, fix on something, make sure your mind's occupied for God's sake.

Evacuee

She's shocked awake, out of her dream – then remembers where she is. Safe: here in 1957 and out of harm's
reach, in her own home.

She falls back on the pillows and smells the cut roses.

She listens to the breathing beside her, regular and assured.
It should inspire confidence in her, that unthinking evenness.
It should do.

What does Norman dream about? Would she really want
to discover, she always puzzles.

She lies, as she always lies on her bad nights, looking up,
trying to identify the geography of the ceiling. She knows she
won't get back to sleep. For one thing, she suspects, the room
is too comfortable: the mattress, the carpet, the thick curtains
at the window, the quiet in the lane. It's odd, that she hasn't
been able to adjust to this life better. But the house doesn't
represent the conditions she was brought up to expect would
be her natural right. She suffers for it: just as the War made
so many suffer in their bodies and minds, she wonders if this
is how people of her own sort have elected to take upon
themselves the guilt of survival. It's a complicated matter,
though, and she doesn't know if she's altogether equipped to
make much sense of it.

She can't sleep, and that perhaps is the beginning and end
of the business.

*

But at the very start of her marriage she'd also tried not to
think about things too much, as if she might be in danger of
undoing the spell, her good fortune.

Of course that had only caused a kind of incidental falseness to develop. Because she felt she was concealing something

288

from herself, that – so she later concluded – must have made her hesitant and uneasy in her relations with Norman. Together they'd always lacked the quality of frankness, perhaps of closeness, and it didn't just have to do with her social elevation and their mutual progress in the material sense.

Their marriage wasn't as 'honest' as it might have been. Somehow that struck her as wholly inappropriate. When *she* tried to be honest and frank with herself, she realised – treachery for a wife – that she had doubts about Norman's professional integrity. She'd picked up enough clues in the past seven years to become aware that he sailed very close to the wind (one of Norman's own phrases) in his business dealings. Commerce (the dealings of manufacturers' agents) was a mystery to her: she was happy enough that it should remain so, but she could guess that, even in business, rules and precepts and (possibly) morality were of some consequence.

They didn't discuss business together. She saw the results of his success: their home, an Armstrong Siddley car parked on the half-moon gravel driveway, the clothes hanging in their wardrobe. Ten years ago the prospect would have seemed not just unlikely, but impossible. Norman's working colleagues struck her as being a little too sharp-eyed for comfort: but what Norman meant by 'comfort' when he said the word only concerned her physical wellbeing, and on that count she could have no uncertainties. She was so comfortable she couldn't will herself back to sleep some nights: that was the crazy thing.

Instead she was remembering running footsteps in the streets – the sooty leaf-mould smell of the underground stations – the wails scoring the sky —

But that was behind her now. She knew that she never needed to remember again.

*

Having children would have helped. They would have grown up with the blithe assumption that all this was their natural, God-given lot in life. She could have viewed her own situation through *their* eyes, and that might have helped her to believe in it more. She would have been able to see herself as a real person, Mrs Norman Hoskins.

Children would have taken up her time, filled her day, been her companions. As it was, she lived a good deal alone.

Norman took business trips about the country – up to Doncaster, Wolverhampton, Bradford, Leeds – but even when he was here with her she felt that their two presences didn't quite fill the house.

It was a very enviable house, of course, as the estate agent had never done reminding them: built in the Jacobean style, with inglenook fireplaces and beams and textured walls, and they were its first owners. But there was a lot of space for two people to occupy – they had four bedrooms, and the morning-room, and a games room above the garage – and she felt less at ease in some rooms than she did in others. That gave rise to a curious sensation: it was as if she were a stranger about to be apprehended, caught red-handed here in her own home – she was passing through on her way to elsewhere, she was only a spectator of her own good luck.

A ridiculous fancy it was, and she did her best to rid herself of it. She listened to long-playing records on the radiogram (Mantovani, Charlie Kunz), she watched the television, she'd developed a taste for gin (topped up with soda from the American syphon). She tried not to be tempted by the selection of unseasonal fruit she kept in the Frigidaire, and she fretted about her waistline. She glanced at newspapers when she could concentrate on nothing else, but more and more she preferred to read of the less weighty matters in daily life's rich you-know-what, the lighter moments.

Everything did its modest little to help the time to pass.

*

Occasionally – once every few weeks, when Norman was away on business – she had a day off, when she left the house to Mrs Minty and took a train up to London.

Then she became a different Mrs Hoskins. She dressed for other people, she smiled, she even indulged in a Senior Service cigarette or two. She let the other passengers in the compartment talk to her if they wanted to, without inviting them.

That was how she got to hear about the station-master's wife at Mindellsham. She'd been a sensitive woman who'd married an older man a little her better, in the old parlance. During the War the sight of the trains rumbling past with their cargo of soldiers had greatly distressed her. At some point she fell for a young man from the district whom she'd known as a child and whose turn came to be called up. She sent him letters when he went off and she posted them herself in the sack that her husband was responsible for putting on to the London train.

The bag that was tossed out on to the platform from the Exeter Night Mail never contained any replies. It was said that the station-master must have known what was going on and he'd taken her letters out of the sack before it was thrown on the train. It was the explanation people favoured, rather than that the young woman should have been intentionally neglected.

After the War the soldier didn't return. He hadn't been reported injured or missing, and there was a rumour that he was living in London. Every morning and evening the station-master's wife used to stand on the platform watching the commuter trains leave and return; her behaviour embarrassed her husband and they had terrible, famous quarrels.

One still June afternoon the woman quite calmly stepped off the platform in the path of an express Pullman train bound for the Devon Riviera. It was agreed afterwards that she must have been more in love than anyone had thought possible: or – maybe – more unhinged than anyone had perceived was the case.

So, Mindelsham station always had a sad association for Norman Hoskins' wife as the train slowed, stopped, took up its passengers, and set off again. It seemed an ordinary, unexceptional station, certainly well kept (the stooped station-master could be seen watering the plants himself and raking the gravel); but a strange sort of quiet made itself felt there, which could have been interpreted (in a wrong frame of mind) as offering no hope, a desperate and frantic stillness, while the country on either side of the station – furrowed fields of chalky earth and grazing pasture with the greenness washed out by the summer's sun, shadowed here and there by an indolent tree with barely the strength to grow – offered its own beguiling, un-English, almost (it struck Mrs Hoskins) *sinister* charm. The sails of an old windmill were always turning, but idly, unindustriously, and she would entertain the same hazy memory of a play she'd heard on the wireless about a Spanish knight of long ago who mistook a host of windmills on a high plain for an imaginary army of foes, and charged them on his slump-backed nag: circumstances weren't at all as he believed them to be, but perhaps a mind that wanders – so Mrs Hoskins argued to herself – can't be wooed back, to a drab, colourless world that isn't able to satisfy its longings.

Deep, disturbing thoughts for early on a weekday morning.

Slowly Mrs Hoskins would lose the recollections of the station-master's wife's story and the Spanish knight's. The train gathered speed, with no more stops left now between Salisbury and London. Later as they approached the metropolis, she would feel that her head was clearing of thoughts; it was a relief not to have to concern herself with the house, with Norman's absences, but – from this point on – just to let the day take her where it would.

Not thinking was her reward on these London excursions, the privilege she paid for with the rest of her life.

*

She starts preparing herself as they roll through the suburbs, past gardens and the backs of terraces and semis. She opens her handbag and – covertly – checks her appearance in the compact, while seeming to be looking at what the windows present of outside, a view of kitchens and living-rooms and little comforts won from the years of austerity and doing without. Cars sit neatly parked on long roads, washing on clothes lines performs optimistic cartwheels. The suburbs celebrate their decent, rather prissy weal and neighbours look over into one another's gardens, squinting through net curtains at that waxed two-tone Hillman drawn up outside next door. (*Or*, Mrs Hoskins asks herself, perhaps after all there *is* more than the eye is met with, there's something unsettling and secretly restive about the torpor such places seem to have?)

The train clatters over points, they slip into the gullies between warehouses and factories. She catches sight of a workman's face watching from a grimy window, and her glimpse is too brief for her to be able to identify its expression: dull indifference maybe – or, she thinks again, could it have been the opposite, a cold look he was applying as a front to his envy? (She knows that look. She sees the give-aways in people's behaviour when they think she doesn't see: eyes in the street failing to notice or sliding to the side and narrowing, words muttered in judgment and the lips scarcely moving, the single second's delay before a shop assistant replies to her.)

Ahead of them, and always before she expects it, looms the hotel of tracery windows and exultant pinnacles – and then, beyond it, the cathedral of vaulting ironwork and miraculously compliant glass. Sounds make vast echoes.

She closes her bag and drapes her coat over her arm. She fits her fingers into, first, one glove, then the other, and flexes them. She tips back her cuff and consults her watch. Her quest today will be for the perfect cup of Kenyan Blue Mountain coffee. (Coffee is one of her new enthusiasms: she will plunder as much of the world as she needs to, in order that her taste buds may be gratified.)

A man in the compartment opens the door and jumps down. She waits for the platform to stop moving before she steps down after him. She catches a whiff of the underground, which always smells of wind and blown dust. She doesn't travel by that means now, but by taxi. These days she doesn't risk what's beneath the pavements: she keeps to street level, to daylight, to everything that floats on the surface of the world.

She follows the other passengers, past the gate where she surrenders half of her ticket, then on to the concourse. She walks forward, ankles balanced on her shoes' heels, but already she's slowing. She can't resist looking, and turns her head on her neck and stares behind her, the way she's come, with her eyes wide. She sees that the station is crowded ...

*

The station was crowded, teeming, she imagined it bulging at the sides with the mass of people packing themselves inside.

Instructions for assembly and anouncements of departures crackled through the tannoy speakers, hardly audible beneath the roar of voices.

Children like herself with scuffed cardboard suitcases and labels tied to their wrists or coat buttons were being shepherded together on the central platform and marshalled into some kind of order.

A hand pushed into her back and a voice, her mother's, told her to go on.

'Platform Eight you've to report to.'

She clasped her fingers tighter on the handle of her case and made for the sign above the gates, carried there by the tide.

On her left and right people heaved, strained, wept, stood stock still, dropped things, remembered things, called good-byes, laughed, peered up at the clock, waved, used cases for battering-rams, shouted over other people's heads, stared into nowhere seeming forlorn and lost.

When she reached the platform, the hand pushed into the small of her back again and she heard her mother start speaking to someone. To a man. She walked on, taking slow, wary steps, towards the end of a crocodile file being got together.

She put her down her case and tried shaking the numbness out of her arm. One of the two girls in front of her looked over her shoulder and nudged the other.

She directed her eyes away, up to the arched roof of sooty glass. Soon her mother would be here to say 'goodbye'. 'Cheerio, Avril, write us a line, won't you?' She wasn't really wanting that moment to happen, although – she supposed – it had to.

From somewhere a grey woman suddenly swooped on her and lifted up the label her mother had tied to the belt of her coat. 'Avril Clancy, is it?' Her name was ticked off on a piece of paper.

In the meantime more bodies had collected behind. Too many to count. The grey woman was calling out, 'In twos!' A boy was propelled by his shoulders into the space beside her. 'We're going into the bloody ark!' someone called out.

The boy – when she looked to see – was pale, foxy-faced, angry-looking. Why was he angry, she wondered. He was so furious he was shaking.

She looked down at her feet in their leaky shoes. Soon her mother would be here, like the other mothers, to say her 'goodbye' to her, and she was wishing she didn't have the ordeal to go through. She didn't think her mother would mean it anyway, not 'good-bye'. Sometimes it seemed to her that the War was suiting her mother quite well, and it didn't matter to her if it carried on and on: the house had been more peaceful with her father away, and – even if she was always being got out of the way, to go and sit at Mrs O'Rourke's or the Roses' – there had been a holiday feeling in the air. Some of the men who visited the house, who said they were her father's pals, they would give her a threepenny bit or a silver sixpence, and so now she had almost nine shillings of her own put away in a secret place in her suitcase. After several years of saving she was rich, she could hold her head up high.

She craned her neck and gazed up at the glass and ironwork arch of the roof. She sensed that the boy beside her continued to be just as angry as before.

She waited for her mother to come, like the other mothers. She waited, without turning her head to look back, until the chain started to move, shuffling, towards the train. 'In twos!' the grey woman was calling.

By then, when she did look back, there was no sign of her mother, no sign anywhere. No hope, even: there were too many people. Couldn't she make her way through the crowd?

She hasn't got through, she decided, she hasn't been able to. The other mothers have, but they've been lucky. Or else *she* doesn't want to have this 'goodbye' happen either: she's sensible and the other mothers (she watched them, crying into handkerchiefs, waving and waving) aren't.

Now it was too late. She was on her own, but – known only to herself – she had the solace of her riches.

*

She found herself in a compartment with nine other children.

Everyone was serious and glum as the farewells were shouted or mouthed and knuckles rapped on the glass. Then the train was pulling out of the station, steam rose from the tracks, arms waved, faces on the platform were indistinguishable.

A boy – he looked the oldest – began speaking, in a loud, unavoidable voice. He told them that he'd been sent away once before but he'd scarpered, made his own way back to London.

'Why'd you let 'em?' someone asked.

'What?'

'Send yer off again.'

The boy had no answer. Another boy, with a wall-eye and

295

an aura of wisdom, said it all depended where they sent you: some kids hated it, others had a ball.

'All depends.'

'What depends?' a voice asked.

'Where they put you.'

'How d'you mean?'

'Who you're with, of course.'

Some folks, he said, were strict. But there were people who were quite the opposite, and you could get away with anything. Murder sometimes. Apparently – Avril learned – the world divided up into those who lived in cold, usually poky houses where everything had to be just so, and those who had nice things but a bit battered, some of them, and easy manners as well, as if they'd stopped worrying about the things getting spoiled or broken.

'That's what you hope for. But it all depends,' he repeated, 'where they farm you out.'

There was silence for several seconds, then – as if on cue – everyone burst into chatter. Voices piled on top of other voices and crowded up to the carriage roof. Avril joined in too, speaking to the girl next to her, who was trying to speak to *her*, but she managed to shout her down, telling her she wanted to be sent somewhere there were soft towels and cakes of scented soap in the bathroom and clean sheets to sleep on, the most perfect things she could think of.

Then, all in a moment, she lost interest in the girl and what the others were shouting over one another's heads. She edged along the seat to a window. She pressed her forehead against the cold glass, and looked in the direction in which they were travelling.

They were rolling past the great grimy flanks of warehouses and works. Grass had seeded in the brickwork; down beneath, grey rats with long tails scurried on the gravel. She lifted her eyes to the wedges of blue sky visible between roofs and walls and chimneys.

Her eyes returned to the brown-and-white photographs in the carriage, set in oval panels above the opposite seat. One showed a windmill, in the other sheep lay in the shade of a gnarled tree which looked scarcely able to support itself in the day's full glare.

The talk was so loud that she couldn't hear the sirens at

first. Then they all seemed to hear them, at one and the same instant.

The train was slowing. Suddenly the brakes were slammed on; everyone was sent flying, suitcases fell off the racks on to whoever was beneath. Somebody was crying as someone else remembered to give the warning. 'Gas masks!'

They'd stopped in a chasm between brick walls, black with soot. No one knew what to do or how to behave: only she, Avril Clancy, and the boy with the wall-eye and the manner of wisdom seemed not to be panicking. Across the carriage in the tumult they caught one another's eye (she just had the choice of his one good eye). The boy winked, and she smiled.

Only a few seconds later their compartment inexplicably went quiet. From the others they could hear rising hysteria, and even singing – 'O God, our help in ages past' and 'My old man said follow the van . . .'

Around her the voices started again, but soberly and composedly. Gas masks were pulled on, all except her own. How ridiculous everyone looked wearing them, goggle-eyed and snouty. She sat leaning against the seat-back thinking, if this is a false alarm it's an awful lot of bother and fuss, and if there really *is* going to be a raid we shall never be saved in a spot like this anyway, it's like the channel between two riverbanks and we're done for. So . . .

So she sat tight instead, but with the semblance of calm, of leisure even, and she lifted her eyes again to the photographs, to the windmill and the lazy summer field in the southern county.

She smiled at the din of panic from the other compartments. Already she was arriving at the house. It was to be found at the end of a long lane overhung with trees. As she walked inside, she felt no stranger to the place, although she had never as much as set eyes on it before.

The rooms smelt of furniture cream and Mansion wax and the white and yellow roses. Every solid thing about her seemed to shine. She saw her reflection repeated, over and over, dozens of herself, Avril Clancy, looking out from the silver and copper and wood and glass as if they had always been there and she were only surprising them now.

She was coming back to reclaim something, without having realised she'd lost it. The house didn't resist her. For a start there were too many Avril Clancys, peering out of all the surfaces with their polished gloss. The shine must have come with generations of applied elbow-grease (her mother's term for it). As for herself, she divined (in a *feeling* rather than in words) that she too would acquire the saving graces and refinement, and the social polish, all in good time.

She started moving through the house in several different directions at once, into each of the waiting rooms, and in those moments she forgot the tousled, anxious nature of the interrupted journey that had brought her here, all overlooked in her new pleasure of possession.

The house was as real as anything she'd ever encountered before. Meanwhile planes roared overhead, from the direction of Kent, but she was already in another, farther county anyway, westwards, and so there was no harm the grieving sky could do to her.

The singing in the carriages stopped, as if everyone was sharing an instinct of what was about to happen to them.

She smelt lavender soap and had the touch of soft towels and freshly-laundered, garden-dried sheets on her skin. There would be enough fresh food to eat, more than she could possibly need. In a time to come the strangers' home would seem just like her own: she would be familiar with every twitch of its floorboards and she'd know where to stand on the staircase so that it didn't creak; she would have the knowledge to calculate how easily a door might swing open or shut. The house would be like all its past, but it would also be able to include *her*, Avril Clancy that was. She wasn't sure what she must do to become the person to whom such things were second nature, but in that gap of silence deep as a wishing-well she was willing to give away her suitcase and all that was in it, her nine-shillings security and her gas mask too, if only she could discover.

The Ghost Cupboard
The Corner Table
Sur la Plage à Trouville
An Evening in Granada

The Ghost Cupboard

When he and Matthew were boys, they used to call it 'The Ghost Cupboard', because of all the dead lives it contained. Really it was the lumber room.

Ghosts can't hurt you, they knew: but still it frightened them, gave them cold shivers.

Matthew, being the younger son, hadn't inherited the house; he, Christopher, had. It had always made him feel guilty, as if he'd been denying Matthew what was also his by rights.

Now Matthew was dead, and it was too late.

Some belongings of Matthew's were still in the house, in the Ghost Cupboard. (Patricia, when she was alive, had always said, just leave them there.) Sometimes he had the prickly feeling these things had no place here now, and he just wanted rid of them. They belonged to a spectre.

One afternoon he went up, settled in his mind to clear out what he could.

Under a skylight was the trunk, stencilled with his own initials, which he knew from memory held Matthew's old school jumble: ties, scarves, cricket balls, a bat, exercise books, text books. He hauled it out into the middle of the floor; it made a shrill complaining noise as he dragged it across the bare boards. The rusty lock 'gave' raspily, and he threw the lid back.

There were no moths inside as he'd expected: he saw they'd decomposed, and it must have been years ago. He picked out the school books first. He banged a couple of them together and choked on the dust they made. He looked through a few: could he possibly sell them when they were so old? Patricia, he thought, *she* would have known what to do.

Or maybe he should just burn them?

He felt, somehow, Matthew was *with* him at that moment, aware of his treacherous thoughts. He looked round sharply, as quickly as his old bones could manage. But there was no one there...

Sorting through the books he couldn't help remembering how lemon-faced outside and vinegary inside Matthew had got in his later years: quite acid and caustic, even about how he and Patricia lived. They might have been brothers, Matthew and himself, but they'd never been alike. Matthew, who'd become a literary journalist, a 'man of letters', always somewhere else in his mind, a helpless bachelor: himself, Christopher, head screwed on the right way (people always said), orderly, scrupulous, made from boyhood to be the banker he became.

Perhaps if we'd gone to the same school, he considered, we would have been more alike? Matthew had been sent to one in the West Country, meant (it was their father's choice) to toughen the boy up, to knock the corners off him, shake the dreams out of his head. Himself, he'd gone to his father's old school – a sound, dependable institution which had provided whole departments of Whitehall with their officials. And it was he, Christopher, when he'd married Patricia, who had inherited their father's house, history and precedent determining who would be the favoured one.

He read the gilt letters on the red spine of one of the school books. '*Attic Lives*', he spoke aloud. Inside were pages of Ancient Greek script: passages of history and biography. (He'd funked classics, couldn't remember a thing now.) Matthew had diligently underlined words, scribbled their meanings in the margins. Subjunctives, optatives, 'should', 'would'. All that supposed wisdom from three thousand years ago...

Three thousand! He sat back on his heels, awe-struck. He picked with his fingers at long strands of dust and cobwebs that had dropped on to the shoulders of his jacket, then started leafing slowly through the pages. The script was like gobbledygook. What good had the discipline of learning it been to Matthew? It had only detached him further from the others in his Form, left him with more dreams and fancies. 'Invite your friends home, Matthew!' their mother would say.

'Like Christopher does.' But he never did, Matthew. (Did he even *have* any friends at school, he used to wonder.)

He'd always felt sorry for Matthew. Being four years older than him had made him protective. He'd still felt compassion even when Matthew became moderately well-known for his newspaper articles. It wasn't natural to live alone as he did: without a person to want to share your life with. That way, you get too inward. If nothing else, your table manners desert you...He'd watched Patricia when they invited him over, how she would sit at the table with her chin in her hands and her eyes rapt, looking unutterably sorry for their guest. It embarrassed him that *she* was embarrassed. At those moments he forgot about Matthew's share of success in life, his reputation, the Christmas cards he remembered peering at in the Shepherd Market sitting-room with the signatures of their distinguished male and (especially numerous) female senders; even his good old-fashioned tweed suits and expensive silk shirts didn't matter, they didn't count, not when he looked so old, so forlorn, and slurped at his soup and dribbled it and forgot they'd provided him with a napkin. A man who'd never married...

He was closing the book, the dog-eared *Attic Lives*, when something fell out of it on to the floor. He felt with his fingertips and retrieved – he held it up for inspection – a postcard. Of Crete. (He blinked with recognition.) The sprawling Minoan palace at Knossos: those not very convincing reconstructions of Sir Arther Evans, which had been such a secret disappointment to him on his honeymoon with Patricia.

He turned the card over and his heart gave a little jump, a judder.

His eyes narrowed, he felt them shrinking in their sockets as he recognised the handwriting.

Patricia's. Patricia's when she was young.

He peered at the postmark. Something or other, '24'. '1924'. The year they'd married and gone on their honeymoon. It was addressed from the hotel to Matthew, at his school in Somerset. He must have been – he counted, as rapidly and precisely as a bank-teller – eighteen years old then. Hardly a schoolboy any more.

He turned the card on its side, to see what it was his young wife of a few days had written to her new brother-in-law.

'*My Dearest Matthew*', it began.

He just stared at the words. Very hard. He didn't know if he should go on. Something warned him against it. A feeling, that had as much to do with his knotted-up stomach as his head. There was a sudden coldness too in the room, like a ghost's chill breath just behind him.

He turned round. But there was nothing, no one...

'*My Dearest Matthew*,' he read again.

He tried to imagine Patricia writing it. The words didn't quite fit with the picture in his head: that decided, no-nonsense woman their friends and his banking colleagues said matched him so suitably. She had always been so, from the beginning.

On the floor of the Ghost Cupboard he focused his mind to remember her in those early days, in the 1920s: cool, collected, in control of herself: a widow's daughter introduced to the two brothers at a dance. Pretty, but not in the usual way: not coy and pleading and winsome as other girls of that 'flapper' era had a fashion of being, but meeting their stares of admiration with a firm, confident return of look belying her years. (In age she'd been between the two of them, Matthew and himself.) Local talk said her mother had great difficulty making ends meet genteelly on an army widow's pension, but she gave nothing of that away. Her eyes hadn't wavered from theirs as the three of them chatted that first night. He was so grateful they'd been fated to meet like this: a few months before, the girl he'd been squiring had abandoned him, and he was still shaken, rocked by it, and deeply hurt.

The truth of the situation was this perhaps: that Patricia that evening had caught him on the rebound. He'd always suspected so, and probably she had too. Not that he hadn't always cared utterly for her, when she became his wife. But there may have been a reason, an ulterior purpose why he'd attached himself to her so readily, at first sight: because she'd given him what he so desperately needed, there and then – the magic solace of an attractive, listening confidante.

For a long time Matthew had looked quite disapproving. 'It's a phase he's going through,' he would tell Patricia. 'Or do you think he's turning into a misogynist?' She would smile, and say something excusing. It was through Patricia he learned for the first time that his quiet younger brother with the slightly haunted good looks and an older appearance than his years didn't go unnoticed by the female company: his reserve marked him out, the women speculated about him, his mystery deepened as each explanation failed to take satisfactory account...

At the social functions where they continued to meet before the engagement, they still made a threesome in the room. Patricia's eyes confronted the two brothers equally – steely blue and without evasion. That had stopped, though, the fraternising – and (he'd been of the opinion) just as well too. Matthew, still at school, struck him as one of that kind, head up in the clouds, who are often least able to look after themselves. It wasn't good for him to be starting on adult relationships so early, he was four years younger than himself: a woman like Patricia could turn that head in the clouds completely...

Up in the lumber room, in the Ghost Cupboard, he wasn't so sure that these arguments he'd once convinced himself with sounded so persuasive. Had he been alarmed that Patricia might *try* to turn his brother's head? That she would have dared to – if only for a kind of game, a dare, a *jeu d'esprit*?

Well, not once they were engaged. Of course not. And after that...

But what about *before*? *Before* they were engaged, and married, and off on honeymoon to Crete and Knossos, and then back to a new house for a while in a different country? In the months *before* all that...

Had she picked up what *he* had – the women's talk about Matthew, the speculation, the fascination?

The postcard shook slightly in his hand. '*My Dearest Matthew*,' he read again. He hesitated – then decided – and lifted the card a little, towards the gauzy grey light from the skylight. He was under instructions from the oculist not to strain his sight, but this occasion was – he had to believe – exceptional.

Fifty years ago, fifty-three, his wife was reporting on their honeymoon.

He read on.

'*My Dearest Matthew*,

305

*Not as bad as you said it would be. Not quite. A little dull,
of course. Which is only to be expected in present company.
Is it not?*

The card wobbled.

*I thought about what YOU would have made of Knossos
as I did my duty and tramped round the site. Lots of old coins
to see, which pleased Christopher no end.*

He's reconciled to being a banker, he told me.

Dust caught in his throat.

*I smiled politely. Think of me, won't you, in our new life.
Come and see us sometimes. Please.*

His throat felt furred.

All my love. Ever, Patricia.'

The card fluttered from between his fingers.

Perhaps he coughed, drily.

Then for a long time he wasn't conscious of anything. It
was as if a very dark, very still stone had been placed in his
head and was filling the space in his brain where his
humming thoughts had been.

It was too late now: for recriminations, blaming. There
was no one left to blame anyway. Except himself:
Christopher, always so trusting, who hadn't noticed, who
hadn't even thought to keep a wary eye open.

He remembered. All those reviews and articles Patricia had
read with such delight: Patricia, hardly 'Brains Trust'
material, who could only read what people of influence in
such matters advised her to read. 'My clever brother-in-law!'
she liked to say for a joke every time Matthew came for
dinner or they visited his bachelor's flat, where he knew she
invariably went to rest on her solo shopping trips to London,
for a shared pot of Lapsang Souchong and pastrymaker's
fancies. 'Clever Patricia, what a meal!' Matthew would reply.
'How very domesticated Christopher has made you!' he'd say
with a sly, secretive smile, dabbing at his mouth with the napkin Patricia would unfold for him and spread across his lap.

Clever them.

*

He picked up the incomprehensible Greek book – *Attic Lives*
– with its crimson binding hardly faded, and found a place
for it at the bottom of the schoolboy's trunk.

The trunk could stay where it was. He hadn't the energy for house-clearing, not at his age. And he might discover something else, worse ...

He stood on the postcard getting to his feet, and happened to look down and see. The blue sky of Crete and the dubious ruins coloured brilliantly with that apricot, eye-stunning dye had a dusty heel-mark stamped on them.

He didn't stoop down to pick up the card, he didn't think, and only remembered when he'd shut the door and locked it and was standing on the top landing, above the deep silence of the house.

The card. Knossos. The fake grandeur. The apricot and blue.

His fingers opened, he dropped the key over the banister. It rattled downstairs, like a coin into a culvert. It disappeared into the silence.

Patricia's photograph awaited, on top of the bureau. And Matthew's, in the bookcase. Watching from different ends of the drawing-room, anticipating footsteps on the staircase, his return.

He laid his hand on the banister rail, took the first step, the second.

The card, he remembered. He paused. Knossos.

But he was too old and it was too late for that to matter, or for attempting to make it matter. Someone else could discover it. Let them have the fun of playing detective, making guesses ...

After all there could be no *wrong* guesses in the Ghost Cupboard.

His handhold tightened on the banister rail. He began his descent.

The Corner Table

For a year once I lived in Italy, in a small medieval city on a hill.

I took breakfast every morning at a particular café, in its busy back room. I work best first thing in the day and I enjoyed the low background rumble of chatter and the constant lifting up and putting down of the coffee cup into my saucer and stirring the teaspoon to pick up the sediment.

The owner quickly caught on to my occupation. 'You're a writer?' Yes, I said, and explained a little, that I wrote stories and articles and travel pieces, whatever I thought I could sell.

He nodded towards the corner of the room and I looked in the same direction. I'd already noticed the three-legged, three-sided triangle of table attached to the wall, but I hadn't paid it any special attention. A single chair stood in front of it – an old-fashioned sort with a wicker seat and half-arms, to rest your elbows on. 'The table was here when I bought the place,' the man said. 'I've just left it as it was. It's not popular, no one sits there.' I looked again. The chair faced into the wall, but I realised it was possible to see the activities of the room reflected in an angled mirror set high up on the wall. Even so, the occupant would have to sit with his back to the company, which wasn't likely to be the reason why customers chose to come to a café.

But, the proprietor said (as if he was reading my mind), the table *had* had a regular occupant. Until maybe three years ago. A retired doctor of the town, a man who kept himself pretty much to himself. After he retired, breakfast at the café started to become a habit with him, much to everyone's surprise. He would stay on from breakfast, till the middle of the morning, then till lunchtime. He'd come in six mornings a week, except on a Sunday, when he went duck-shooting with his sister and brother-in-law.

He'd had no wife, the man explained (although perhaps he did once, a long time ago, before he came to the town, there had always been rumours). He hadn't been able to hold on to his housekeepers, he never had, and he would vacate the house while a girl came in to clean and scrub and wash.

So the café had become his refuge, the proprietor said: and it was at *that* table he'd seated himself with his briefcase. Inside the case there were always books and sheets of paper and pens, with a bottle of ink. The old doctor would proceed to read, and he also wrote: just like that, he'd read and write, and sip at his coffee, read some more, write some more, and sip again. (He'd always had three cups of sugary black coffee in the morning, at regular intervals between quarter-to-nine and half-past-twelve, and he liked to gnaw at a wedge of bread – always the same size and type of flour, so he insisted – which he spread with honey.)

Finally they discovered, the proprietor said – lowering his voice a little, as if it had been a great and subterfuge feat of deduction – they discovered what his business was about. About collecting fables: stories he found in old books, to do with people's sightings of mermaids and satyrs and goblins and other extraordinary phenomena. These witnesses' accounts – so I gathered – referred to such matters as levitation, the sprouting of wings on mortal shoulders or horns on brows or tails on rumps, the metamorphosis of a person into a being that was part-human and part-animal (a cat, a sheep, a wolf). So the doctor had conceded to the proprietor after he summoned courage to ask him one morning. He said he would be interested to hear from the man any stories that came his way, and he did indeed pass them on to him, when he was able to: all manner of tales and legends, about an old woman who could survive just by chewing grass, a tyrant of a father who went up in flames in front of his family, a young grieving widow who grew a beard like her dead farmer husband's, two hating twin-brothers who each – because they could only inherit together – coincidentally committed suicide to spite the other, a maiden centuries ago kept prisoner on her family's estate who had herself fired from a cannon so that she could clear the park's high wall into her lover's arms, an astronomer who floated off in a gas balloon into infinity, a meek young woman who kept breaking into the voice of her murdered grandmother, a chemist who bottled sunshine and sold it and died the most contented of men.

The doctor had continued with his reading, but at the end of the second year he suddenly stopped bringing the books in his battered and bulging briefcase. Instead he wrote: not from his pages of notes (it was observed), but composing sentences and paragraphs straight out of his head, covering the top side of sheet after sheet, as many as forty at a single sitting (so they'd once counted). Most mornings the doctor had no difficulty in writing: the café was always nicely warm, as the proprietor reminded me, no one dared to trouble him at his work, even with complaints about their painful ailments – for a long time the man had been well-known in the district for being taciturn, not much disposed to speak. But at the corner table the words seemed to escape freely from him, and his hand holding the pen had a hard job to keep up as it skimmed over the whiteness of each new sheet.

A book it must be, everyone agreed. At first, when they realised, voices were dropped, perhaps in embarrassment. But a comment from the doctor to the proprietor soon after-wards amended the situation, and the company in the café returned to their usual ways, much relieved. The proprietor had always wondered quite how this most reclusive customer concentrated: owing to the room's acoustics, the table – although it was in a corner – actually caught more of the noise than, say, *my* table did, which was directly beside the open doorway from the front room. But the doctor had continued, somehow, even with so much chatter swilling about him.

Certain questions were politely asked of him on days – saints' days, holidays – when people felt they could. A book? they'd say. And the doctor would nod, pleasantly enough (for him) but giving away nothing. 'A book, I hope,' was as much as he would reply. The proprietor had naturally assumed that it must be about the matter of his research, which he'd caught sight of over the doctor's shoulders on many occasions serving him coffee: all those tomes about extraordinary pheno-mena. (Not – he fumbled for a word as he tried to explain to me. Not – A bestiary? I suggested. No, he said, not that. Old books about people and – I paraphrase him – about the strange sights they set eyes on or the wonders that befell them.)

Then, during the very cold winter still raw in everyone's memory, the doctor took a bad chill. It developed into pneumonia. With all his knowledge both medical and of other things, he couldn't save himself in that damp house in its wild garden, and he died in the first week of the new year.

His sister and brother-in-law, the duck-shooters, came to the town to settle everything. They cleared out the house, and lawyers attended to all the official business.

And the book? I asked, when the café owner didn't mention it. What about that? Anything? The man shrugged his shoulders. No one had heard, not so much as a whit or a jot: perhaps he hadn't written so much of it after all. What a pity, I said, and we were both silent for a few moments, thinking of all that sad waste of knowledge.

Then he left me to my own work. I sat for a long while, toying with the spoon in my saucer and looking over at the corner table, within easy, comfortable viewing distance of the angled mirror on the wall. If I had sufficient strength of purpose, I told myself, I would claim the table for myself. But neither on that day nor any other did I pull out the chair and sit down. In a way I wanted to, but the Scottish Calvinistic spirit in me reprimanded me sharply, it instructed me that I hadn't yet earned the right. *One* day, maybe, if I stayed here long enough and made anything at all of my writing.

*

It was at the end of the same year, as I was making plans to leave Italy and move on, that I chanced to read the early reviews of a novel that had been published in Turin. The author's name translated – rather archly, I thought – as 'Enigma'. The novel was called *The Table in the Corner*. It took the form of many conversations overheard by an anonymous observer sitting in the back room of a café in an unnamed small city. It was a chance quotation in a review – a description of a three-sided triangular table with (a prudent invention) a marble top – which brought me up short, with a jolt of recognition.

I invested some of my hard-earned cash in a copy of the book. I even took it with me into the café to read, to the warmest place I could find that November. No one glanced at the cover, it didn't appear to mean anything to them. Maybe none of this café's customers read in a city with dozens of cafés? How many other cafés had triangular tables, though? I looked into several, as casually as I could feign, but didn't see any other specimen.

The events the novel told of took place in this same region of the country. The dialect matched our local one: reviewers commented on the author's unique ability to catch its flavour. The stories were mainly of the doings of shopkeepers and those on a social par, except where they were records of (or speculations about) other people in the town not in the speakers' own social orbit.

The reviewers' praise was unanimous. I read that the novel was selling well from high piles in the bookshops of the big cities. Even the bookshops in our town were doing brisk business. The author called 'Enigma' was one of the arts world's favourite names that season, but the publishers resolutely kept his identity a mystery. Their confidentiality of course guaranteed even more interest and conjecture.

In the end I stayed on for another season in the town, partly to see what its reaction would be to the success of *The Table in the Corner*. Apparently – so I surmised – it saw nothing in the book that might refer to itself. Life in the café continued just as before, with nothing to interrupt the dependable routine. I was served my coffee and I heard nothing in the everyday commotion to indicate that anyone was any the wiser. As before, my own literary efforts – spread before me on the (square, wooden) table-top – brought no one's attention. The triangular table in the corner of the room continued to be unused: because – of course – the occupant must sit with his back to the company, and maybe because even café tables can carry their own ghostly legend, as much as any castle rampart or dungeon.

I read the book again, from cover to cover. This time I recognised particular traits of certain persons' speech which I'd already caught for myself. Then, a little slowly admittedly, I cottoned on.

I remember after that second reading how I sat listening much more carefully to the voices round about me, to what was being said and how it was being said; I listened for several hours in toto. By now I could have identified the speakers with my eyes shut: the owner of the 'Meteor' garage, the off-duty police sergeant, the hatter, the fruiterer, the typewriter dealer.

Tactfully everyone 'Enigma' mentioned had been granted a different calling in life: the people they told their stories about, the clerics and social upstarts and faded pedigree aristocrats, they all swapped physical characteristics and quirks of personality in the book.

Also, inevitably, I was set wondering what had caused the doctor to stop work on the study of bizarre phenomena, and to embark on a novel. Unless, to a mind which had travelled the spectrum of human experience, there seemed less and less distinction to be made between singing mermaids and the dentist's wife who put on dark glasses and went hitching lifts from unknown men; between the godly, suddenly raptured with the mysterious, blessed gift of wings beneath their shoulder blades, and the young teenage lovers and middle-aged adulterers who disdained mortal danger to stay with each other and attain eternal bliss together; between the wolf-men and vengeful landlords; between the walkers-on-water and those smitten with ambition, to whom nothing was an obstacle, who had the faith to ride on their dreams.

*

The book was reprinted, several times, and the author's name passed into quite common currency: nonetheless his identity continued to be – and remains – the publishers' secret. (I *have* tried to find out, but I've drawn a blank.) It even happened that a film was made of the book at Cinecitta and on location (the wrong one, though – Tuscany); it must have been shown in one of the local cinemas, and perhaps it has also had a run or two on television.

Last summer I revisited Umbria and the town, after seven or eight years away. I made my way back to the café. I spotted from the clean zinc finish that the espresso machine was new, and maybe the walls were painted a different colour. But the owner was still there, the same man, wearing glasses now: he claimed to recognise me, after I'd re-introduced myself and told him my name. I asked if much had changed. No, he said: he didn't think so. When I'd asked a number of questions I nodded at the vacant three-sided table in the corner of the back room and enquired about the old doctor. He told me what I remembered him telling me before, a more or less identical story, with nothing of significance added or taken away. It seemed that he knew nothing that he hadn't known and told me then.

Some of the faces in the back room I recognised, only they'd grown seven or eight years older. Customers stood in groups, in knots, always talking and gesticulating: sometimes laughing, sometimes making long faces.

I sat down at the corner table for a little while. I watched in the mirror angled high on the wall, but no one looked over. The table was out-of-bounds in the proprietor's mental geography, because no one ever sat there. He didn't come across to serve me, and after five or six minutes I got up and left, through the chatter, apologising as I went. A few old regulars – woolgatherers – smiled, vaguely, and moved a few inches to make way. The talk closed over behind me, as if I hadn't been in that room at such a moment on such a day, the voices, hardly put out at all, settled again, as do even and untroubled waters.

Sur la Plage à Trouville

The year is 1876. The scene is a beach on the coast of Normandy, at Trouville. High clouds chase across a blue, scrubbed summer sky. The waves froth as they run for the shore.

Along the beach, sensibly distant from the sea and each other, families have arranged themselves for the afternoon, sheltered from the sun and breeze by umbrellas and parasols. One particular group occupies the foreground. It comprises ten persons altogether. There are four children, somewhere between six or seven years old and the early teens, dressed in pinafores and sailor suits and digging in the sand with spades. They're being watched by a governess, perched on a low canvas stool beneath a frilled beach umbrella. Next to her, more upright, sit a couple in their late forties or early fifties: the woman is apparelled in colours mid-way between city and resort, the man – the 'paterfamilias' – wears conservatively grey trousers and a dark blue yachting jacket: they talk, but each with an attentive eye cast on whoever is passing by. (Everyone here in Trouville on this summer's day in 1876 belongs to the well-heeled Paris world '*en vacances*', taking the salt sea air but ever mindful of the social disciplines – propriety and precedence.) Another figure of much the same age as the parents sits a little removed from them: a woman dressed in shades of black or dark purple, in a high mulberry hat with the veil pulled up: she's holding a black fringed parasol as she reads her book.

There are two other members of the party. A young woman, perhaps a girl in her late teens, the eldest child of her parents, wears a striped blouse buttoned to the cuffs and a long white linen skirt; on her lap lies a straw hat with a bright daffodil-yellow ribbon and bow. Behind her stands a young man, dressed – like the woman who's reading the book – in sober subfusc colours. He is positioned – possibly – several feet behind the girl, and looks towards her. She holds a white parasol, and doesn't see, or affects not to see, the man. He holds himself tall and erect with his two thumbs stuck into the pockets of his waistcoat; he has a rash of sidewhiskers and a smudge of moustache. His attention is all for one person on this high-summer's day in 1876 much like all the other days in the season, with a light breeze ruffling the parasols and fast, fleecy clouds scudding up the Channel towards England.

*

What is to be discovered?

At a guess, it is the woman in stern black and purple who offers an entrée to the situation. Why is she seated that slight but judicious distance apart from the children's parents?

Is she a family friend – why then apart? She doesn't have the confidence in her manner that a *sister* of the parents would be possessed of. She might instead be a *cousin*. So much black in her beach attire – that and the veil folded back – indicate a summer version of widow's weeds. Perhaps financial and social anxieties have brought her here to Trouville, at her cousins' invitation of course: her son is the one means she has of securing a safe and dependable and respectable future for them both. And isn't it a most fortuitous coincidence that her cousins' attractive daughter is as yet unspoken for...

Or perhaps the situation is really rather different? Her only son, with almost indecent haste after his father's recent decease, has shown himself smitten by the girl. What insensitivity! But the mother cannot afford to lose the sympathy of her son, so she has followed him here, having played on her cousins' respectful sentiments and solicited an invitation from them. Such behaviour on her part is untypical but, in the circumstances, expedient. She is neither her cousins' social superior nor inferior: it is enough that she believes an attachment between their respective progeny is not at all suitable or seemly at this juncture. Anyway, who knows what the future might offer her son in the way of introductions to other young women, perhaps of a higher social placing on the

Parisian pyramid? So she determinedly sits as one of the company in her widow's mourning, to remind them all: we must show restraint in my dear lost husband's name, for his hallowed memory's sake, please!

*

The widow is the clue to the meaning. But the *reason* for the artist's notice and the resulting tableau of the group, committed to canvas, *that* lies elsewhere. It resides in the comely representation of the girl, sitting at an angle to the others, eyes tantalisingly shaded under a trim white parasol, with her sleeves minutely buttoned to her wrists and a straw hat sporting a bright yellow ribbon resting on her lap.

*

The figures exist both in *their* moment – of that year, 1876 – and also in this freeze-frame present, above the heads that stop to look at them in the French Room of an art gallery far from Normandy and Trouville. More than a century has gone by, but – as the watchers' eyes look – that interlude of one hundred and ten years seems neither here nor there.

*

The picture poses a question, several questions, and the artist – only a few years older than the girl at the time he painted it – lures us into the web of hypotheses he's spun.

He comes to the beach every day. In the mornings and evenings he works on his canvas in the studio of the house he has rented for the summer. After lunch he leaves the house and comes to the beach to replenish his imagination, to study the same faces he sees every day, to – surreptitiously – sketch, sitting low in his canvas chair with his knees raised both to stop the pages fanning in the breeze from the sea and to protect his own secrecy. Perhaps even the sketching is a pretence, to himself if not to them, who may have failed as yet to notice him.

But he doesn't believe that his presence has gone wholly unnoticed, not by everyone. Why does the young man so seldom sit? – thumbs in his waistcoat pockets, is he afraid of losing what he feels is his advantage of height over the girl, and over anyone who may be watching? Can his mother be

317

quite so absorbed in her book? – why are her mouth and jaw quite so restive? Is it merely chance that the girl sits where she does – on the perimeter edge of the group, with her chair turned at such a telling angle away from her parents and the others, facing towards himself, the stranger?

*

What happened to them all after Trouville, when the summer was done?

If the widow's heart was set on a marriage, perhaps it did take place? Or – by an alternative reading – maybe she saved her son from making a terrible mistake by persuading him that the girl was too wilful, too coquettish almost, and she convinced him he should seek elsewhere? In which case, marriage being an expectation and obligation, he wed someone else, not quite so handsome or showy but rather more predictable, and he doted on his new wife: for a while, that is, until his spaniel eyes were turned by another woman of a stronger character. An indiscretion (or several) may have been committed on his part, but most likely the relationship survived, just, with its open secrets – a touch-and-go marriage.

Unlike *hers*, the girl with the crocus-yellow ribbon on her hat. Very probably in the years that followed she caught the attention of an older man, one who appreciated the virtues of the fresh and spring-like in a young woman, plus a frisson of the surprising. He was a well-to-do widower perhaps, who – a decorous interval having now passed since his first, tubercular wife 'passed over' – decided that his children should have another, healthier mother and that *he* might dare to be a little more adventuresome in his choice this time.

His second wife was admired by all, and he soon realised she required careful handling: not to be put on too tight a rein, but neither should she be given her head. Married to him, and not unhappily, she inherited a family, and subsequently added more offspring of her own. The family came back to these beaches of her youth, not to a rented villa but to one they owned, and in the sad and fateful far future it was in the same war-ravaged Normandy that she lost two of her four sons. But that was a long way off: Time taking from her as it had given, history's malison on two, three generations. In the years before, she forgot – as well as she could – about

318

wars, as they'd tried to forget about the fighting with Prussia in the early days when she'd come with her family and Governess Doury, to take the bracing air of Trouville into their lungs, as recommended to them by their doctor.

Her parents' cousin's son never entered her thoughts either, then – when she was beside the sea with her husband and their children – or at any other time: except once, once only, one night in Paris when she caught sight of him from a cab and recognised him, leaving a restaurant among a party of men in evening capes: they were fawning on the woman who led the way, like a pied piper, a temptress, charming them from their wives and homes, a famous luminary of the dramatic stage in a blue velvet fish-tail gown and ostrich feathers. Apart from that one incident, she had no cause to remember.

And perhaps had no cause to remember someone else from that period in her life – 'seventy-five or 'seventy-six – the man with the sketch pad who'd presented himself on the beach every day, always *after* the family had settled beneath their umbrellas and parasols, sitting low in his chair and watching. Always watching. While she – coyly shading her eyes against the sun – smiled in his direction so inscrutably.

But afterwards, the august painter preferred to think, she *couldn't* have forgotten. Why else, on that August morning in Trouville almost twenty years later when he recognised her leading a family party from the gate of a villa, out on to the promenade, why did she hesitate, pause, turn to him as he stood to attention, canvas and portable easel tied with ropes to his bicycle, his breath caught in his throat, his heart hurting on his ribs?

*

There is the possibility that, when the artist had earned his fame and she could only walk with the aid of a stick – long after the deaths of her soldier sons – she saw the picture in one of the Paris shows of his work.

After the War she'd never returned to Normandy, to Trouville Plage. Conceivably her eyesight was too poor for her to see more of the picture than the sky, clouds, breeze, a blur of people: too many people.

*

And the artist, whose shoulder we're looking over, whose eyes we're seeing through, how did *he* view the scene when the clothes and parasols had become quaint and Trouville town had slipped out of fashion again?

He hardly remembered. He saw a straw hat with a yellow ribbon and a girl sitting alone with her unconcern, whose best years are still ahead of her; he saw the widow's dark-clad son in the throes of first love. He failed to see himself: all his life and work had been a statement of the wish to be *included* – but he'd always known better, that if he *were* to be included, drawn in and defined, he must cease to paint and cease to be his own true self. Whenever he looked at that early painting – 'Sur la Plage à Trouville' – he preferred to concentrate on the features of its composition, on the colours, the quality of the brush strokes. If the picture and its subjects had ever meant more to him than that, he told himself he'd forgotten; and so – with time – he'd passed from such a youthful exercise to other, greater things.

An Evening in Granada

Seen from the window the garden is still, composed,
as if it's only waiting. Waiting for...? Nothing stirs, she
might be looking at a photograph. She lays her hands on the
window glass. Her eyes are fixed on the entrance from the
street, between gateposts. 'A drink, Louise?' She tucks back a
loose strand of hair. 'So, what kind of day have you had?' She
watches the traffic on the street, seeing through herself, sea-
cotton blouse, silk scarf, neat cuffs, gold chain. 'Whisky,
please.' She's running downstairs, like a girl, hair flying and
heels screeching, laughing. The car door slams. A blue car,
hidden in shrubbery. Is everything to be secret? She half-
wishes otherwise. 'What kind of day have you had, Louise?'
She might be looking through the window at a photograph.
She lays her hand on the pane of glass. A white car, Paul's
car, sprawls on the gravel. On the trees leaves are budding,
showing green, *another* spring and she can laugh at it. 'You
make me young, Lou, you *do!*' Hair flying and heels screeching, to hell with secrets. 'How long have we got?' 'Six
o'clock, we eat at seven, Paul and I, we live by the clock,
you've no idea...' Running downstairs, laughing. 'Relax!
Listen, there's a hotel I know...' 'But this is better. In my
own home. This scares me.' 'You're crazy, Lou, you know
that? A mad lady.' She tucks back a loose strand of hair. 'Six
o'clock, we have a drink, we eat at seven, Paul and I, you've
no idea...' She smiles. 'What do you *do* all day?' She laughs.
'I watch the garden.' She lays her hand on the window glass.
'I just watch, and I wait.' She sees through herself. Unbuttons
the cuffs. The sea-cotton blouse slips from her shoulders. He
tucks back a loose strand of her hair. She rolls her head on
her neck. '*Belle de Jour, n'est-ce pas?*' 'But what on earth do
you *do* all day?' She unlinks the chain. 'I watch the garden.'

She smiles. 'I just wait.' She looks over her naked shoulder. There's green on the trees. 'A drink, Louise?' *Louise*, that name, it belongs with his other possessions in this house, not her own home at all. She tucks back a loose strand of hair. 'Whisky, Paul. Please.' In the garden nothing stirs, it might be a photograph. 'So, what kind of day have you had?' She fingers the cuffs of her blouse, she walks over to the shelves of records. Not her own home at all. 'Is there anything you want to hear?' She turns on the lamp. She smiles. 'Whisky, please.' Running downstairs. '... anything you want to hear...' '*You* choose, Louise.' Running like a girl. Debussy: *Soirée dans Grenade*. 'Six o'clock, we have a drink, eat at seven, Paul and I, we live by the clock.' 'Is there anything you want to hear?' '*You* choose, Louise.' She smiles. She turns on the lamp. *Soirée dans Grenade*. She tucks back a loose strand of hair. '*Belle de Jour, n'est-ce pas?*' A blue car, hidden in shrubbery. 'This is better, this scares me.' She watches him leave. Seen from the window, the garden is still, composed. A white car, Paul's, sprawls on the gravel at an angle. She lays her hand on the window glass. 'Between six o'clock and seven.' 'Whisky, Paul. Please.' She watches the traffic on the street. She sees through herself. Sea-cotton blouse, silk scarf. She smiles. Neat cuffs, gold chain. 'So, what kind of day have you had?' The garden is still, composed, as if it's only wait-ing. Waiting for...? The tumbler is in her hand, shattered crystal. A stone breaks the window, the rug glitters with splinters of glass. She smiles. The stone is wrapped in paper. She laughs. Like a girl. 'A STEPPING-STONE TO YOUR HEART.' 'A drink, Louise?' She lays her hand on the window glass. Seen from the window, the garden ... She turns on the lamp. She sees through herself. 'Whisky, please. Paul.' Run-ning downstairs. ' – drink, eat at seven – ' *Soirée dans Grenade*. ' – we live by the clock – ' Her eyes are fixed on the entrance from the street, between the gateposts. 'I watch, and I wait.' A blue car, his, hidden in shrubbery. '*Belle de Jour, n'est-ce pas?*' A white car, her husband's, claiming the driveway. 'This is better, this scares me.' He tucks back a loose strand of her hair. 'What kind of day have you had, Louise?' She smiles. She turns on the lamp. She walks over to the shelves of records. 'You're crazy, Lou, like a mad lady.' She smiles. 'Is there anything you want to hear?' She touches the gold chain at her throat. '*You* choose, Louise.' That name. A stone breaks the window. Debussy. Glass splashes on the rug. 'Listen, there's a hotel I know ...' *Soirée dans Grenade.* 'Relax!' She laughs like a girl, unwraps the stone. 'A STEPPING-STONE TO YOUR HEART.' She turns on the lamp. 'I watch. And I wait.' The tumbler is in her hand, shattered crystal. From the window the garden is very still, composed, as if ... She lays her hand on the window glass. 'I just wait.' Nothing stirs, she might be looking at a photograph. 'What kind of day have you had, Louise?' She smiles. '*Belle de Jour, n'est-ce pas?*' Living by the clock, Paul and she. She watches the traffic on the street. A white car, Paul's car, sprawling on the gravel. Leaves are budding on the trees, she smiles, showing green. 'I just wait.' Another spring, and she can laugh at it. She lays her hand on the window glass. The tumbler is in her hand, in Granada, shattered crystal. '*You* choose, Louise.' A stone wrapped in paper breaks the window. First, she smiles. She tucks back a loose strand of hair. The window pane explodes, shards fly. Then, like a girl, she laughs. Shards like snapped icicles, the rug glitters, now she's walking on glass.

Begun at Midnight
Divertissement
Fludde's Ark

Begun at Midnight

Correspondence of an Intimate Nature
from the Sender Mr J.S. to Mr Trotwood
Copperfield Esquire

'Daisy', I was going to call you, *Dear Daisy, My Dearest Daisy*, as if you were my property, but No, it doesn't seem right that I should do so now, not now. Those We Were seem stranger to me than if they were lodging with me here in this most dismal rooming-house (called the Anchor, if you will believe it), & they are the queerest bunch and what jinx we might have had!! at their expense if things had been the way they used to be, in that
  'dark backward and abysm of time'
We were indeed such Good Friends, Daisy – or Trotwood, or David or Davy should I call you as My Poor Wife did sometimes of an evening when the mood caught her just so and she could not stay her mind from taking that track back. I think I must call her My Wife too, because if I say Emily or Em'ly the word is salt in my wound, and Davy, you must believe me, I am a carcass riddled with those wheals that shall never close, and if you could feel burning on your skin, Daisy, even one-hundredth of those distractions it drives me to, the worst unspeakable horrors, you might be moved to feel sorrow and pity for your Old Friend James Steerforth, who can be your Friend no more, which makes him fear himself and suffer his frenzys over doubly so.

And this night, Daisy or Davy should I say, if it rains like this in London I fear the streets really must be mud slides & the city will tilt into the river. In Calais the windows and doors shake as if a fist beats on them & hail rattles down the chimney and falls hissing on the grate. Its the most God-less night, and the birds don't fly – even the Storm Petrels of that name – and if I ever wished (As I did oftentimes, and you to hear me Davy) I had the coat-tails of some Faith to hold on to, then it surely is this night.

In an inn once, Daisy, where we met — it was a fortuitous Accident, that one, oh the happiest!! —
> *''Tis far off, and like a dream ...'*
— and I called that your room should be exchanged for one next to mine and I came in when you were settled, and we talked, Daisy, for how long into the night was it? You knew then that your friend J.S. was a castaway — 'a lone lorn Creatur' — and he was complicated by the *emptiness* that was inside him. I told you then that a parent of indomitable will (as the writers say) is a very Devil to live your life with & steals from you your spirit back as if it was a forfeited gift. And yet I wonder too if you plumb'd fully down to the depths of J.S.'s nature?

> 'There was a boy went into a barn,
> He lay down on some hay;
> An owl came out and flew about ...'

—Daisy, *I wanted to stay with you that night*. And now you know it. But even that confession brings only a wistful smile to your face as you peruse this by a comfortable fire, a disposition such as yours is can not see the harm I might have been intending you. Its the very harmlessness I wish back, to *turn my-self to You*, by some Alchemy, but I meant to destroy you too. Emily was as close as I might reach to you, but Daisy I ruined her, and it is what I wd have done to you also. She was my Mother, and she was Rosa, and she was all the Young Ladies of quality coaxed out to Highgate that I should learn to make love to them, and also she was You, Daisy, more than any of them. I say it so no one else can hear, with the wind rumbling in the chimney's belly & the sea spray spewing down the windows and the caterwauling inn-sign turning cartwheels on its pole. When we were a-bed even, Emily and I, and it should shame me to write you that, but you were the flesh I played between my fingers.

So now you know it, the worst there is to tell. I suffered that child Emily, not for love of her But because in her thankful and wondering eyes like a glass I saw a boy on Yarmouth sands. In Rome she watched with care the women with their painted faces (I speak of my Emily again) but there was the bloom of springtide life in her too, the swell of all fresh growing things, & to me yr innocence is truly *daisy*-like, you are compleat in yr Being, perfectly.

But I by the mischance of my birth and father-less condition am not so. In Cambridge my dark days began, or just before, escaping the house with Littimer's contrivances and staying out later and later on the Heath lured into compy of the basest kind. I discovered currents beneath the flow of ordinary things, v. dangerous swift-running tides, & I tell you a man can lose his strength in these. 1stly I went to loud, riotous taps, and Littimer directed me to houses where I met some pretty boys & learned how the Mandarins in China smoke their bubble pipes, and from there it was an easy decline. Sometimes she saw the prodigal's return, Rosa, like a nightgown'd sentry at her window, watching how I sailed in a fog; and her mouth threw me an ugly smile as if she could know what I was suffering.

I bought boys in Oxford, Davy. And I did it with no more thought than I bought an apple or an orange when I went strolling through the market, and my appetite was an ache and my eye saw what it liked. A lad cost me 6d, and I might have had a basket of Bartlett's for that, or *Cox's*, or the seeds that put me to sleep when I couldn't sleep, but no taste seemed comparable to me with that sweetness of a young streetboy's c—k.

My mouth could never have said these truths to you, Daisy, and I shall regret p'haps this Confidence *Begun at Midnight*, a Hell-hag of a night with a tempest howling at my door, But it was needing to be told to you. So maybe it is, for that, the wind claws underneath the eaves & bites & tears & tries to rip the roof from over my head. And this infernal moaning always in the flu, like a terrible thing bricked up there, the Hell-kite. Remember, *You kill what you hold most dear for very love of it.* We Steerforths are stern and solid (and so, secretive stock), and I think we suffer wonderfully. Now I ask myself, did we say an honest word to each other in that big, bald, bleak barracks of a house on the hill? I speak of it as if it were a time of memory only, & there is nothing to come and

329

so it can not be reclaimed. I fear that it is too late, and the Steerforths will not surrender to superstition now and say a miracle is possible. I think, Daisy, it would need that – a miracle.

The French are famous for their *Letters*, although I doubt that the report has reached you yet. (I pray it has not; & very earnestly. I time my jokes badly.) I also hear it said, the delivery of foreign correspondence is not to be trusted to the services of riders in this country. That certainly is no fiction. I mean to carry you with me, Daisy, tucked beneath my waist-coat; wrapt snug beneath my shirt. You shall nestle warmly there, on the hairy hummock of my breast, til I charge you go with speed and the safe conduct of a sturdy, sober English-fellow, a 2nd Mr Barkis if another exists like that good soul you made me think I knew as a friend.

And THEY have appeard again in the fire, all those worthy faces, and the fine places you took me to. Til the sea-coal shifts in the grate and a lump at the back splits, and the rush of sparks is doused by a drenching of rain. It was a happy time, Davy, & I wrecked it – because that is all there is left to do to happiness. I saw it becoming a heavy sickness, a great leaden fever that must sap the life from us. Or else I would have believed we might have continued just like that, for ever; and I had to discover what were the weaknesses it contained. Emily it was who was the most frail link, not so strong even as Mrs Gummidge with her handkerchiefs, & then my evil seemed not that at all but a functioning of nature as the old Order crumbled in, like a bank of coal in a hearth, as if it was obliged to happen and only the occasion had lacked.

Dont blame me all you might, Daisy, I beg you not to; for the sake of the Friends we were. I did so much Harm, to preserve what so transcended even that excellent life you brought me to, down there in what you called your Old Country; I mean to say, what lifted us beyond that simple joy of theirs, the Love that we bore to each other.

And if only now I learn we weren't apart from it, but *a part* of it (that charm'd ring), spare one single second's kind thought in a day of reviling me, and believe (if you ever could) that I acted for the only good I knew, which was to quiet the torments racking your chastened friend, like a head-ful of scorpions which come snapping and snarling —

Jesus wept, I did it because I took the thing you loved (because you knew no better) & meaning us to become two, her and me, I thought I must become the object that YOU loved, your Love-Object. Men who have the fault which I have, Daisy, frequently they desire to become that object of their Affection, so they might impersonate him, as well as they can. In our intimate act which satisfied me very little, I had yr Emily call me 'Daisy'; she imagined it was just a whim, and she played on it because it seemed to rouse me when nothing else would, But I disturbed her when I called out 'Ah Davy!!' once, shooting my seed into her faster than I had ever done.

She couldn't know the tunnels of love (as they are called) I had travelled before, and it was as well she did not. I pre-ferred to take my laddies, when we had our commerce in little lanes, arse out, c——k firm against a wall. But she thought I was a gentleman. And – strangest of all to say – looking up into my eyes from underneath she really did see YOU, because you were always whom we talked about afterwards. So, you were with us all the time when you couldnt have known it, in our minds, and in the unsteady trading of our bodies that was a torture to me but thus gratefully done.

I write this by a hurricane lamp. There are no ships to sail from this harbour til Friday, and it is Tuesday now.

> *'Eeny, weeny, winey, wo,*
> *Where do all the Frenchmen go?'*

Unless I find one from Spain or Portugal that shall, and they say I can. The wine would kill a dog, but it is the loneliest place in the world, and sometimes I imagine that where England is – or where we are told it is – there is really nothing. Then I think that would be better than my returning there. My going is as futile as a moth's path to this flame would be; but it is nature, and I can not resist it. I think the wine must also clear my head, Daisy, I see that going to or coming from – England or any place on the earth's skin – its all one, and I am the bearer of my ill-fortune like a shell on my back, I sail my own little bark.

> *'I see the moon, and the moon sees me,*
> *God bless the men who sail out to sea.'*

But I don't like the wee fiendies' zeal, Daisy, pricking at me with their toasting forks because they think I'm coming down to stay. Ppooooff!! There are angels, too, although I do not know the words they speak and the light must burn my eyes to look at them; constant and true, not sputtering as this flame does because suddenly we have moved into the teeth of the storm and it slams down on us, the sea is hungry, and I can feel the walls are buckling outwards and the floor is splitting under me —

And I wonder, Daisy, if it is not too late to do a shining thing, before the candl

Divertissement

This story belongs to the topsy-turvy days of a new age, the 1950s.

Every Sunday afternoon and three evenings in each week 'entertainments' took place in the main lounge of the hydropathic hotel, situated somewhere in a Scottish county of rolling heather-hills.

The previous entertainments manager, the aptly-named Mr Moody, had had too much of the actor about him ('Ac-tor', as he had pronounced it), and in the end people hadn't been able to feel they quite *trusted* him. He'd become the living subject of umpteen stories, apocryphal and otherwise. Latterly his failings had been rather more on display, and ceased to be purely apocryphal. He had a talent for employing the untalented, or the inappropriate, or the downright dregs. For instance, a husband and wife garbed in Highland dress were explaining the rudiments of the 'Duke of Perth' reel when they begged to differ with each other over one of the steps, and the difference of opinion flared into a quarrel: the husband lapsed into guttural, pulled the skean-dhu from his stocking, brandished it at his wife's frilly jabot in a most alarming manner, and the police had to be called. Sometime later the famous Mr Moody hired a lieder singer to help improve his kudos in the hydro, but her lot was at an even lower ebb than his and in the course of her third recital, as her audience fidgeted and as library books were cracked open and the bits shaken out of scrabble bags, the poor harassed soprano succumbed to a very public nervous breakdown: her face had to be slapped, repeatedly, before she could be brought under anything like control. The piper at a Burns' Night Supper stood too close to a candle, and his kilt took the flame and caught fire – the din as the bagpipes were dropped and trodden on in the stampede was never to be forgotten. The entertainments manager, further down on his luck, intrepidly tempted fate by devising a very ambitious project, a pantomime, and attending to the casting in April: come rehearsals in December, his Cinderella was found to be eight months pregnant, and in performance she needed the help of the Ugly Sisters and Buttons *and* the Prince to rise from the milkmaid's stool in the ashes of the fireplace to try on the glass slipper, in a scene of agonising longevity and suspense.

Mr Moody had had to go. Mr Gilfillan, permitting the Cinderella pun, was a new broom. Under his regimen Scottish country dancing was still a very dependable attraction. New acts had been introduced: a comic monologuist, a flower-arranger, a mind-reader, a pair of Old Time dancing experts hired for an exhibition display, a paper-folder, a conjurer in top-hat and opera cloak, a husband and wife comic turn ('Mr and Mrs Aberdeen') who attempted impersonations of 'The McFlannels' and others. The palm court trio was the staple, of course: no self-respecting hydro with standards to maintain would have allowed itself to be without one. Tenors, unlike women singers, were always popular (Scottish songs and, if possible, one or two Neapolitan lollipops: 'Funiculi, Funicula' complemented 'Flow On, Sweet Afton' very nicely). Failing that, a pianist helped to fill in most people's time quite pleasantly. Unfortunately, holding an audience's concentration was always a problem with a solo instrument: the piano tended to fare better than a harp or a clarsach, or a clarinet, or the less refined accordion (Mr Gilfillan had once mistakenly called on the services of kilted 'Jock Dalrymple and His Auld Squeezebox', but never again).

Curiously, it often happened that the performances which went down best were those the audience and Mr Gilfillan had least hopes for: the ventriloquist, for example, or the balloon man, or the two Rumanian acrobats (brothers, they'd claimed, but some of the audience, like Mr Gilfillan, had clearly had their doubts as they sat watching their contorted pairings, with their hearts in their mouths).

Mr Gilfillan was a young-ish man who told himself he had

the confidence to take (and survive) risks. His latest booking was also a first-time novelty for the hydro: a hypnotist.

*

Mr Farrell was from England. His stage name was 'The Mesmerising Dr Mesmer'. He turned out to be a meeker and more reserved man than expected; unflamboyant, decidedly untheatrical even with his height. He had a vague face, and vague mannerisms, nothing at all about him was insistent. Clutching his well-travelled suitcase, he seemed – he *seemed* – the sort of person destined to be forgotten. During his brief overnight stay for his engagement at the hydro he spoke to none of the staff or guests, and was indistinguishable from his background.

Mr Gilfillan had questioned him a little on the telephone beforehand, about what he – and an audience – might expect.

'My act is psychological,' Mr Farrell told him.

The entertainments manager nodded his head to give himself encouragement.

'I see,' he said, but failed to see.

'An intimate act of regression, back to the true self. And after the hypnosis my subjects, they will feel – relieved.'

Hmm. Well, that *could* be baloney, but reports he'd picked up on had been favourable.

'Do they remember anything of what's happened?' Mr Gilfillan asked.

'I trust not. But they'll believe they've made some kind of mental journey in the absence of consciousness, one which causes them a sense of satisfaction – fulfilment.'

'I see.'

'No one can be hypnotised who does not want to be.'

'I see.'

Mr Gilfillan did *not* understand: but then how could he, if the man was claiming his skill was in the way of a science? All that concerned him, he told himself, was that an audience should enjoy itself. Would Mr Farrell be esteemed a success?

*

The principal management were somewhat alarmed at the prospect, Mr Gilfillan could tell: but he had, as the saying goes, a good track record.

335

'Let us wait and – and see,' he advised, figuratively crossing his fingers.

On that particular Sunday afternoon there was an impressive turn-out, so considerable in fact (fifty or thereabouts) that the lounge became quite crowded and every window had to be opened, for what air could be coaxed in from the garden.

The audience consisted not only of guests; the staff had been discussing the event days in advance and Mr Gilfillan watched as between a dozen and twenty of them entered the room and stood at the back when most of the guests were already settled. The under-manager was there, and Mrs McArdle the secretary, and the overseer of catering; collectively, and diplomatically, they turned blind eyes to the two chefs in white hats and the two uniformed under-housekeepers and assorted maids and the representative of the laundry women and the handful of waiters and the second porter from the hall, all of them unable to suppress their curiosity.

When the trio had stopped playing, Mr Gilfillan made the short opening announcement in his 'front-of-house voice'; and at the end of it (as he always declaimed) dared to hope that the audience would enjoy the 'diversion' that had been arranged for them. Then, as welcoming applause rippled round the room, he positioned himself against a wall to watch.

Farrell appeared (to the immediate disappointment of those anticipating a vizier) wearing a lounge suit and looking very insignificant. His first words were softly pitched but, at the same time, they were distinct and articulate; so much so that the general disappointment at his appearance mysteriously and rapidly ebbed, to be replaced by that initial curiosity and interest. Farrell, or 'Dr Mesmer', spoke a little about the ease with which mental resistance could be overcome in the matter of hypnosis. He told his audience that a sleeping spell could be brought on in the middle of the waking state: what was required was applied concentration on absolutely nothing at all, and the eyes' fixing on any suitably neutral, lulling, almost-inert object: say, the grandfather clock, or the grate in the fire (had it been lit), or the convex fish-eye of mirror above the fireplace, or the watery, dapple-like glare from the gilt fittings on the centre lights above them, as the sun shone reflections on to the ceiling.

There was silence in the room as all the heads turned, including Mr Gilfillan's, to regard what had previously been no more than the most ordinary artefacts and effects.

'But this is the favourite of all,' Farrell announced, drawing a gold watch and chain from his waistcoat pocket.

Some of the audience murmured recognition.

Farrell, 'The Mesmerising Dr Mesmer', then offered assurances that his intent was not to embarrass or cause distress: that sensitivity was a byword with him, that no one in the room had any cause to be fearful. Rather, they were all in safe hands (at the word 'all' there was a pronounced shifting of bodies and limbs in chairs).

'Your safety is in your *own* hands, ladies and gentlemen.'

(Further creaks of limbs and furniture.)

Several heads were already on the point of nodding off in the intense heat of the afternoon; some other guests were waving lace handkerchiefs in front of their faces, or fanning themselves with newspapers. Farrell must have taken that as a broad hint that he should begin.

The volunteers were first: a man seated beside his resolutely-unbelieving wife, then a doughty, dauntless widow normally never done telling of her travels, to the Orinoco and beyond, and thirdly a teenage girl who'd seemed anxious all week to have nothing whatsoever to do with her family. The process of catalepsy took no more than seconds for each of them. The room was hushed as Farrell then started to move from the front seats towards the next row, watch and chain held high in front of him. More heads dropped forward or rolled back. Behind those heads, others succumbed: like – like a rush of some – some tropical sleeping-sickness, it woozily occurred to Mr Gilfillan as he fought to keep his eyes open. Row by row, on and on, the heads gently tipped this way or that. Row by row by

Mr Gilfillan saw the under-manager staring at the swinging watch on its chain – the light was catching the gold case in such a way, at such an angle, that there seemed to be the strength of the sun contained in it. Sunspots danced in front of Mr Gilfillan's eyes: he couldn't hear the words, he only knew they were perfectly soothing. Some of the maids seemed to be asleep on their feet. One of the two housekeepers was trying to resist as Farrell came closer but the other had her hand on her friend's arm, and its contact appeared to still her.

No one out of all their number had keeled over, and it was the last thing Mr Gilfillan felt he was conscious of: that, and seeing how the room, the whole room was succumbing, in no time at all, as if time had lost its meaning...and noticing, just, the beads of perspiration on the temple of an elderly woman guest's face, watching them trickle slowly, so slowly...

*

A very strange sight it must have been, but neither Mr Gilfillan nor anyone else witnessed it.

As the temperature soared on this baking mid-July afternoon the hydro lounge seemed to be time-frozen, just like a photograph. Outside the windows birds sang, a fountain gently poppled water into a stone bowl sculpted like a raised clam shell; further off a car engine whined to life, there was the crack of an axe splitting wood, once, twice, three times.

The rose-patterned curtains blew at the open windows. The leaves of the standard palms in their brass pots flexed. Insects hovered in draughts of air. Otherwise all appeared still, without movement. Time was on the blink.

The room's quietude might have been declaring the very end and cessation of the mortal world.

Here seemed to be the stasis of death itself.

But only 'seemed to be', however, because the repose was that of a deep, numbing slumber: not the ultimate, marble-cold oblivion of death.

Gradually limbs twitched, bodies agitated in the hold of their chairs, eyelids fluttered, life pulsed back into veins and ventricles, wrists throbbed, hearts stuttered, the pumping mechanism was triggered, slowly the feeling returned to extremities. Eyes opened, the room displayed its curious panorama of discomposed bodies and general torpor. The first thoughts struggled to rise from the brain's mud-slurp sloth, the first words floated up like bubbles.

It was like the return to the element of the living, from nirvana or from limbo.

Mr Gilfillan fumbled towards daylight, consciousness, prising his eyes open, catching his breath.

What had happened? How could he have lost consciousness, when *he'd* had responsibility for the afternoon?

He remembered ... the gold watch on its chain, the beads of perspiration ... and then ... nothing ... nothing ...

*

No one knew how long had passed.

An automatic gesture was to consult a watch, watch*es*, your own, the next person's.

Each timepiece in the room told the time as approximately fourteen minutes after the point at which the session of (voluntary? involuntary?) mass hypnosis had started.

Later the rest of the world caught up with them, or vice versa, wrist and pendant and waistcoat watches were checked against Big Ben's peals on the wireless. Unless there was a greater temporal conspiracy afoot, the watches showed the true time by Greenwich. Why then should so many of the persons present suspect that a longer lapse of time had occurred than fourteen minutes or so? (Some of them still felt dazed and befuddled the next day, as if they'd woken from a long deep sleep of hours on end.)

A total of fourteen minutes had passed. In the lounge watches were double-checked against the grandfather clock, then against one another. No, that was all. Fourteen minutes, almost exactly: eight hundred and forty seconds, give or take a dozen or a score. An unexplained interval of time, but surely not long enough to have caused this ocean-drop into a night's sleep? A gap that puzzled reason, and also no time at all really.

Everyone was waking, in a room they recognised, in company they were familiar with, another fourteen minutes further on. After a nap they were ready to begin again, to take up the cudgels of ordinary breathing life on whichever side of the divide they belonged, guests or staff, although everyone – doesn't the Bible say? – serves in their own way. All just as before, and waking revived, refreshed.

And yet ...

*

And yet everything was slightly, but crucially, different.

On the dais behind the palms the violinist realised he was holding the cellist's bow, and the cellist his. In front of the pianist a different piece of music lay on the lid than had been there before. And hadn't he *opened* the lid to play?

A young woman looked down and saw she was wearing someone else's shoes. Her elderly neighbour discovered that the library book in her hands wasn't the one she'd been reading, and had been issued not in Perth but in Edinburgh.

Two men managed to take in, but only just, that they were wearing each other's crested ties.

A grande dame woke to find herself lolling against a wall instead of seated in state in her usual chair, which was now occupied by a maid. When the same distinguished lady turned her head she saw that she was in the company, not of those with whom she might deign to engage in conversation, but of other common maids and serving-hands.

A child was sitting on the fireplace fender with his feet in the empty, ornamental coal-bucket, but remembered – dimly – crouching behind a chair, preparing to ambush a tea-trolley.

A waiter jerked awake, put his hand in his back trouser pocket to cover his perplexity, and felt with his fingers the unaccustomed bulk of bank-notes. A woman guest's first instinct was to open her handbag, which was filled – not with what she expected to see, compact, handkerchief, emery board, keys, the ration card she took everywhere – but a weight of glass marbles, staring up at her like sheep's eyes.

A teenage girl was startled out of sleep by the under-manager's trousered leg grazing hers, and she immediately blushed, incredulous how she could have reached the sofa and dumb with embarrassment because there was no more handsome man in the hotel to be sitting beside.

A chef used to wrestling with the shortages of rations was holding a room key (to one of the best rooms, at that), and when the rear-admiral's widow opened her hand she disclosed to all and sundry who chanced to see – a pastry brush like those of her long-gone housekeeping days.

A father's head – until he knocked the sleep out of it and some sense and decency in – was resting on his pubescent daughter's shoulder. A teenage boy slumbered on on his mother's ample chest, while her guilt made her gasp to think what the company might be imagining.

Two husbands, business colleagues who came with their respective families every year, woke side by side, in the full consciousness that their flies were gaping open.

A maid sensed that her breasts were bare beneath her blouse, bare and aroused, and her eyes immediately sought the desired culprit – the porter called 'Jimmy'.

A grey-haired, granite-faced gentleman of the cloth found a girl's cheap crucifix and chain hanging from his dog-collar.

A kitchen orderly stared at the fashion magazine in her hands; she turned some pages and blinked at the shots of haughty, tippy models daring the camera lens.

A most demure, whey-faced young woman opened her embroidered lap-bag and gawped at the lipstick and face-paint stashed inside.

It dawned on a suffering husband that the car keys in his pocket weren't his, and he wished he could keep the fact from his wife.

A tight-skinned woman sitting alone found herself with a child's colouring-book on her lap and started to weep silent tears. Simultaneously the hydro's odd-job man sat holding a rag doll with rosy cheeks and a sunshine smile sewn to the face, and he looked dejected beyond words.

A male guest in too sharp country tweeds and too new brogues saw another person's blood oozing between his fingers and he blanched, not knowing how his secret could have been discovered.

Mr Farrell, 'The Mesmerising Dr Mesmer' – when everyone remembered to look – had gone.

*

No more hypnotists were engaged: neither Farrell, who'd simply disappeared (without being paid, which put a certain onus on the hotel), nor any other.

The event – whether openly referred to or not – quickly became apocryphal. The nervous management clung to the hope that, eventually, time would bring forgetfulness. In the meanwhile some guests who'd been in the lounge at the entertainment merely chose not to believe that any of it could

341

have taken place. Others – including a number of the staff – thought the experience almost mystical, in hindsight.

*

Ten or eleven days later a chambermaid called Bridie claimed she'd sighted the Holy Mother of Jesus in Room 316, stepping into the wardrobe. The girl had to be urgently despatched home, all the way back to County Wexford in Ireland.

*

Two of the guests, 'regulars', returned home to Troon on the Ayrshire coast, with the hypnotist's visit no more than an anecdote of memory for social conversation.

One was a woman in her seventies, whom the chambermaids referred to behind her back as 'The General'; the other was her daughter, called 'Wee Slavey', who functioned as her mother's eyes and (increasingly) her ears.

Marjorie was in her forties. She'd never *had* a life, she sometimes thought. She didn't blame anyone for that. Somehow everybody had just *presumed*, because her mother had such an invincible will . . .

She'd always existed merely in her mother's shadow. When he was alive her father hadn't been allowed to matter either; her mother had conducted a cold war with him for many years. He hadn't been a weak man, but he'd had an eye for the ladies.

That had turned her mother against men. She had only ever entertained her *female* friends in the spruce grey sandstone house an avenue back from the sea-front. She'd told Marjorie that men would only double-cross her and make a mess of everything. At no time had any young men been encouraged about the house, whatever their social credentials, and in those days her mother had had her spies planted everywhere.

Marjorie realised too well that she had missed out all along: too old during the War to lose her head, and ten years older now, past the age of men's interest. Quite often she wondered what would happen to her, with no one to care for, and no one to care for *her* once her mother . . .

At nights she had dreams, dreams of desire, and sometimes she was afraid to fall asleep. Her dreams would be there, she

342

knew, waiting: and the phantom lovers would be there too, waiting for their virginal inventor. Once she'd read about an author who'd written seven novels set in America and who, because of a childhood injury to her spine, had never been outside Kent in her life. *It may be*, the author had said, *that what you imagine is more true than any of the doing and going.*

In the third month succeeding the hypnotist's and her own visit to the hydro, Marjorie – her mother's 'Wee Slavey' – was obliged to make an appointment with a doctor, the private sort of course, and to travel up to his consulting rooms in the West End of Glasgow.

A further appointment was necessary. In the course of their second conversation the consultant announced to her what was an indisputable fact, that she was expecting a child.

She sat forward in her chair and stared at him, the famously virtuous and selfless Miss McQuarrie. She shook her head, from side to side, in the face of the doctor's reputation and knowledge. Technically it wasn't possible, such a thing, because she hadn't ever given herself to a man, or come anywhere near. Not ever in her life. So it just wasn't possible, it couldn't be.

By early January she was convinced her mother must soon see her condition for herself, even with her dimmed and failing sight. She already felt she was swollen like a tent, filled with wind.

Her muddle was such that she all but forgot about her annual summer's holiday at the hydro, although (if she'd thought about it) that was when the impossible must have happened. She all but forgot about the hypnotist, 'The Mesmerising Dr Mesmer', and his performance that was going to 'divert' them, and the unexplained loss of those fourteen minutes in the lounge, and everyone's groggy confusion at first. She almost forgot that her mother had woken with a pair of sugar tongs hanging from her deaf ear, and how very tactful she'd been in removing them, only wondering how she alone was more or less just as she had been before (except that she seemed to be as much *lying in* the sofa as *sitting on* it). But every new day for Marjorie McQuarrie had seemed destined to be the same as all those that had preceded it.

Until now.

She quite forgot that as she'd started awake beside her mother (*in* or *on* the sofa) she'd felt in those initial moments of awareness – she hadn't been quite sure *what* exactly, it was an unknown sensation – somehow uneasy in her stomach, unsteady, raw. The tubes at her fork were straining, quietly aching. Through tiredness? Or was it because of how she'd been positioned, as she slept, legs a little splayed? Or had it been the heat's doing, it must have been, the heat.

But now all that was forgotten too in the current train of events; in one sense it was lost time to her.

She was determined to disbelieve, only to accept this 'mountain' inside her belly as being a spoof, hocus-pocus, a trick of her body or a sleight of her imagination. The doctor must have made a dreadful, heedless mistake in his diagnosis.

But then one day she felt its first kicks. All that night she had to suffer its punches, as if it was waking from a long, long deep sleep.

Thereafter her thoughts turned to those pregnant women in the Bible, coming into the natural condition of God's ordained span. On that account, she told herself, everything *must* be under control: even if she did suspect she was going to be the exception to the rule.

She took to wearing full smocks and kept the house in as much darkness as she could, and didn't echo her mother's words and sympathise whenever she lamented the awfulness of old age, seeing and hearing so little.

Every morning and evening Marjorie McQuarrie would calculate and double-check how many weeks until the thirty-ninth, and the number of days left, and quite often in her sleep, in her sunken dreams, the faceless single men who stood on afternoon street corners waiting for her checked the time by fob watches on chains, which seemed to have the strength of the sun garnered in the gold.

344

Fludde's Ark

shooes from Mogull
shooes from Barbery
shooes to walk on Snow without finking

In the basement he diligently checked from the catalogues —
Tradescant's own of 1656 and a later one — as he packed the
objects away. Every day he filled a cardboard box with them
to take home. Even in Oxford, even in the Ashmolean — a
functioning museum, which made it a kind of miracle in 2017
— plundering the artefacts of the foremost Caroline collector,
he got away with it.

skades to flide with
sandals made of twigs

His superiors must have known, but they chose to say
nothing.

choppenes for ladyes from Malta and Venice
boxwood combs
Babylonian combs

He looked upon it as a last desperate, required act of pre-
servation.

Nunnes penitentiall Girdle of Haire
A lacrymaticall Urne for Teares, of glasse

He was well qualified to handle them at least, he knew what
he was doing, although old-fashioned newspapers — they'd
really only been bulletin sheets for political spiel once most of

the news had been censored out — these would have been useful and would have saved him the inevitable accidents.

> iron band worn by Cranmer
> charred end of a martyr's stake
> a Buddha — 'bhumi sparsa', calling the Earth to witness. under Bodhi-tree at Bodhgaya, when set on by hosts of Mara — a witness to his unshakable determination to find path of salvation for all sentient beings

He tried above all else to keep his mind resolute.

*

He'd reverted to the spelling of his name his ancestors used: *John Fludde*. He liked the look of it on letters he wrote. He seldom saw it on envelopes, though, because very few replies came back to him. Motor-cyclists carried the mail and often they were attacked by riders like modern highwaymen on faster, nimbler bikes. It was a sorry state of affairs and just part of life, but it was the reason he continued, keeping up the old forms, and now doubly so. A woman corresponded with him from the British Museum — the 'People's Palace' it had been for a decade — and when her one letter in every four got through he felt the sight of his name spelt like that, *John Fludde Esquire*, lifting his heart.

*

Oxford was in its dog days. A new Dark Age was upon them, and they wouldn't weather this one out in honeystone retreat.

Another volcano had burst the earth's skin and erupted, in the Caucasus this time, and the sky was noticeably darker than the last series of American explosions had turned it. It was several degrees colder too. Wars had become an anachronism with this new resentment against nations which haplessly showered the stratosphere with sulphur dust and blackened all their days.

He tried to imagine the skies before California and then Colorado blew up and, much longer ago than that, before engines and machines sent up their chemical ooze. The high vaulted sky of medieval Oxfordshire must have seemed like a

346

tunnel to those who were fated to live under it: for some an inspiration and spur to their curiosity and learning, and for others – the most of any age – a wonder they had to neglect, except for those brimstone hours on Sundays.

*

Every evening there were bonfires in Jericho, where the allotments used to be. He didn't like to think what was being burnt. Three times he'd seen dead babies floating in the canal from the little dutch bridge behind Kingston Road. Dogs howled, those that ran loose and had trained their sight to hunt by dusk and later. *To hunt and not be hunted*: the world had so vastly uncomplicated itself in his lifetime.

He did a detour with his cardboard box as he always did and lost the children on his tail. Sometimes they were very old children, with their heads shaved and painted and wearing their uniform of jerkins spiked with nails. It kept him fit for his fifty-plus years, jumping the broken spars of fences and the ditches like moats people dug around themselves, and even – twice it had happened, when the gangs came down from the north – picking his unsteady way along the roof on his terrace. Only the truly lithe and sure-footed deserved to survive.

Safe home, his life was as disciplined as a monk's in another century. He ate what there was to eat, still wrapped up in his coat and muffler; smoked a cheroot if he had one; played a record – Taverner, Byrd, Purcell – if there was current and enough of it; then, when it was darker, he double-locked the back door and padded down the garden in his slippers – he was particular to be quiet about it – to the old brick warehouse he used to rent until the landlord disappeared.

Inside he got down to his job. He was building a boat, though no one was meant to know in this time of no-secrets. He took the historical perspective as always: ages ago the lathe and wood-turning had been gentlemanly pursuits, and he dared to think he kept a convention alive. He banged as noiselessly as he could, swathing his hammer-blows with blankets. It was a queer vessel: an old holiday cabin-cruiser he and a couple of colleagues had dug out of the canal mud and then hauled back here on ropes one night, between midnight and dawn. The other two, Jarvis and Pearce, had smiled at his plans, in time they'd learned to call it 'a noble venture' to please him. (And then one night, quite suddenly and unannounced, they'd both made their get-away from Oxford with their families, and he hadn't heard from either of them since.)

The boat had a comically top-heavy look. He'd extended the little cuddy back to the rudder and enclosed it; he'd taken off the roof and built another which doubled its height. Inside he'd fitted up a single berth for himself and tilted shelves for the things he was taking with him. The navigation was simple, primitive. He was only a carrier after all, a preserver, and his destination was unimportant. He would make for higher ground, but it scarcely mattered where.

*

From the window at the back of the house he could see by the fires' light the canal slopping between its banks, spilling over in places where the ground had crumbled away or been sabotaged. Already a couple of the lowest-lying terraces down beneath the shell of Saint Barnabas' were under water and abandoned, and he'd seen the looters begin their vulture work there. Everyone seemed to get to hear the bad news and they responded by instinct, hiding themselves away or ganging together to make a stake. Nerves were raw and fretted, and the ends were becoming desensitised with their exposure. From behind a curtain he'd watched some of the groups fighting for their patch, the booty they'd recovered forgotten about – or they'd deliberately smashed it up, so no one would have a claim on it.

In the mornings they were always gone and he'd look again from behind the curtain's cover. He'd adjusted to the permanently soupy twilight they lived in, just as he had to the cold and the chilblains and mouth sores. He watched as smoke curled across the waste of allotment ground, wreathing it like river mist. The brilliantly green profusion of scrub in the sooty dawn half-light told him Oxford was returning again to its endemic condition, marsh and bog. He must always be oddly satisfied by what he saw at the start of every day, knowing history with its symmetries and ironies hadn't forgotten them yet and that they merely moved according to a patient plan.

*

More and more the radio news couldn't be proved or disproved. Mostly it was statistics and what official reports had concluded and information about food availability which must alter from hour to hour.

He heard other things in the museum. These had more the flavour of their age. An entertainer was on tour with a tribe of his followers, who slept on wet grass and rooted vegetables from fields and made pillaging expeditions into villages; someone had seen him hacking a girl's hand off during a performance. A duchess in her seventies stripped for male callers in her Belgravia drawing-room. They were eating their own turds down in the country. One of the Royals had escaped from detention at Balmoral. In July snow had blown blizzards in Spain. *My Fair Lady* was being revived to satisfy the 'aristocracy' craze. Cattle grazed in the lush and weedy centre of Gloucester. Shopping in Knightsbridge required pass-discs. You couldn't travel north on the motorway beyond Penrith. Scotland was owned by a consortium of Dutch millionaires. There would be no trawlers out fishing this winter – anywhere. A plane had crashed over East London, but there'd been no emergency services and the news was suppressed to stall a panic. The Severn Bore wasn't running any more. White ermine was being worn in London, another whimsical consequence of the 'aristocracy' craze. Literature was dead because there were no publishers to publish it, but a scholar in Chicago had unearthed a new Shakespeare play. They were re-mooting the idea of a papacy – a secular one this time, and Swiss. Herds of wild pigs had moved into Surrey. The waiting-time for an urgent, life-saving operation was eighteen months – if you could find a hospital. A woman had borne a whelp by a dog. The fashionable faces were green this season. A Japanese hologram-computer almost perfected would let you be in two, three, three dozen, three hundred places at one and the same time.

And so it went on.

*

Sometimes he heard the pealing of cracked bells; he didn't know what message or warning it was they carried. On tiptoe he could see the gentle rise of Wytham Hill, like the arched back of a crouching beast: beyond that, on the other side, he'd heard that it was possible to have a life of comparative order, if you stockaded yourself and were sensible about protection. Now he never saw those people, the intelligentsia herded in their rural pounds. Only the rich colleges with independent means had survived the onslaughts of jealous politicians, and companies of private guards covered all the comings and goings in plated vehicles. Security made living in Oxford perilous for families: he'd known of people kidnapped shopping for food, their cars had been attacked manoeuvring the obstacles in Woodstock Road, gangs lay in wait and threw bricks over the screens of meshing into the couple of private schools that had started up again in Summertown. In the country, he'd been told, you could still play tennis and cook a stockpot on an Aga and hear birds singing, you could shut your eyes and believe none of the rest had really happened.

But it had. And he was simply being expedient now, and to-the-point. Even if no one would thank him for it he was paying the debt he felt his humanity owed. When the waters finally broke... and he only saw what came after that in the abstract, as his 'mission'.

*

He continued his cataloguing by night. He pulled the curtains across the windows for a little warmth and for the privacy he needed. He used candles to write by, because they induced an intimacy with the things and what he sympathised were their collector's intentions.

> A glaffe-horne for annointing Kings
> rhino horn cup (Chinese) – as poison detector,
>   then aphrodisiac

Tradescant had raked as much of the globe as was known then for a trove to fill his house, and from it he'd furnished his imagination like a complete little room, *Soe that I am persuaded a Man might in one daye behold and collecte into*

*one place more Curiousities than hee should see if hee spent
all his life in Travell.* He felt it was even so in his own case,
that the earth and the millenia had shrunk to fit the tiny
compass of his own mind, *beasts, fowle, fishes, serpents,
wormes, pretious stones and other Armes, Coines, shells,
feathers, etts. of sundrey Nations, Countries, forme, Collours.*

Upstairs and downstairs the objects were ready for loading. In the museum basement there were another two-dozen
empty tea-chests, but he hadn't space to carry more than a
fraction of what they must contain.

> Dodar, from the Ifland Mauritius, it is not able
>   to flie being fo big
> Munkyes fceleton
> cat-a-mountaine
> alegator from Ægypt
> sunfifh and starrefifh

Whatever journeyed with him — before the trouble-makers
could discover the underground cache and break into the
museum and go charging through the cellars on a rampage —
it could only be a token of all the rest. The collection was
such a bizarre miscellany anyway, he didn't need to try to be
representative in his choice.

> hand of a mermaid
> Blood that rained in the *Ifle of Wight*, attefted by
>   Sir Jo: Oglander
> A Virginian habit of Beares-skin
> an *Umbrella*

For Tradescant the world had been one — a marvellous round
whole — in the unity of its emblems, and any point on the cir-
cumference might have suggested another, another, another.

> Russian abacus
> pocket Runic calendar — symbols of lunar cycle &
>   princ. saints' days
> wooden statue of (?) juggler
> Virgin of the Adoration
> Playing-card from a pack sent by Laud (d.1645)
>   Chancellor of Oxon. Univ. to Vice-Chancellor

Simple and profound touched, in a cheering way.

> the Passion of Christ carved very daintily on
>   a plumftone
> a Gamaha, a stone found in the West Indies in the
>   water, whereon were graven Jesus, Mary & Joseph
> A Hand of Jet usually given to Children, in *Turky*,
>   to preferve them from Witchcraft
> small relief carving in soapstone of Ganesa, the
>   elephant-headed god, a son of Siva famed for his
>   wisdom in practical affairs and particularly
>   popular among merchants of Western India.

Tradescant had netted the truths of life on a planet, and was only touched to inquire further and extend the grid. Time and place were utterly false distinctions to him.

> Spanish manacle
> a scourge with wh. Charles V is said to
>   have scourged himself
> Henry the VIII his Stirrups and Hawkes-hoods
> Moorish horse-bit – Iron curb bit, commonly
>   recognised by Europeans as unduly fierce
> ball-headed clubs – tamahacks (Algonquinian)
> A *Damafcus* knife perfum'd in the casting

When a civilisation was in its dying days, the earth could still keep spinning, and a man like Tradescant – worm-picked in his stone – became a global hero.

*

The news crackled on the radio. Nothing, as usual. But a visitor to the Western Art Library had told him the river-wall was broken in half-a-dozen places on the stretch between Gravesend and Sheerness. The Medway had swollen over its banks and surged inland, until now it covered Hoo. Gillingham was under nine feet of water. The pressure had burst open the west doors in Rochester Cathedral.

Remembering Rochester sent him to Dickens. *A monotonous, silent city, deriving an earthy flavour throughout from its Cathedral crypt, and so abounding in vestiges of* romantic graves, that the children grow small salad in the dust of abbots and abbesses, and make dirt-pies of nuns and friars...And further back, to *David Copperfield*. He had little room on board for books and he'd already selected *Great Expectations* to take with him, so he read with more sadness than he usually did David's troubled passage to Dover because it must be the last time that he made the journey with him. He experienced again that genius gift of Dickens to capture a life with its coincidences made credible, and shames and follies so ridiculous and excusable together, and its joy and pain seeming to be dependent.

And for the last time too he read the paragraphs that begin *Our Mutual Friend. He had no net, hook, or line, and he could not be a fisherman...His boat was too crazy and too small to take in a cargo for delivery, and he could not be a lighterman...*

The tide had turned an hour ago, was running down...

*

He'd heard the sirens wailing down-river for two nights in a row. They sounded like exotic, very perplexed birds.

Another six or seven days more – once the lagging was finished and the cock-stops were working properly and the bias in the rudder had been corrected – then he'd be prepared for any contingency. Already great pools of water had collected in the swampland where people used to garden and when the smoke blew across it was like the steaming heart of Africa without the heat – or a time when human life was still several stages off and monkeys lived in trees.

Tonight there was dancing on the radio. The murky moon coasting in the sky shone dimly in some broken windows in one of the vandalised terraces. A gilt harp sat in the street among broken lumps of tarmac, too cumbersome to be carried off and defying destruction. In a respectable house a woman and a man heard the same programme and shuffled in an attic room. Next door to them a tree reached out of a first-floor bay window. For a short time a dog barked terribly somewhere, and then mysteriously the din stopped. A bird flew out of a hole in a roof. He thought he heard the siren call again, from closer to. The oblong of outhouse at the bottom of the garden kept its secret guarded. There was the gleam of fresh snail-slime on the path.

He sat it all out at his window. Then he started suddenly, catching a movement among the vegetation.

It seemed to be the shadow of a man, turning away.

In the next few seconds other shadows claimed the human one, and the watcher at his window couldn't distinguish any more. He searched with his eyes and lost consciousness of himself, neglecting to hear that the radio was silent, as if there was no more music for dancing, it had played itself out.